Make History with this fantastic CGP book...

OK, so the latest GCSE History exams are pretty tricky... but with this brilliant CGP Revision Guide, you'll be ready to go into battle!

It's packed with everything you need to get your head around the subject, including crystal-clear notes, maps, diagrams and photos for each topic.

We've also included exam-style practice questions throughout the book, plus plenty of advice on how to pick up top marks. After all that, you'll be like an heir to the throne — destined to succeed.

CGP — still the best! ☺

Our sole aim here at CGP is to produce the highest quality books — carefully written, immaculately presented and dangerously close to being funny.

Then we work our socks off to get them out to you — at the cheapest possible prices.

CONTENTS

Published by CGP

Editors:
Emma Cleasby, Catherine Heygate, Jack Perry and Rebecca Tate.

Contributor:
Peter Callaghan

With thanks to Louise McEvoy for the proofreading.
With thanks to Ana Pungartnik for the copyright research.
Coordinated by Paddy Gannon.

Acknowledgements:

With thanks to The Art Archive / Palazzo Barberini Rome / Collection Dagli Orti for permission to use the image on page 1.
With thanks to Photo Researchers / Mary Evans Picture Library for permission to use the images on pages 2, 23, 39 and 61.
With thanks to Mary Evans Picture Library for permission to use the images on pages 5, 14, 19, 24, 71, 82, 90 and 93.
With thanks to Historic England / Mary Evans for permission to use the image on page 7.
With thanks to INTERFOTO / Bildarchiv Hansmann / Mary Evans for permission to use the image on page 9.
With thanks to Mary Evans / Everett Collection for permission to use the images on pages 11, 47 and 103.
With thanks to iStock.com/MikeLane45 for permission to use the image on page 13.
With thanks to iStock.com/GeorgiosArt for permission to use the image on page 17.
Poll from public survey on page 29 from King's Fund analysis of NatCen Social Research's British Social Attitudes survey data.
With thanks to Mary Evans/Interfoto for permission to use the image on page 38.
With thanks to Mary Evans/Classic Stock/C.P. Cushing for permission to use the image on page 42.
With thanks to Illustrated London News Ltd/Mary Evans for permission to use the images on pages 46 and 91.
With thanks to The Art Archive / Granger Collection for permission to use the images on pages 51, 55, 56, 58, 74 and 137.
With thanks to Mary Evans / Iberfoto for permission to use the images on pages 66 and 126.
With thanks to National Museums NI / MARY EVANS for permission to use the image on page 72.
Image on page 74 copyright Anthony Masi. This file is licensed under the Creative Commons Attribution 2.0 Generic license.
https://creativecommons.org/licenses/by/2.0/deed.en
With thanks to Mary Evans Picture Library/DOUGLAS MCCARTHY for permission to use the image on page 77.
With thanks to Thaliastock / Mary Evans for permission to use the image on page 99.
With thanks to Mary Evans / Sueddeutsche Zeitung Photo for permission to use the images on pages 102, 110 and 131.
With thanks to Mary Evans / SZ Photo / Scherl for permission to use the image on page 106.
Extract on page 107 from 'School for Barbarians: Education Under the Nazis' (Dover Books on History, Political and Social Science). Dover Publications Inc.; Reprint edition (28 Mar. 2014).
With thanks to Mary Evans / Imagno for permission to use the images on pages 113 and 129.
With thanks to Everett Collection / Mary Evans for permission to use the image on page 116.
With thanks to Mary Evans Picture Library/Imagno for permission to use the image on page 122.
First extract from history textbook on page 136. Layton, G. (2000). Access to History: Germany the Third Reich 1933-1945 2ED.
London: Hodder Education. © Geoff Layton 2005. Reproduced by permission of Hodder Education.
Second extract from history textbook on page 136. © Ian Kershaw, 2015, The Nazi Dictatorship, Bloomsbury Academic, an imprint of Bloomsbury Publishing Plc.

Every effort has been made to locate copyright holders and obtain permission to reproduce sources.
For those sources where it has been difficult to trace the copyright holder of the work, we would be grateful
for information. If any copyright holder would like us to make an amendment to the acknowledgements,
please notify us and we will gladly update the book at the next reprint. Thank you.

ISBN: 978 1 78294 608 3
Printed by Elanders Ltd, Newcastle upon Tyne.
Clipart from Corel®

Based on the classic CGP style created by Richard Parsons.

How History Works

For GCSE History, <u>you</u> have to <u>become</u> a historian, so you'd best be sure what they <u>really do</u>.

Historians use Sources to Find Out about the Past

<u>Sources</u> are things that historians use to <u>find out about</u> and <u>make sense of</u> the past. They can be <u>written</u> (e.g. newspapers, government reports) or <u>visual</u> (e.g. photographs, maps, films).

<u>**Primary sources**</u> are evidence <u>from the period</u> you're studying. E.g. a <u>newspaper report</u> on the First World War from 4th September 1914, or a <u>picture</u> of Henry VIII that was painted during his reign.

<u>**Secondary sources**</u> are evidence about (but <u>not from</u>) the period you're studying. E.g. a <u>1989 book</u> called 'Origins of the First World War', or a <u>website</u> providing information about <u>portraits</u> of Henry VIII.

Historians have to Interrogate and Interpret every source

1) Historians have to be <u>careful</u> with sources. To make sure they're using sources <u>accurately</u>, they <u>interrogate</u> every source they use. This means they ask themselves <u>questions</u> about the source's <u>background</u>.

King Henry VIII, 1540

© The Art Archive / Palazzo Barberini Rome / Collection Dagli Orti

- <u>**What**</u> is this source? *E.g. It is a painting of King Henry VIII.*
- <u>**Who**</u> made this source? *E.g. It was produced by the King's official painter, Hans Holbein.*
- <u>**Why**</u> did they make the source? *E.g. He was asked to paint it by the King.*
- <u>**Where**</u> and <u>**when**</u> was it made? *E.g. It was made in the Palace of Whitehall in 1540.*

2) Historians use their answers to work out <u>how useful</u> and <u>how reliable</u> a source is.

- This is a <u>professional</u> painting made <u>during</u> Henry's reign (meaning the painter could have <u>met</u> Henry). So this should be a <u>useful</u> source for finding out what Henry looked like.
- BUT perhaps the painter would have been <u>punished</u> if he didn't show Henry looking good, so it may not be entirely <u>reliable</u>.

A source that presents a one-sided view is <u>biased</u>.

3) After they've interrogated a source, historians <u>interpret</u> it. This means deciding <u>what it tells them</u> about what they're studying.

For example, Henry was probably quite a <u>big man</u> with <u>fair hair</u> and a <u>beard</u>. But the painter may have been told to make the picture to <u>Henry's liking</u> — based on just this picture, you can't really say for sure <u>how big</u> he really was.

4) Historians look at <u>lots of</u> sources, and <u>compare</u> them against each other. If sources <u>contradict</u> one another, they'll try to work out <u>why</u>, and what this tells them about the past.

Historians study Change, Continuity, Causes and Consequences

- <u>**Change**</u> is when something happens to make things <u>different</u>. Changes can be <u>quick</u> (e.g. a law making secondary education free) or <u>slow</u> (e.g. a gradual change in a society's literacy levels).
- <u>**Continuity**</u> is the <u>opposite</u> of change — it's when things stay the <u>same</u>.

The <u>most important</u> changes in history are called <u>turning points</u>. After a turning point, life might never be the same again.

1) Change and continuity can happen <u>at the same time</u> in different parts of society. For example, when the <u>Normans</u> conquered England in 1066, many of the <u>richest</u> people in English society lost their <u>jobs</u> and <u>status</u> (= change). But life didn't actually change very much for <u>peasant farmers</u> (= continuity).

2) Historians are often interested in whether <u>everyday</u> aspects of society are showing change or continuity — e.g. attitudes, lifestyles, beliefs, fashions, diets... the list is endless.

- <u>**Cause**</u> means the <u>reason</u> something happened — e.g. the causes of World War Two.
- <u>**Consequence**</u> means what happened <u>because</u> of an action — it's the <u>result</u> of an event. E.g. a consequence of World War Two was that a lot of young men were killed.
- Causes and consequences can be <u>short-term</u> or <u>long-term</u>.

If you have an event in history, think about <u>what caused it</u> and <u>the effect it had</u> — it's a good way to show the examiner how different events are <u>linked</u> to each other.

3) Historians also think about how causes and consequences <u>interact</u>. For example, there might be a <u>chain</u> of causes that lead to an event, or one consequence might be <u>more important</u> than all the rest.

And if you're really good at history — they'll let you on the telly...

As you use this book, think about the 'four Cs' of history — change, continuity, causes and consequences.

Disease and the Supernatural

In medieval England (and for the purposes of this section we're talking roughly 1000 to 1500), treatment of disease was a bit... medieval. The key problem was a lack of understanding of the causes of disease.

Disease was thought to have Supernatural Causes

1) Many people believed that disease was a punishment from God for people's sins. They thought that disease existed to show them the error of their ways and to make them become better people. Therefore, they thought that the way to cure disease was through prayer and repentance.

2) Disease was also thought to be caused by evil supernatural beings, like demons or witches. Witches were believed to be behind outbreaks of disease — many people were tried as witches and executed.

3) People believed that some diseases could be caused by evil spirits living inside someone. Members of the Church performed exorcisms, using chants to remove the spirit from the person's body.

The Church had a big Influence on medieval medicine

1) The Roman Catholic Church was an extremely powerful organisation in medieval Europe. It dominated the way people studied and thought about a range of topics, including medicine.

2) The Church encouraged people to believe that disease was a punishment from God, rather than having a natural cause. This prevented people from trying to find cures for disease — if disease was a punishment from God, all you could do was pray and repent.

3) The Church made sure that scholars of medicine learned the works of Galen (see p.3) as his ideas fit the Christian belief that God created human bodies and made them to be perfect. It also stopped anyone from disagreeing with Galen.

4) The Church outlawed dissection. This meant that medieval doctors couldn't discover ideas about human anatomy for themselves — they instead had to learn Galen's incorrect ideas.

Comment and Analysis

The Church's influence over medieval medicine meant that there was very little change in ideas about the cause of disease until the Renaissance — the Church and its messages were so influential that people were unable to question them.

Astrology was used to Diagnose disease

1) Astrology is the idea that the movements of the planets and stars have an effect on the Earth and on people. Astrologers in medieval England believed that these movements could cause disease.

2) Astrology was a new way of diagnosing disease. It was developed in Islamic medicine and brought to Europe between 1100 and 1300.

3) Medieval doctors owned a type of calendar (called an almanac) which included information about where particular planets and stars were at any given time. The doctor then used this information to predict how patients' health could be affected.

4) Different star signs were thought to affect different parts of the body.

A woodcut from 1490 showing two astrologers looking at the positions of the Sun and Moon.

The medieval period — a dark age for medicine...

Look at the woodcut of the astrologers above. Scribble down a few sentences explaining how useful you think it would be to a historian studying medieval beliefs about the causes of disease.

REVISION TASK

Natural Explanations

Some treatments in medieval Britain were based <u>less</u> on <u>religious faith</u> and <u>more</u> on <u>natural theories</u> and observation of the physical world. But a reason-based theory can still be <u>wrong</u>.

Medicine was dominated by the Four Humours Theory

After the fall of the <u>Roman Empire</u>, much Ancient <u>Greek</u> and <u>Roman</u> medical knowledge was <u>lost</u> in the West. The <u>Theory of the Four Humours</u> was eventually brought back to western Europe via the <u>Islamic world</u> (see p.4). Many medieval doctors based their <u>diagnosis</u> and <u>treatment</u> on this theory.

1) The Theory of the <u>Four Humours</u> was created by the Ancient Greek doctor <u>Hippocrates</u> (c.460-c.377 BC). Hippocrates believed that the body was made up of <u>four fluids</u> (or <u>humours</u>) — <u>blood</u>, <u>phlegm</u>, <u>yellow bile</u> and <u>black bile</u>. These were linked to the <u>four seasons</u> and the <u>four elements</u>. They needed to be in <u>balance</u> for good health.

> E.g. in <u>winter</u> we get <u>colds</u>. So Hippocrates thought that in winter the body created an excess of <u>phlegm</u>. Sadly, Hippocrates failed to see that a bunged up nose, fevers, etc. are <u>symptoms</u> of the disease — he thought they were the <u>cause</u>.

> E.g. someone with a <u>cold</u> (too much cold, wet <u>phlegm</u>) could be given chicken, pepper or wine (all considered <u>hot</u> and <u>dry</u>) to correct the <u>imbalance</u>.

2) The Theory of the Four Humours was developed further by another Greek doctor, <u>Galen</u>, who was born in AD 129 and worked for much of his career in <u>Rome</u>.

3) Galen believed that diseases could be treated using <u>opposites</u>. He thought that different foods, drinks, herbs and spices had a <u>humour</u>, which could <u>balance</u> the excessive humour that was causing the disease.

The Miasma Theory blamed Bad Air for causing disease

1) The <u>miasma</u> theory is the idea that <u>bad air</u> (or miasma) causes disease when someone breathes it in. This bad air may come from human <u>waste</u> or <u>dead bodies</u> — anything that creates a <u>bad smell</u>.

2) The miasma theory originated in Ancient <u>Greece</u> and <u>Rome</u>, and was incorporated by <u>Galen</u> into the Theory of the Four Humours. The idea became extremely popular in medieval Britain.

3) The miasma theory was so influential that it lasted until the <u>1860s</u>, when it was replaced by the <u>Germ Theory</u> (see p.15). Miasma often prompted people to do <u>hygienic</u> things, like cleaning the streets, which sometimes helped to stop the spread of disease (but for the wrong reasons).

> **Comment and Analysis**
>
> The Four Humours and miasma were both <u>incorrect</u> theories. But they assumed disease had a <u>natural</u> cause, rather than a supernatural one. This was important, as it suggested that people weren't <u>powerless</u> against disease — they could <u>investigate</u> and <u>take action</u> against it.

Hippocrates and Galen were very Influential

The work of <u>Hippocrates</u> and <u>Galen</u> was extremely influential in medical diagnosis and treatment.

1) Hippocrates and Galen wrote down their beliefs about medicine. These were <u>translated</u> into Latin books, which were considered important texts by the <u>Roman Catholic Church</u>. Like the Bible, Hippocrates' and Galen's ideas were considered the <u>absolute truth</u>.

2) Many of their ideas were taught for <u>centuries</u> after their deaths, including the <u>incorrect</u> ones. For example, Galen only ever dissected <u>animals</u> — animal and human bodies are very different, so some of his ideas about <u>anatomy</u> were <u>wrong</u>. Medieval doctors were <u>not allowed</u> to perform their own dissections, so they continued to learn Galen's incorrect ideas.

3) Some of Hippocrates' and Galen's ideas were so influential that they continue to be used <u>today</u>. The <u>Hippocratic Oath</u> is the <u>promise</u> made by doctors to obey rules of behaviour in their professional lives — a version of it is still in use today. Hippocrates and Galen also believed that doctors should <u>observe</u> their patients as they treat them.

The four humours — it's totally hilarious...

In the exam it's important to take a couple of minutes before the start of longer questions to plan your answer. This will make sure that you answer the question and don't veer off topic.

Islamic Medicine

In the medieval period, <u>Islamic</u> medicine was <u>miles ahead</u> of European medicine. Islamic ideas eventually made their way to Europe — including knowledge of the all-important <u>Galen</u> and <u>Hippocrates</u>.

Islamic doctors kept Classical Knowledge alive

1) While a lot of <u>medical knowledge</u> was <u>lost</u> in the West after the fall of the Roman Empire, medical ideas like the <u>Four Humours</u> and <u>treatment by opposites</u> (see p.3) were <u>kept alive</u> by Islamic scholars.

2) In the <u>9th century</u>, Hunain ibn Ishaq (also known by his Latin name <u>Johannitius</u>) travelled from <u>Baghdad</u> to <u>Byzantium</u> to collect Greek medical texts. He translated these into <u>Arabic</u>.

3) This classical knowledge was eventually brought to Europe by <u>Avicenna</u> (or Ibn Sina), a Persian who lived from around <u>AD 980-1037</u>. Avicenna wrote the '<u>Canon of Medicine</u>', which brought together the ideas of <u>Galen</u> and <u>Hippocrates</u>, and was the most important way that classical ideas got back into <u>Western Europe</u>.

4) This work and other Islamic texts were <u>translated</u> into <u>Latin</u> in <u>Spain</u> (which was partly Christian and partly Islamic) or <u>Italy</u>. The <u>Crusades</u> also made Europeans aware of the scientific knowledge of Islamic doctors.

> **Comment and Analysis**
>
> Islamic medicine was generally more <u>rational</u> and <u>evidence-based</u> than European medicine, partly due to their knowledge of classical (Ancient Greek and Roman) medical texts.

> The <u>Crusades</u> were a series of <u>wars</u> fought by Christian Europeans against Muslims. They were an ultimately <u>unsuccessful</u> attempt to retake <u>Jerusalem</u> and the surrounding areas associated with the early history of Christianity.

Islamic doctors made several New Discoveries

1) <u>Albucasis</u> (or Abu al-Qasim, born <u>c.AD 936</u>) wrote a well thought-out book describing <u>amputations</u>, the removal of <u>bladder stones</u> and <u>dental surgery</u> — as well as methods for handling fractures, dislocations and the stitching of wounds.

2) In the <u>12th century</u>, <u>Avenzoar</u> (or Ibn Zuhr) described the parasite that causes <u>scabies</u> and began to question the <u>reliability</u> of Galen.

3) <u>Ibn al-Nafis</u>, who lived in the <u>13th century</u>, also questioned Galen's ideas. He suggested (correctly) that blood flows from one side of the <u>heart</u> to the other via the <u>lungs</u> — and doesn't cross the <u>septum</u> (the dividing wall between the left and right sides of the heart). Ibn al-Nafis' work wasn't recognised in the West until the <u>20th century</u>.

> **Comment and Analysis**
>
> In the Islamic world, as in Western Europe, <u>religion</u> strongly influenced the development of medicine. For example, Islam, like Christianity, <u>prohibited dissection</u>.

> The autobiography of <u>Usama ibn Munqidh</u>, a 12th century Muslim doctor, suggests the <u>difference</u> between <u>Islamic</u> and <u>European</u> medicine. Usama describes how he treated a knight with a sore on his leg by using a <u>poultice</u>, and a woman who was 'feeble-minded' by advising a <u>new diet</u>. Then a <u>French doctor</u> arrived and claimed Usama <u>knew nothing</u>. He <u>cut off</u> the knight's leg with an axe, and cut the woman's head with a <u>razor</u> and rubbed the skull with <u>salt</u>. Both patients died.

Alchemy helped to develop New Drugs

1) Alchemy was the attempt to turn <u>base</u> (ordinary) metals into <u>gold</u> and to discover the elixir of <u>eternal life</u>.

2) <u>Alchemy</u> traces its origins back to the <u>Egyptians</u> and it was preserved in the Islamic world.

3) Unlike modern chemistry, much <u>superstition</u> was included — an unsuccessful experiment was as likely to be blamed on the position of the <u>stars</u> or the spiritual purity of the <u>alchemist</u> as anything else.

4) Even so, Islamic alchemists invented useful <u>techniques</u> such as distillation and sublimation, and prepared <u>drugs</u> such as laudanum, benzoin and camphor.

Who needs gold when you've got health?

Imagine that you've been tasked with 'selling' Islamic medicine to Europe. Write an advert for Islamic medicine, including a list of the ways it was more advanced than European medicine.

Treating Disease

As the Middle Ages went on, medical treatments continued to be based on ideas we'd nowadays consider very <u>unscientific</u>. <u>Treatments</u> were <u>ambitious</u> though, and <u>theories</u> quite <u>sophisticated</u> in their <u>own ways</u>.

Prayer and Repentance were major treatments

1) Disease was believed to be a punishment from God, so sick people were encouraged to <u>pray</u>. The sick often prayed to <u>saints</u>, in the hope they would intervene and stop the illness. Medieval people also believed that <u>pilgrimages</u> to <u>holy shrines</u> (e.g. sites containing the remains of saints) could cure <u>illnesses</u>.

2) Others took their <u>repentance</u> one step further. <u>Flagellants</u> were people who whipped themselves in public in order to show God that they were sorry for their past actions. They were particularly common during <u>epidemics</u>, such as the Black Death (see p.8).

3) Many <u>doctors</u> had <u>superstitious beliefs</u> — e.g. some used <u>astrology</u> to diagnose and treat illness (see p.2), or believed that saying <u>certain words</u> while giving a treatment could make that treatment more effective.

Bloodletting and Purging aimed to make the Humours balanced

1) <u>Bloodletting</u> and <u>purging</u> were popular treatments because they fitted in with the <u>Four Humours Theory</u> (see p.3).

2) If someone apparently had too much blood inside them, the doctor would take blood out of their body through <u>bloodletting</u> — they might make a small <u>cut</u> to remove the blood or use blood-sucking <u>leeches</u>.

3) Some people were accidentally <u>killed</u> because too much blood was taken.

4) <u>Purging</u> is the act of getting rid of other fluids from the body by <u>excreting</u> — doctors gave their patients <u>laxatives</u> to help the purging process.

> **Comment and Analysis**
>
> <u>Bloodletting</u> caused more deaths than it prevented, but it remained a popular treatment. This shows the strength of medieval people's <u>beliefs</u> in the face of <u>observational evidence</u>.

Purifying the Air was thought to Prevent Disease

1) The <u>miasma</u> theory (see p.3) led people to believe in the power of <u>purifying</u> or <u>cleaning</u> the air to prevent sickness and improve health.

2) Physicians carried <u>posies</u> or <u>oranges</u> around with them when visiting patients to protect themselves from catching a disease.

3) During the <u>Black Death</u> (see p.8), <u>juniper</u>, <u>myrrh</u> and <u>incense</u> were burned so the <u>smoke</u> or <u>scent</u> would <u>fill the room</u> and stop bad air from bringing disease <u>inside</u>.

> Purifying the air was also seen as important for helping with <u>other health conditions</u>. In the case of <u>fainting</u>, people <u>burned feathers</u> and made the patient <u>breathe in their smoke</u>.

Remedies were Early Natural Medicines

1) Remedies bought from an <u>apothecary</u>, local 'wise woman' or made at <u>home</u> were all popular in medieval Britain and contained <u>herbs</u>, <u>spices</u>, <u>animal parts</u> and <u>minerals</u>.

2) These remedies were either <u>passed down</u> or <u>written</u> in books explaining how to mix them together. Some of these books were called '<u>Herbals</u>'.

3) Other remedies were based on <u>superstition</u>, like <u>lucky charms</u> containing '<u>powdered unicorn's horn</u>'.

This medieval print shows a doctor and an apothecary. The plants in the middle show the importance of herbal remedies.

Medieval medical treatment was varied and diverse...

Look at the print of the doctor and apothecary above.
How useful would this source be to a historian investigating medieval medicine? [8]

Health and Medicine in Britain, c.1000-present

Treating Disease

If you were ill in the Middle Ages, you <u>couldn't</u> just go to your <u>local GP</u>. But as there were <u>various</u> kinds of medical healers, there could still be an element of '<u>patient choice</u>'...

People used lots of Different Healers

1) <u>Physicians</u> were <u>male doctors</u> who had trained at <u>university</u> for at least <u>seven years</u>. They read <u>ancient texts</u> as well as writings from the <u>Islamic world</u> (see p.4) but their training involved little <u>practical experience</u>. They used handbooks (vademecums) and <u>clinical observation</u> to check patients' conditions. But there were fewer than <u>100</u> physicians in England in 1300, and they were very <u>expensive</u>.

2) Most people saw an <u>apothecary</u>, who prepared and sold <u>remedies</u> (see p.5), and gave <u>advice</u> on how best to use them. Apothecaries were the most <u>common</u> form of treatment in Britain as they were the most <u>accessible</u> for those who could not afford a physician.

3) Apothecaries were trained through <u>apprenticeships</u>. Most apothecaries were men, but there were also many so-called '<u>wise women</u>', who sold <u>herbal remedies</u>.

There were Few Public Hospitals

1) Most <u>public hospitals</u> were set up and run by the <u>Church</u>. There were relatively <u>few</u> such hospitals, but they were very <u>popular</u> and <u>highly regarded</u>.

2) The main purpose of hospitals was not to treat disease, but to <u>care</u> for the <u>sick</u> and <u>elderly</u>. The hospital provided its patients with <u>food</u>, <u>water</u> and a <u>warm place to stay</u>. Most hospitals were also more <u>hygienic</u> than elsewhere, because they had developed <u>water</u> and <u>sewerage</u> systems.

3) Some <u>monasteries</u> also cared for the <u>sick</u>, the <u>elderly</u> or the <u>poor</u> (see p.7).

4) Most sick people were treated at <u>home</u> by members of their <u>family</u>.

> Famous <u>hospitals</u> like St. Bartholomew's and St. Thomas' in London started life as <u>church establishments</u>. The <u>monastery</u> at Canterbury Cathedral already had a complex <u>water</u> and <u>sanitation</u> system by 1250.

Surgery — work for Barbers, not doctors

1) Medieval surgery was very <u>dangerous</u> — there was no way to prevent <u>blood loss</u>, <u>infection</u> or <u>pain</u>. It was therefore only attempted <u>rarely</u> and for very <u>minor procedures</u>, e.g. treating hernias or cataracts.

2) There were a few <u>university-trained</u>, <u>highly paid</u> surgeons, but surgery as a whole was <u>not</u> a <u>respected</u> profession in medieval times — most operations were carried out by <u>barber-surgeons</u> (who also cut hair).

Some Progress was made in Surgery

1) <u>Hugh of Lucca</u> and his son <u>Theodoric</u> worked as surgeons in Italy in the early <u>13th century</u>. They recognised the importance of practical experience and observation, and <u>questioned</u> some of Galen's ideas — their thoughts appear in Theodoric's <u>textbooks</u>.

2) They began <u>dressing wounds</u> with bandages soaked in <u>wine</u>, because they noticed that the wine helped to keep wounds <u>clean</u> and <u>prevent infection</u>. They made this discovery by <u>chance</u>.

3) They also realised that <u>pus</u> was not a healthy sign, unlike other doctors at the time who might try to <u>cause</u> wounds to pus because they believed it would <u>release toxins</u> from the body.

4) Some surgeons tried to find ways to reduce <u>pain</u> during operations. For example, <u>John of Arderne</u> created a recipe for an <u>anaesthetic</u> in 1376 which included hemlock, opium and henbane (a relative of deadly nightshade). In carefully controlled doses this may have worked — but was very likely to <u>kill</u>.

Comment and Analysis

Hugh and Theodoric's approach was <u>unusual</u> in the Middles Ages. It wasn't until the <u>Renaissance</u> that people started to question widely-held beliefs about the <u>causes</u> of disease, and to carry out <u>experiments</u> to find <u>more effective</u> methods of treatment and prevention.

Get the terminology right — no funny spellings...

Some of the marks in the exam are for using specialist terminology — so make sure you know it.

Health and Medicine in Britain, c.1000-present

Health in Towns and Monasteries

In the medieval period, how <u>healthy</u> people were had a lot do with the area <u>where they lived</u>.

Living Conditions in Towns were pretty Poor

1) Most towns were <u>small</u>, especially after the <u>Black Death</u> when a lot of people died (p.8). Houses were usually made of <u>wood</u> and were <u>crammed together</u> — <u>overcrowding</u> and <u>fires</u> were common problems.

2) A lot of <u>towns</u> didn't have <u>clean water supplies</u> or <u>sewerage systems</u> — waste was chucked into the <u>street</u> or into <u>rivers</u> to be washed away. Sewage from <u>latrines</u> (pits with wooden seats) leaked into the <u>ground</u> and got into <u>wells</u>.

3) Businesses and homes <u>weren't separated</u> — butchers, tanners and dyers threw <u>toxic waste</u> into rivers and residential streets. People had to get their <u>drinking water</u> from rivers and wells that were <u>contaminated</u>.

4) In the <u>13th century</u>, a <u>water channel</u> called the <u>Great Conduit</u> was built to bring <u>clean water</u> into London, as the Thames was getting <u>too toxic</u>.

> 'When passing along the water of Thames, we have beheld <u>dung</u> and lay stools and other filth accumulated in <u>diverse places</u> within the city, and have also perceived the <u>fumes</u> and other <u>abominable stenches</u> arising therefrom...'
> King Edward III commenting on the state of the Thames in London in 1357.

5) In <u>1388</u>, the <u>government</u> ordered <u>town authorities</u> to keep the streets <u>free of waste</u>. Towns introduced <u>public health measures</u> to tackle waste, sewage and pollution and to create a <u>clean water supply</u>.

York and London both <u>banned</u> people from <u>dumping waste</u> in the street. These cities also built <u>latrines</u> over <u>rivers</u> so that sewage could be <u>carried away</u>.

London eventually banned <u>any waste</u> from being thrown into the Thames — <u>carters</u> were hired to <u>collect waste</u> and take it <u>out</u> of the city.

Many towns, like York, ordered <u>toxic businesses</u> like butchers, tanners, fishmongers and dyers to move <u>outside</u> the <u>city walls</u>.

Comment and Analysis

People <u>broke these rules</u> and officials struggled to <u>enforce</u> them. People knew that <u>dirty water</u> and <u>bad health</u> were <u>linked</u>, but <u>they didn't</u> really <u>understand</u> the <u>risks</u>. Town authorities didn't have enough <u>money</u> or <u>knowledge</u> to <u>properly</u> fix these public health issues.

Monasteries were Healthier than Towns

Monasteries had <u>cleaner water</u> than towns and had good systems for getting rid of <u>waste</u> and <u>sewage</u>. Monks also had access to <u>books</u> on healing and they <u>knew</u> how to <u>grow herbs</u> and make <u>herbal remedies</u>.

This is what historians think <u>Fountains Abbey</u> in Yorkshire might have been like.

<u>Sick monks</u> were cared for in <u>infirmaries</u>. These <u>infirmaries</u> normally had their own <u>kitchen</u> that served <u>good meals</u> and <u>meat</u> to help sick monks to <u>recover</u>.

Monasteries <u>separated</u> clean and dirty <u>water</u>. They had one water supply for <u>cooking</u> and <u>drinking</u> and one for <u>drainage</u> and <u>washing</u>, so people didn't have to drink <u>dirty water</u> like they did in towns.

Some monasteries had <u>hospitals</u> that <u>cared</u> for <u>poor people</u> from the <u>local community</u> when they were sick and gave shelter to <u>travellers</u>. <u>Benedictine</u> monks believed <u>caring</u> for the sick was the <u>most important</u> Christian duty.

Most monasteries were built near <u>rivers</u>. If there was no river, <u>man-made waterways</u> were built to supply <u>clean water</u>.

<u>Latrines</u> were put in <u>separate buildings</u>, which were often built over streams of <u>running water</u> that <u>carried sewage away</u>.

Infirmary

Kitchen

Guest Houses

It was <u>easier</u> to create <u>healthy living conditions</u> in <u>monasteries</u> than it was in towns.

1) Monasteries were <u>wealthy</u>, so they could <u>afford</u> to build <u>infrastructure</u> like latrine buildings and waterways to keep their water <u>clean</u>. Towns had to rely on <u>wealthy individuals</u> to <u>fund</u> these kinds of projects.

2) Monastery <u>populations</u> were small and had one leader (the Abbot) — he had the <u>power</u> to <u>enforce</u> rules about cleanliness and waste disposal. Getting <u>hundreds</u> of <u>townspeople</u> to adopt cleaner habits was <u>trickier</u> — towns didn't have one person <u>in charge</u> who could easily <u>enforce</u> public health measures.

City livin' ain't all it's cracked up to be...

Draw two boxes — one with the heading 'Towns' and the other with the heading 'Monasteries'. Fill in the boxes with bullet points about health and living conditions in each location.

The Black Death in Britain

The <u>Black Death</u> first struck in the <u>14th century</u>. People tried to limit its <u>spread</u>, but couldn't <u>stop</u> the disease.

The Black Death was a devastating Epidemic

1) The <u>Black Death</u> was a series of <u>plagues</u> that swept Europe in the <u>14th century</u>. It was really two illnesses:

- <u>Bubonic plague</u>, spread by the bites of fleas from rats carried on <u>ships</u>. This caused <u>headaches</u> and a <u>high temperature</u>, followed by pus-filled <u>swellings</u> on the skin.
- <u>Pneumonic plague</u> was <u>airborne</u> — it was spread by coughs and sneezes. It attacked the <u>lungs</u>, making it <u>painful to breathe</u> and causing victims to cough up <u>blood</u>.

2) The disease first arrived in Britain in <u>1348</u>. Some historians think at least a <u>third</u> of the British population died as a result of the Black Death in 1348-50. There were <u>further outbreaks</u> of the Black Death throughout the Middle Ages.

People Didn't Know what Caused the Black Death

No-one at the time knew what had <u>caused</u> the plague.

1) Some people believed that the Black Death was a <u>judgement from God</u>. They thought the cause of the disease was <u>sin</u>, so they tried to <u>prevent</u> the spread of the disease through <u>prayer</u> and <u>fasting</u>.

2) Some blamed <u>humour</u> imbalances (see p.3), so tried to get rid of the Black Death through <u>bloodletting</u> and <u>purging</u>. Those who thought that the disease was caused by <u>miasma</u> carried strong smelling <u>herbs</u> or lit <u>fires</u> to <u>purify</u> the air.

3) Some people also carried <u>charms</u> or used 'magic' <u>potions</u> containing <u>arsenic</u>.

> **Comment and Analysis**
>
> One of the main reasons why the Black Death killed so many was because people <u>didn't know</u> what caused the disease. Their ideas about the cause of disease were <u>wrong</u>, so their attempts at prevention and treatment were mostly <u>ineffective</u>.

Local Governments tried to Prevent the spread of the disease

1) Some people in Winchester thought that you could catch the plague from being <u>close</u> to the <u>bodies of dead victims</u>. When the town's cemetery became <u>too full</u> to take any more plague victims, the townspeople refused to let the bishop extend the cemetery in the town centre. Instead, they insisted that <u>new cemeteries</u> be built outside of the town, away from the houses.

2) The town of Gloucester tried to <u>shut itself off</u> from the outside world after hearing the Black Death had reached Bristol. This suggests that they thought the plague was spread by <u>human contact</u>. Their attempt at prevention was <u>unsuccessful</u> — many people in the town <u>died</u> of the Black Death.

3) In November 1348, the disease reached London. In January 1349, King Edward III <u>closed Parliament</u>.

The Black Death caused Social Change

1) After the Black Death, there were <u>far fewer workers</u> around. This meant that they could demand <u>higher wages</u> from their employers, and <u>move around</u> to find better work. The <u>cost of land</u> also <u>decreased</u>, allowing some peasants to buy land for the first time.

2) These changes threatened the power of the elites. The government created <u>laws</u>, such as the <u>1349 Ordinance of Labourers</u>, to try and stop peasants moving around the country.

3) Some people think the Black Death helped cause the <u>Peasants' Revolt</u> in 1381, and, eventually, the collapse of the <u>feudal system</u> in Britain.

Don't plague aims — this Black Death is serious stuff...

In the exam, remember to check the number of marks each question is worth. If a question's worth double the marks of another question, you'll need to give it double the time.

The Renaissance

The Renaissance was a time of <u>new ideas</u> and fresh <u>thinking</u>. People began to <u>challenge</u> old beliefs, and there were many <u>new developments</u> in doctors' <u>knowledge</u> and <u>skills</u>.

The Renaissance was a time of Continuity and Change

1) In the Renaissance there was a <u>rediscovery</u> of knowledge from classical <u>Greek</u> and <u>Roman</u> times. Western doctors gained access to the original writings of <u>Hippocrates</u>, <u>Galen</u> and <u>Avicenna</u> (a Persian physician who lived between 980 and 1037 AD). These <u>hadn't been available</u> in the medieval period. They led to <u>greater interest</u> in the <u>Four Humours</u> Theory and <u>treatment by opposites</u> (see p.3).

2) But the Renaissance also saw the emergence of <u>science</u> as we know it from the <u>magic</u> and <u>mysticism</u> of medieval medicine. People thought about how the human body worked based on <u>direct observation</u> and <u>experimentation</u>.

3) This was partly because many of the new books that had been found said that <u>anatomy</u> and <u>dissections</u> were very important. This encouraged people to <u>examine</u> the body themselves, and to come to their <u>own conclusions</u> about the causes of disease.

4) People began to <u>question</u> Galen's thinking and that of other ancient doctors. However, his writings <u>continued to be studied</u>.

<u>Protestant Christianity</u> spread across Europe during the <u>Reformation</u>, reducing the influence of the <u>Catholic Church</u>. Although <u>religion</u> was still <u>important</u>, the Church no longer had so much control over medical teaching.

This woodcut shows physicians debating over a medicine book.

The Medical Knowledge of doctors Improved

1) Many doctors in the Renaissance trained at the <u>College of Physicians</u>, which had been set up in <u>1518</u>. Here they read books by <u>Galen</u>, but also studied <u>recent</u> medical developments. <u>Dissections</u> — showing how the body actually worked — also became a <u>key part</u> of medical training.

2) The College of Physicians encouraged the <u>licensing</u> of doctors to stop the influence of <u>quacks</u>, who sold <u>fake medicines</u> (see p.12). Some of the college's physicians (such as <u>Harvey</u> — see p.11) made <u>important discoveries</u> about disease and the human body.

3) New <u>weapons</u> like <u>cannons</u> and <u>guns</u> were being used in <u>war</u>. This meant that doctors and surgeons had to treat injuries they <u>hadn't seen before</u>, forcing them to quickly find <u>new treatments</u>.

4) <u>Explorations</u> abroad brought <u>new ingredients</u> for drugs back to Britain, including <u>guaiacum</u> — believed to cure syphilis — and <u>quinine</u>, a drug for <u>malaria</u> from the bark of the <u>Cinchona</u> tree.

There were some <u>technological</u> developments too. <u>Peter Chamberlen</u> invented the <u>forceps</u> (probably at some point in the 1600s), which are still used today to help with <u>childbirth</u>.

5) In the <u>1530s</u>, Henry VIII closed down most of Britain's <u>monasteries</u> (this was called the '<u>dissolution of the monasteries</u>'). Since most hospitals had been set up and run by monasteries (see p.7), this also led to the <u>closure</u> of a large number of <u>hospitals</u>. The sudden <u>loss</u> of so many hospitals was <u>bad</u> for people's <u>health</u>.

6) The monastic hospitals were gradually <u>replaced</u> by some <u>free hospitals</u>, which were paid for by <u>charitable donations</u> (see p.16). Unlike the monastic hospitals, which had been run by monks, these new hospitals were run by trained <u>physicians</u>, who focused more on <u>getting better</u> from <u>illness</u>.

Vesalius and Sydenham

Vesalius and Sydenham believed that <u>direct observation</u> was the best way to learn about the body. They encouraged people to gain <u>practical experience</u>, and to use <u>dissection</u> to understand <u>anatomy</u>.

Vesalius wrote Anatomy books with Accurate Diagrams

1) <u>Vesalius</u> was born in <u>1514</u> and was a medical <u>professor</u> in Padua, Italy. He believed that <u>successful surgery</u> would only be possible if doctors had a proper <u>understanding</u> of the human <u>anatomy</u>.

2) Vesalius was able to perform <u>dissections</u> on <u>criminals</u> who had been <u>executed</u>. This let him study the human anatomy more closely.

3) He wrote books based on his observations using <u>accurate diagrams</u> to illustrate his work. The most important were '<u>Six Anatomical Pictures</u>' (<u>1538</u>) and '<u>The Fabric of the Human Body</u>' (<u>1543</u>).

4) His works were <u>printed</u> and <u>copied</u> (see the <u>printing press</u>, p.12), allowing lots of people to read about his ideas.

> Vesalius' work helped point out some of <u>Galen's mistakes</u>. For example, in the second edition of 'The Fabric', Vesalius showed that there were <u>no holes</u> in the septum of the heart.

5) Vesalius's findings encouraged others to <u>question Galen</u>. Doctors also realised there was <u>more to discover</u> about the body because of Vesalius' <u>questioning</u> attitude.

6) Vesalius showed that <u>dissecting bodies</u> was important, to find out exactly how the human body was <u>structured</u>. Dissection was used <u>more and more</u> in medical training for this reason.

Comment and Analysis

The work of Vesalius <u>didn't</u> have an immediate impact on the <u>diagnosis</u> or <u>treatment</u> of disease. However, by producing a realistic description of the human <u>anatomy</u> and encouraging <u>dissection</u>, Vesalius provided an essential <u>first step</u> to improving them.

Thomas Sydenham used Practical Experience

1) <u>Thomas Sydenham</u> (1624-1689) was a <u>Renaissance physician</u> who worked in London. He was the son of a <u>country squire</u>, and fought in the <u>English Civil War</u> before becoming a doctor. He has been called the '<u>English Hippocrates</u>' because of the big impact of his medical achievements.

2) Sydenham didn't believe in the value of <u>theoretical knowledge</u>. Instead he thought that it was more important to gain <u>practical experience</u> in treating patients. As a doctor, he made <u>detailed observations</u> of his patients and kept <u>accurate records</u> of their symptoms.

3) Sydenham thought that diseases could be <u>classified</u> like animals or plants — the <u>different types</u> of disease could be <u>discovered</u> using patients' <u>symptoms</u>.

4) Sydenham is known for showing that <u>scarlet fever</u> was different to <u>measles</u>, and for introducing <u>laudanum</u> to relieve pain. He was also one of the first doctors to use <u>iron</u> to treat <u>anaemia</u>, and <u>quinine</u> for <u>malaria</u> (see p.9).

5) Sydenham wrote a book called '<u>Medical Observations</u>' (published in <u>1676</u>), which was used as a textbook by doctors for <u>200 years</u>. His descriptions of medical conditions like <u>gout</u> helped other doctors to <u>diagnose</u> their patients more easily.

Comment and Analysis

Sydenham's work on classifying diseases helped make <u>diagnosis</u> a more important part of doctors' work. Before, the emphasis had been on <u>prognosis</u> — predicting what the disease would do next.

Sydenham and Vesalius believed in direct observation...

Scribble down the main achievements of both Sydenham and Vesalius. Then note down the impact of their ideas — did they change things? Think about short-term and long-term effects.

Harvey and Paré

William Harvey and Ambroise Paré were key individuals in the history of Renaissance medicine.
Harvey discovered how blood circulates around the body, and Paré made surgery safer and more effective.

Harvey discovered the Circulation of the Blood

1) William Harvey was a British doctor, born in 1578. He
studied medicine at Padua University, Italy, then worked
in London at the Royal College of Physicians (see p.9),
before becoming Royal Physician to James I and Charles I.

> Harvey was one of many British doctors who studied
> medicine at a university in Italy or France. During
> the Renaissance, major new discoveries were being
> made at these European universities — the discoveries
> of Vesalius (see p.10) were made at Padua University.
> British doctors who studied in Europe learnt the latest
> ideas in medicine and brought them back to Britain.

2) Harvey studied both animals and humans for his work.
He realised that he could observe living animal hearts in
action, and that his findings would also apply to humans.

3) Before Harvey, people thought that there were two kinds of blood, and that they flowed
through two completely separate systems of blood vessels. This idea came from Galen.

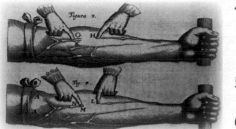

*A diagram from Harvey's book 'On the
Motions of the Heart and Blood' (1628),
showing blood circulation in the arm.*

4) Harvey realised Galen's theory was wrong. From experiments, he
knew that too much blood was being pumped out of the heart for
it to be continually formed and consumed. Instead he thought
that blood must circulate — it went round and round the body.

5) Harvey's ideas, shown in his books, gave doctors a map of how
the body worked, changing their understanding of anatomy.

6) However, not everyone believed his theories, and it took a long
time before doctors used them in their treatments. For example,
people continued to perform bloodletting (see p.5), even though
Harvey had shown the reasoning behind it to be wrong.

Paré improved Surgical Techniques

1) Ambroise Paré was a French barber-surgeon born in 1510. Surgery was still a low
status profession. Paré worked for a public hospital, then became an army surgeon.

> Paré also designed
> quite sophisticated
> artificial limbs.

2) As an army surgeon, Paré treated many serious injuries caused by war. His experience
treating these wounds led him to develop some improved surgical techniques.

- At this time, gunshot wounds often became infected. Doctors didn't
understand why this happened or how to treat it. The usual treatment was to
burn the wound with a red hot iron, or to pour boiling oil onto it. This may
have worked in some cases, but it often did more harm than good.

  > A cool salve is a
  > type of ointment.

- During one battle, Paré ran out of oil and resorted, by chance, to a simple cool salve instead.
To his surprise the patients treated in this way did better than the ones scalded with oil.

- Paré also improved the treatment of amputations. Before Paré, the severed blood vessels left by
amputation were sealed by burning their ends with a red hot iron (cauterisation). Paré invented a
method of tying off the vessels with threads (ligatures). This was less painful than cauterisation, so
it reduced the chances of the patient dying of shock. However, it did increase the risk of infection.

3) Paré published his ideas to enable other doctors to
read about them — British surgeons used the methods
of Paré and took inspiration from his work. Over
time, his ideas helped improve surgical techniques.

> Paré's ideas were resisted by doctors who felt that a lowly
> surgeon shouldn't be listened to. He eventually became
> surgeon to the King of France, and it was only with the
> King's support that his ideas started to be accepted.

The circulation of the blood goes round and round...

*Look at Harvey's diagram of the blood circulation in the arm above. How useful
would this source be to a historian investigating Renaissance medicine? [8]*

Continuity and Change

Change was pretty rapid during the Renaissance — <u>new technology</u> allowed ideas to be circulated more easily, making change <u>even quicker</u>. Even so, there was still <u>continuity</u> in many aspects of medical care.

The Spread of New Ideas accelerated Change

1) The invention of printing accelerated the <u>rate of progress</u> in medicine (and everything else).

2) Printing meant that books could be <u>copied</u> more <u>easily</u> — in the past, new ideas had to be <u>widely accepted</u> before anyone would bother copying them by hand. <u>Students</u> in <u>universities</u> could have their own <u>textbooks</u> for the first time, letting them study in detail.

3) People could also question <u>existing</u> ideas and have scientific <u>debates</u>.

> At least <u>600</u> different editions of <u>Galen's</u> books were printed between 1473 and 1599. Lots of people <u>knew</u> his theories, but with so many different versions around, it was <u>unclear</u> what Galen had originally written — this made his writings seem <u>less reliable</u> and easier to <u>question</u>.

4) The <u>Royal Society</u> was founded in <u>1660</u>. Its motto was '<u>Nullius in verba</u>', which means '<u>take no-one's word for it</u>' — the society wanted to encourage people to be <u>sceptical</u> and to <u>question</u> scientific ideas.

5) The Royal Society helped to spread <u>new scientific theories</u> and got people to <u>trust new technology</u>. Its scientific journal '<u>Philosophical Transactions</u>' allowed more people to read about new inventions and discoveries.

> The <u>first British</u> printing press was set up in the <u>1470s</u>.

> **Comment and Analysis**
>
> Huge <u>progress</u> was made in the Renaissance — and the <u>printing press</u> and the <u>Royal Society</u> helped spread the <u>new ideas</u>. But most people <u>couldn't read</u>, so new ideas only had an impact on a <u>small part</u> of society.

People continued to use Old treatments

1) Many doctors were reluctant to accept that <u>Galen</u> was <u>wrong</u>. This meant that they continued to use similar treatments to the Middle Ages, like <u>bloodletting</u> and <u>purging</u> (see p.5).

2) Doctors were still very <u>expensive</u>. As a result, most people used <u>other healers</u> (e.g. apothecaries and barber-surgeons — see p.6), like in the <u>medieval period</u>. Some people turned to <u>quack doctors</u> who sold <u>medicines</u> and <u>treatments</u> in the street. Their cures were often <u>fake</u>, though some may have worked.

3) <u>Superstition</u> and <u>religion</u> were still important. People thought the <u>King's touch</u> could cure <u>scrofula</u> (a skin disease known as the '<u>King's Evil</u>'). <u>Thousands</u> of people with scrofula are thought to have visited King Charles I (1600-1649) in the hope of being cured.

4) <u>Wise women</u>, who were skilled in <u>herbal remedies</u>, carried on providing medical attention in the community. <u>Wealthy ladies</u> sometimes took this role — they would care for <u>local families</u>.

> Lady Grace Mildmay (1552-1620) was a wise woman who was <u>highly educated</u> and read lots of medical books. She used her knowledge to <u>help patients</u>. She also kept <u>detailed records</u> of her treatments.

Poor living conditions had a Bad Effect on people's Health

1) Living conditions in Renaissance towns were <u>terrible</u> — they were <u>less healthy</u> than medieval ones.

2) <u>Overcrowding</u> was a big problem and there was a lack of <u>light</u> and <u>fresh air</u> in houses. <u>Streets</u> were <u>unclean</u> — there weren't any <u>sewerage systems</u> or any sort of <u>rubbish collection</u>. Finding <u>clean water</u> could be quite hard.

3) <u>Local authorities</u> began to <u>improve</u> conditions. They used <u>Acts of Parliament</u> to get <u>power</u> to do things like <u>keep roads clean</u>. <u>Housing improved</u> and some <u>towns</u> were planned with living conditions in mind.

> Poor living conditions meant <u>disease</u> spread <u>quickly</u> around towns. Since towns were becoming more <u>closely connected</u> through trade, disease also began to spread <u>easily</u> around the <u>country</u>.

Change and continuity — just a fancy 'spot the difference'...

Make two lists of the key features of medieval and Renaissance medicine — how much had changed? Think about the experience of the average person, as well as new scientific discoveries.

The Great Plague

The continuity in Renaissance medicine was felt most when the Great Plague struck London in 1665. From prayers to bloodletting, people's responses were eerily similar to the reaction to the Black Death (see p.8).

The Great Plague hit London in 1665

1) In 1665, London was struck by the Great Plague. This was a rare but deadly recurrence of the medieval Black Death.

2) London's death toll was about 100,000 — this was around underline{20%} of the city's population.

3) Many people fled the city, but only richer people had this option.

4) Doctors and priests were often most affected because the sick went to them for help.

Like the Black Death, the Great Plague was spread by the bites of fleas from rats. The people at the time didn't know this, though.

Superstition still dominated Treatment

Just like responses to the Black Death 300 years before (see p.8), most treatments for the Great Plague were based on magic, religion and superstition.

1) This included wearing lucky charms or amulets, saying prayers and fasting.

2) Special remedies were made using ingredients like dried toad.

3) Bloodletting was still used, even though this probably made the plague worse — it created wounds which could become infected.

4) Other people thought that miasma caused the disease (see p.5). They carried around posies of herbs or flowers to improve the air.

5) Perhaps the most extreme treatment was strapping a live chicken to the swellings — people thought the disease could be transferred from the plague victim to the chicken.

Comment and Analysis

Living conditions were very poor in Renaissance England, so it isn't a surprise that the plague came back. Death records show that the poorest, most crowded areas of London were worst hit.

People tried to Prevent the plague from Spreading

Local councils took measures to try to stop the spread of the plague. They were largely ineffective because they didn't know the cause of the disease.

1) Councils tried to quarantine plague victims to prevent them passing on the disease to others. The victim's house was locked and a red cross was painted on their door, along with the words "Lord have mercy upon us".

2) Areas where people crowded together such as theatres were closed.

3) People tried not to touch other people. E.g. if someone had to give money in a shop, the coins might be placed in a jar of vinegar.

4) The dead bodies of plague victims were buried in mass graves away from houses. Carts organised by the authorities roamed the city to the infamous cry of "bring out your dead!", collecting corpses for burial.

5) Local councils paid for lots of cats and dogs to be killed, because they thought they carried the plague.

Comment and Analysis

The responses to the plague came from local councils — they did more to try to combat the Great Plague than they had done for the Black Death 300 years previously. But there were no national government attempts at prevention.

The plague gradually began to disappear. Many people think the Great Fire of London in 1666 helped wipe it out, by effectively sterilising large parts of London — it burned down the old, crowded houses, killing the plague bacteria.

Those Renaissance doctors — stuck in the past...

How were the responses to the Great Plague and the medieval Black Death similar? Explain your answer and refer to both epidemics. [8]

EXAM QUESTION

Vaccination

Until the 1700s, people had <u>few</u> effective ways to <u>prevent</u> the spread of <u>disease</u>. <u>Edward Jenner's</u> discovery of the <u>smallpox vaccine</u> was a <u>landmark</u> in the development of <u>preventive medicine</u>.

Before Jenner the only way to prevent Smallpox was Inoculation

1) In the 1700s, <u>smallpox</u> was one of the most <u>deadly</u> diseases — in 1751, over 3500 people died of smallpox in London alone.

2) At the time, the only way to prevent smallpox was through <u>inoculation</u>. This was introduced into Britain from Turkey by Lady Mary Wortley Montagu in 1718.

3) Inoculation involved making a <u>cut</u> in a patient's arm and soaking it in pus taken from the swelling of somebody who already had a <u>mild form</u> of smallpox.

> Inoculation was successful in preventing the disease, but it meant patients had to <u>experience smallpox</u> before they could become immune — some <u>died</u> as a result.

Jenner discovered a link between Smallpox and Cowpox

1) <u>Edward Jenner</u> (born in 1749) was a country doctor in <u>Gloucestershire</u>. He heard that <u>milkmaids</u> didn't get smallpox, but they did catch the much milder <u>cowpox</u>.

2) Using careful <u>scientific methods</u> Jenner investigated and discovered that it was true that people who had had <u>cowpox</u> didn't get <u>smallpox</u>.

3) In 1796, Jenner <u>tested</u> his theory. He injected a small boy, <u>James Phipps</u>, with pus from the sores of <u>Sarah Nelmes</u>, a milkmaid with cowpox. Jenner then infected him with smallpox. James <u>didn't catch</u> the disease.

4) Jenner <u>published</u> his findings in <u>1798</u>. He coined the term <u>vaccination</u> using the Latin word for cow, <u>vacca</u>.

> **Comment and Analysis**
>
> Jenner was important because he used an <u>experiment</u> to test his theory. Although experiments had been used during the Renaissance, it was still <u>unusual</u> for doctors to <u>test</u> their theories.

Jenner's vaccination was Successful despite Opposition

1) Some people <u>resisted</u> vaccination. Some <u>doctors</u> who gave the older type of inoculation saw it as a <u>threat</u> to their livelihood, and many people were <u>worried</u> about giving themselves a disease from <u>cows</u>.

2) But Jenner's discovery soon got the approval of <u>Parliament</u>, which gave Jenner <u>£10,000</u> in 1802 to open a vaccination clinic. It gave Jenner a further <u>£20,000</u> a few years later.

3) In 1840 vaccination against smallpox was made <u>free</u> for infants. In 1853 it was made <u>compulsory</u>.

4) The vaccine was a <u>success</u> — it contributed to a big fall in the number of smallpox cases in Britain.

A cartoon from 1802 by James Gillray, with cows bursting out of vaccinated patients' sores. Vaccination was met with a lot of <u>opposition</u> — some groups in Britain published pamphlets against vaccination.

> **Comment and Analysis**
>
> The government's attempts to get people vaccinated against smallpox were <u>surprising</u> given attitudes at the time. People believed in a <u>laissez-faire</u> style of government — they thought that government <u>shouldn't get involved</u> in people's lives. The vaccination policy <u>went against</u> this general attitude.

> Jenner didn't know why his vaccine worked. This <u>lack of understanding</u> meant Jenner <u>couldn't</u> develop any other vaccines. This was only possible after the Germ Theory was published (see p.15), when <u>Pasteur</u> and others worked to discover vaccines against other diseases, like chicken cholera and anthrax.

Jenner's vaccine got things mooving on disease prevention...

'The smallpox vaccination was the most important medical discovery in Britain between the years 1700 and 1900.' To what extent do you agree? Explain your answer. [16]

The Germ Theory

Although people's understanding of <u>anatomy</u> had improved greatly during the Renaissance, there was still plenty to learn. The <u>causes of disease</u> was an area that still needed proper explanation.

Pasteur was the first to suggest that Germs cause disease

1) Germs and other <u>micro-organisms</u> were discovered as early as the 17th century. Scientists thought that these microbes were <u>created</u> by <u>decaying matter</u>, like rotting food or human waste — this theory was known as <u>spontaneous generation</u>. It led people to believe that <u>disease caused germs</u>.

2) In 1857, the French chemist <u>Louis Pasteur</u> was employed to find the explanation for the <u>souring</u> of sugar beet used in fermenting industrial <u>alcohol</u>. His answer was to blame <u>germs</u>.

3) Pasteur proved there were germs in the air — he showed that sterilised water in a closed flask <u>stayed sterile</u>, while sterilised water in an open flask <u>bred germs</u>.

4) In <u>1861</u>, Pasteur published his <u>Germ Theory</u>. In it he argued that <u>microbes</u> in the air <u>caused decay</u>, not the other way round. He also suggested that some <u>germs caused disease</u>.

> Pasteur's discovery was partly due to Antonie <u>van Leeuwenhoek's</u> invention of the <u>microscope</u> in the 17th century. <u>More advanced microscopes</u> were developed during the 1800s. They allowed scientists to see much <u>clearer images</u> with a lot <u>less light distortion</u>.

It took Time for the Germ Theory to have an Impact

1) The Germ Theory was first met with <u>scepticism</u> — people <u>couldn't believe</u> tiny microbes caused disease. It didn't help that the germ responsible for each disease had to be identified <u>individually</u>, as this meant it was several years before the theory became useful.

2) The Germ Theory soon gained popularity in Britain:

- The theory inspired <u>Joseph Lister</u> to develop <u>antiseptics</u> (p.19).
- It proved <u>John Snow's</u> findings about <u>cholera</u> (p.20).
- It linked disease to <u>poor living conditions</u> (like squalor and contaminated water).

> This put pressure on the government to pass the <u>1875 Public Health Act</u> (see p.21).

Robert Koch used dyes to identify microbes

1) The German scientist <u>Robert Koch</u> built on Pasteur's work by linking specific diseases to the particular <u>microbe</u> that caused them. Koch identified <u>anthrax</u> spores (<u>1876</u>) and the bacteria that cause <u>septicaemia</u> (<u>1878</u>), <u>tuberculosis</u> (<u>1882</u>) and <u>cholera</u> (<u>1883</u>).

2) Koch used revolutionary <u>scientific methods</u>:

- He used <u>agar jelly</u> to create solid <u>cultures</u>, allowing him to breed lots of bacteria.
- He used <u>dyes</u> to stain the bacteria so they were more visible under the microscope.
- He employed the newly-invented <u>photography</u> to record his findings.

3) Other scientists used Koch's methods to find the <u>germs</u> that caused other diseases — they became known as <u>microbe hunters</u>. They included <u>Edwin Klebs</u>, who discovered the <u>diphtheria</u> germ in 1883.

Pasteur developed Vaccines for Anthrax and Rabies

In <u>1877</u>, <u>Pasteur</u> came out of retirement to find and combat <u>new microbes</u>. Pasteur's team found that if they injected chickens with a <u>weakened</u> cholera culture, followed by some <u>newly cultured</u> cholera, the chickens survived. The weakened (<u>attenuated</u>) cholera had made them <u>immune</u>.

> The team produced an <u>attenuated</u> version of the <u>anthrax</u> bacteria to make <u>sheep</u> immune. They then used a similar method to find a vaccine for <u>rabies</u>.

Pasteur's theory — more than the germ of an idea...

Split your page into three sections, with the headings: individuals, technology and changing attitudes. Under each heading, list the ways in which that factor contributed to the Germ Theory.

Surgery and Hospitals

Over time, surgeons became <u>more important</u> and developed their approach to surgery. From the 18th century, hospitals also focused more on <u>treating</u> patients (rather than just <u>caring</u> for them) as well as <u>teaching</u>.

Surgeons became more Important

1) In the Middle Ages, there were <u>two types</u> of surgeons. There was a small group of <u>professional surgeons</u>, who <u>trained</u> at university and were <u>highly paid</u> by their rich patients. Then there were unqualified <u>barber-surgeons</u> (see p.6). In general, surgeons <u>weren't respected</u> compared to doctors.

2) In the 1700s and 1800s, surgeons began to gain the same <u>status</u> as doctors.

> In 1800, the <u>London College of Surgeons</u> (later the Royal College of Surgeons) was created, which <u>set training standards</u> for surgeons for the first time.

John Hunter was a well-known Surgeon and Scientist

1) Hunter (1728-93) joined his brother William, a doctor, at his <u>anatomy school</u> in London where they <u>dissected human corpses</u>. Over 12 years, Hunter developed an <u>unrivalled knowledge</u> of the human body.

2) Hunter became an <u>army surgeon</u> and a popular <u>teacher</u>. He made several important <u>medical discoveries</u>. He learned more about <u>venereal disease</u> (sexually transmitted infection), a major cause of illness at the time, and introduced a new approach to the treatment of <u>gunshot wounds</u>.

3) In <u>1785</u>, Hunter introduced a <u>new</u> way to treat an <u>aneurysm</u> (a bulge in a blood vessel) in a man's thigh. He <u>tied off</u> the blood vessel to encourage blood to flow through <u>other vessels</u> in the leg, stopping it from having to be <u>amputated</u>.

4) Hunter encouraged <u>better approaches</u> to surgery. This included <u>good scientific habits</u> like <u>learning</u> about the <u>body</u> to understand illness, <u>experimenting</u> to find better ways to treat disease, and <u>testing</u> treatments (e.g. on <u>animals</u>) before using them on people.

> **Comment and Analysis**
>
> Hunter's <u>pupils</u> included doctors like <u>Edward Jenner</u> (see p.14), so his methods and ideas were <u>passed on</u>. This improved the way people conducted <u>scientific research</u>.

Hospitals focused more on Treatment and Learning

1) From the early 18th century, several <u>charity hospitals</u> opened, including The London Hospital and Guy's Hospital. They were funded by the <u>rich</u>, and offered <u>largely free</u> treatment to the poor. Some <u>specialised</u> in treating certain illnesses, or provided somewhere for mothers to <u>give birth</u>.

2) Only those who were likely to <u>recover quickly</u> were admitted. This was because of a <u>lack of space</u> and the risk of illnesses <u>spreading</u>. The '<u>deserving</u>' poor (those who led hardworking, respectable lives) had more chance of being admitted.

3) <u>Dispensaries</u> provided <u>free non-residential care</u> to poor people. <u>Medicines</u> and <u>non-surgical</u> services from people like <u>dentists</u> and <u>midwives</u> were given without charge.

4) Most poor people were treated in <u>workhouses</u> — large buildings that people went to if they couldn't look after themselves (e.g. because of unemployment, illness or old age). <u>Conditions</u> were <u>poor</u>, but from the 1850s a partially successful movement began to <u>improve conditions</u> in <u>workhouse infirmaries</u>.

5) In the 19th century, some hospitals were founded alongside <u>universities</u> or <u>medical schools</u>, including Charing Cross Hospital, University College Hospital and King's College Hospital. These hospitals were used as <u>training schools</u> for doctors, and for conducting <u>scientific research</u>.

6) <u>Cottage hospitals</u>, run by <u>GPs</u>, opened from the 1860s. They provided care for people in <u>rural</u> areas.

> **Comment and Analysis**
>
> Before the 18th century, many hospitals focused only on <u>caring</u> for people. In the 18th and 19th centuries, <u>treating</u> diseases became more important.

Hunter's ideas were surgeon up in the medical world...

Make some notes comparing surgery between 1500 and 1800 with surgery in medieval times. Keep adding to your notes as you read on — things got pretty fancy in the 20th century.

Developments in Nursing

Before the 1800s, hospitals were often <u>dirty</u> places that people associated with <u>death</u> and <u>infection</u>. <u>Florence Nightingale</u> helped change that — by improving <u>hospital hygiene</u> and raising <u>nursing standards</u>.

Florence Nightingale improved army hospitals

1) <u>Florence Nightingale</u> (1820-1910) brought a new <u>discipline</u> and <u>professionalism</u> to a job that had a very <u>bad reputation</u> at the time. Despite <u>opposition</u> from her family, she studied to become a nurse in <u>1849</u>.

2) When the <u>Crimean War</u> broke out in 1853-54, <u>horror stories</u> emerged about the <u>Barrack Hospital</u> in <u>Scutari</u>, where the British wounded were treated.

3) <u>Sidney Herbert</u>, who was both the <u>Secretary of War</u> and a friend of her family, asked for Nightingale to go to Scutari and sort out the hospital's <u>nursing care</u>.

4) The military <u>opposed</u> women nurses, as they were considered a distraction and inferior to male nurses. Nightingale went anyway, with <u>38 hand-picked nurses</u>.

5) Using methods she had learned from her training in Europe, Nightingale made sure that all the wards were <u>clean</u> and <u>hygienic</u>, that water supplies were adequate and that patients were fed properly.

6) Nightingale improved the hospital a lot. Before she arrived, the <u>death rate</u> in the hospital stood at <u>42%</u>. Two years later it had fallen to just <u>2%</u>.

> <u>Mary Seacole</u> (1805-1881) also nursed in the Crimea.
>
> 1) She learnt nursing from her mother, who ran a boarding house for soldiers in <u>Jamaica</u>.
>
> 2) In 1854, Seacole came to England to <u>volunteer</u> as a nurse in the Crimean War. She was rejected (possibly on <u>racist</u> grounds) but went anyway, paying for her <u>own</u> passage.
>
> 3) Financing herself by <u>selling goods</u> to the soldiers and travellers, she nursed soldiers on the <u>battlefields</u> and built the <u>British Hotel</u> — a small group of makeshift buildings that served as a hospital, shop and canteen for the soldiers.
>
> 4) Seacole couldn't find work as a <u>nurse</u> in England after the war and went <u>bankrupt</u> — though she did receive support due to the press interest in her story.

Nightingale used her fame to Change Nursing

1) In 1859, Nightingale published a book, '<u>Notes on Nursing</u>'. This explained her methods — it emphasised the need for hygiene and a professional attitude. It was the standard <u>textbook</u> for generations of nurses.

2) The public raised <u>£44,000</u> to help her <u>train nurses</u>, and she set up the <u>Nightingale School of Nursing</u> in <u>St. Thomas' Hospital</u>, London. Nurses were given three years of training before they could qualify. Discipline and attention to detail were important.

3) By <u>1900</u> there were <u>64,000</u> trained nurses in Britain from colleges across the country.

4) In <u>1919</u> (after Nightingale's death) the <u>Nurses Registration Act</u> was passed. This made training <u>compulsory</u> for all nurses.

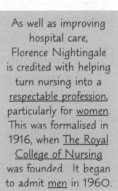

As well as improving hospital care, Florence Nightingale is credited with helping turn nursing into a <u>respectable profession</u>, particularly for <u>women</u>. This was formalised in 1916, when <u>The Royal College of Nursing</u> was founded. It began to admit <u>men</u> in 1960.

The 1800s also saw a massive increase in <u>hospital building</u>. Hospitals became <u>cleaner</u> and <u>more specialist</u>, catering for rich patients as well as the poor.

Comment and Analysis

The Germ Theory wasn't published until 1861, so initially Florence Nightingale <u>didn't know</u> what the cause of disease was — she believed in the <u>miasma theory</u>. But her teachings suggested that good <u>hygiene</u> could prevent the spread of disease.

Nightingale swooped in and improved the hospital...

Write a list of all of Florence Nightingale's achievements. At the end of your list, write a sentence explaining what you think was her most important achievement.

REVISION TASK

Anaesthetics

Improving the hygiene and sanitation of hospitals helped to prevent many unnecessary deaths. But the two problems of pain and infection were yet to be solved. The answer to the first of those was anaesthetics.

Anaesthetics solved the problem of Pain

Pain was a problem for surgeons, especially because their patients could die from the trauma of extreme pain. Natural drugs like alcohol, opium and mandrake had long been used, but effective anaesthetics that didn't make the patient very ill were more difficult to produce.

- Nitrous oxide (laughing gas) was identified as a possible anaesthetic by British chemist Humphry Davy in 1799 — but he was ignored by surgeons at the time.
- The gas had been dismissed as a fairground novelty before American dentist Horace Wells suggested its use in his area of work. He did a public demonstration in 1845, but had the bad luck to pick a patient unaffected by nitrous oxide — it was again ignored.

- In 1842, American doctor Crawford Long discovered the anaesthetic qualities of ether, but didn't publish his work. The first public demonstration of ether as an anaesthetic was carried out in 1846 by American dental surgeon William Morton.
- Ether is an irritant and is also fairly explosive, so using it in this way was risky.

- James Simpson was a Professor of Midwifery at Edinburgh University. Looking for a safe alternative to ether that women could take during childbirth, he began to experiment on himself. In 1847, he discovered the effects of chloroform.
- After Queen Victoria gave birth to her eighth child while using chloroform in 1853, it became widely used in operating theatres and to reduce pain during childbirth.
- Chloroform sometimes affected the heart, causing patients to die suddenly.

> General anaesthesia (complete unconsciousness) is risky, so local anaesthesia (numbing of the part being treated) is better for many operations. In 1884, William Halsted investigated the use of cocaine as a local anaesthetic. His self-experimentation led to a severe cocaine addiction.

Early Anaesthetics actually led to a Rise in death rates

1) Anaesthetics led to longer and more complex operations. This was because surgeons found that unconscious patients were easier to operate on, meaning they could take longer over their work.

2) Longer operating times led to higher death rates from infection, because surgeons didn't know that poor hygiene spread disease. Surgeons used very unhygienic methods.

- Surgeons didn't know that having clean clothes could save lives. Often they wore the same coats for years, which were covered in dried blood and pus from previous operations.
- Operations were often carried out in unhygienic conditions, including at the patient's house.
- Operating instruments also caused infections because they were usually unwashed and dirty.

Comment and Analysis

Anaesthetics helped solve the problem of pain, but patients were still dying from infection. This meant the attempts at more complicated surgery actually led to increased death rates amongst patients. The period between 1846 and 1870 is sometimes known as the 'Black Period' of surgery for this reason.

Anaesthetics revision — don't let it put you to sleep...

In the exam remember to be specific about the information you use. For example, rather than writing about anaesthetics in general terms, try to use specific types to explain your answer.

Health and Medicine in Britain, c.1000-present

Antiseptics

Anaesthetics had solved the problem of pain, but surgeons were still faced with a high death rate from operations due to the amount of infection. Antiseptics and later asepsis helped prevent this by killing germs.

Antisepsis and Asepsis reduce infection

There are two main approaches to reducing infection during an operation:

- Antiseptic methods are used to kill germs that get near surgical wounds.
- Aseptic surgical methods aim to stop any germs getting near the wound.

Joseph Lister pioneered the use of Antiseptics

1) Ignaz Semmelweis showed that doctors could reduce the spread of infection by washing their hands with chloride of lime solution between patients. However, it was very unpleasant, so wasn't widely used.

2) Joseph Lister had seen carbolic acid sprays used in sewage works to keep down the smell. He tried this in the operating theatre in the early 1860s and saw reduced infection rates.

3) Lister heard about the Germ Theory in 1865 — he realised that germs could be in the air, on surgical instruments and on people's hands. He started using carbolic acid on instruments and bandages.

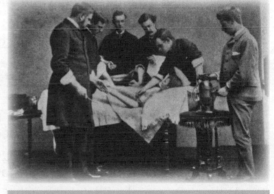

A photograph of a surgical operation taken in the late 1800s. You can see Lister's carbolic spray on the table on the right. The operating theatre isn't aseptic though — the surgeons aren't wearing sterile gowns or surgical gloves.

4) The use of antiseptics immediately reduced death rates from as high as 50% in 1864-66 to around 15% in 1867-70.

5) Antiseptics allowed surgeons to operate with less fear of patients dying from infection. The number of operations increased tenfold between 1867 and 1912 as a result.

Comment and Analysis

Antiseptics (and later asepsis) solved the problem of infection. This, combined with the use of anaesthetics (see p.18) to stop pain, improved British surgery — many deaths were prevented as a result of antiseptics and anaesthetics.

Asepsis reduced the need for Nasty Chemicals

Since the late 1800s, surgeons have changed their approach from killing germs to making a germ-free (aseptic) environment.

1) Instruments are carefully sterilised before use, usually with high temperature steam (120 °C).

2) Theatre staff sterilise their hands before entering — and wear sterile gowns, masks, gloves and hats. Surgical gloves were invented by William Halsted in 1889.

3) The theatres themselves are kept scrupulously clean and fed with sterile air. Special tents can be placed around the operating table to maintain an area of even stricter hygiene in high risk cases.

4) Aseptic surgery reduced the need for a carbolic spray, which is unpleasant to get on your skin or breathe in — many doctors and nurses didn't like to use it.

Make a Lister them facts — then germ up on them...

Write a paragraph summarising whether you think anaesthetics or antiseptics were a greater breakthrough for 19th century surgery.

REVISION TASK

Public Health

The industrial revolution began in the 18th century. Lots of people moved into cities like London to work in the factories. The places they lived were cramped, dirty and great for spreading diseases like cholera.

Overcrowding in Towns led to Poor Living Conditions

1) During the 18th and 19th centuries, lots of people moved from the countryside to towns to work in factories. The towns grew so quickly that good housing couldn't be built fast enough — instead, houses were built as close together as possible, with little outside space and poor ventilation.

2) Overcrowding was a big problem. Workers had little money, so tried to live in the smallest possible space — families with four or more children often lived in a single room. The poorest lived in cellars.

3) People didn't understand the need for clean water or good sewerage systems. Most houses had no bathroom — they instead shared an outside toilet, called a privy.

4) Each privy was built above a cesspit. Cesspit and household waste was collected by nightmen, who threw the waste into rivers or piled it up for the rain to wash away.

5) Water companies set up water pumps in the streets, which were shared between many houses. The pumps' water supply was often contaminated by waste from the cesspits or rivers.

Cholera epidemics Killed Thousands of people

1) Cholera reached Britain in 1831. By 1832 it was an epidemic — over 21,000 people in Britain died of cholera that year.

2) Cholera spreads when infected sewage gets into drinking water. It causes extreme diarrhoea — sufferers often die from loss of water and minerals. Both rich and poor people caught the disease.

3) At the time, people didn't know what caused cholera — the best theory was miasma (see p.3). The government started regulating the burial of the dead, but this did little to halt the spread of cholera. The 1832 epidemic declined and interest was lost.

4) Cholera epidemics recurred in 1848, 1853-54 and 1865-66.

Chadwick's Report led to the 1848 Public Health Act

1) In 1842, the social reformer Edwin Chadwick published a report on poverty and health. The report showed that living conditions in towns were worse for people's health than conditions in the countryside.

2) Chadwick's report suggested that the government should pass laws for proper drainage and sewerage systems, funded by local taxes.

3) Chadwick's report and another cholera epidemic in 1848 (which killed 53,000 people) put pressure on Parliament to pass a Public Health Act.

4) The 1848 Act set up a central Board of Health (which included Chadwick as a member) and allowed any town to set up its own local board of health as long as the town's taxpayers agreed.

Comment and Analysis

The impact of the 1848 Act was limited — towns could set up health boards but very few chose to, and those that did often refused to spend any money to improve conditions. Chadwick annoyed a lot of people, and was forced to retire in 1854. The central Board of Health was dismantled in 1858.

Snow linked Cholera to Contaminated Water

John Snow showed that there was a connection between contaminated water and cholera in 1853-54. He studied a cholera outbreak in the Broad Street area of London and noticed that the victims all used the same water pump. So he removed the handle from the pump and ended the outbreak.

Snow's work received little attention at first. Most people still believed diseases were spread by miasma ('bad air').

I hope you're not Bored of Health, as there's more to come...

Explain the differences between public health in the Middle Ages and public health during the industrial revolution. [8]

EXAM QUESTION

Public Health

Despite the work of Chadwick and Snow, public health <u>didn't improve</u> — <u>cholera returned</u> to Britain in 1865. But then, thanks to <u>several factors</u>, things began to change and the <u>government</u> took action.

The 'Great Stink' struck London in 1858

1) As in other towns, a lot of <u>waste</u> in London drained into <u>water sources</u>, including the <u>River Thames</u>.

2) In the summer of 1858, the hot weather caused the river's <u>water level to drop</u> and <u>bacteria</u> to grow in the waste. This produced a <u>smell</u> that was so bad it affected large parts of London and <u>stopped Parliament</u> from meeting.

3) To reduce the stink, engineer Joseph Bazalgette was appointed in <u>1859</u> to build a new London <u>sewer system</u>. The sewers transported waste that was normally dumped into the Thames away from heavily populated areas to the <u>Thames Estuary</u>. About 1300 miles of sewers were built.

4) The sewer system was officially opened in <u>1865</u>. Bazalgette's design became the blueprint for most cities in Western Europe.

Comment and Analysis

When Bazalgette started work on his sewers, people still <u>didn't understand</u> how diseases spread. They were trying to get rid of the <u>bad smells</u> coming from the Thames. The fact they stopped cholera by cleaning the drinking water was <u>unintended</u>.

Public Opinion began to Change

For most of the 19th century, people believed in a <u>laissez-faire</u> style of government — they thought the government <u>shouldn't intervene</u> in public health. But then things began to <u>change</u>.

1) Evidence from Chadwick and Snow (see p.20), and Pasteur's <u>Germ Theory</u> (see p.15), showed that cleaning towns could <u>stop</u> the spread of disease.

2) In 1867, the <u>Second Reform Act</u> was passed giving nearly <u>1 million more men</u> the vote, most of whom were industrial <u>workers</u>.

3) Several <u>reformers</u> helped <u>change attitudes</u> towards health. <u>William Farr</u> was a statistician who recorded <u>causes of death</u>. He used his statistics to press for reforms in areas where death rates were <u>high</u>.

> Now they had the vote, <u>workers</u> could put <u>pressure</u> on the government to listen to concerns about health. For the first time, politicians had to address workers' <u>concerns</u> in order to <u>stay in power</u>.

The 1875 Act improved Public Health

In the 1870s the government finally took action to improve public health.

1) In 1871-72, the government followed the Royal Sanitary Commission's proposal to form the <u>Local Government Board</u> and divide Britain into '<u>sanitary areas</u>' administered by officers for public health.

2) In 1875, <u>Benjamin Disraeli's</u> government passed another <u>Public Health Act</u>. It forced councils to appoint <u>health inspectors</u> and <u>sanitary inspectors</u> to make sure that laws on things like <u>water supplies</u> and <u>hygiene</u> were <u>followed</u>. It also made councils <u>maintain sewerage systems</u> and keep their towns' <u>streets clean</u>.

3) The 1875 Public Health Act was <u>more effective</u> than the one passed in 1848 because it was <u>compulsory</u>.

4) Disraeli also brought in the <u>Artisans' Dwellings Act</u> in 1875. This let local councils <u>buy slums</u> with poor living conditions and <u>rebuild them</u> in a way that fit new government-backed housing standards.

> <u>Few</u> councillors used the Artisans' Dwellings Act. An exception was <u>Joseph Chamberlain</u>, who became Mayor of <u>Birmingham</u> in 1873. Chamberlain persuaded the city authorities to buy the local <u>gas</u> and <u>water</u> companies to make sure people had <u>good supplies</u> of both. In <u>1875</u>, he cleared an area of the city's <u>slums</u> and built a <u>new street</u> in their place. He also <u>improved</u> some of the slum housing.

Comment and Analysis

There were several changes to public health during the industrial revolution, and the <u>1875 Public Health Act</u> was the biggest. The work of the <u>government</u> and <u>individuals</u> like Chadwick, Snow and Farr were key to these changes. <u>Technology</u> (like Bazalgette's sewers), the <u>1867 Reform Act</u> and the <u>cholera epidemics</u> were other factors that prompted improvement.

Turns out laissez-faire had made things less fair...

Write a list of the factors which led to the 1875 Public Health Act. For each factor, write a sentence explaining how that factor helped cause the Act.

Modern Ideas about the Causes of Disease

The Germ Theory (see p.15) was a major breakthrough in identifying the causes of disease, but identifying bacteria couldn't explain every disease. Viruses, genetics and lifestyle were all found to impact on health.

Viruses were discovered at the turn of the century

Despite their successes with bacteria, Pasteur and Koch (see p.15) were unable to find the cause of some diseases, as they were caused by microbes called viruses, which were too small to see under a microscope.

1) In 1892 the Russian microbiologist Dmitry Ivanovsky investigated mosaic, a disease that was killing tobacco plants. He found that the cause was an extremely small microbe that remained in water even after bacteria were removed. In 1898, the Dutch scientist Martinus Beijernick found that these microbes had different properties to bacteria — he labelled these microbes viruses.

2) The discovery of viruses led to their successful treatment. Unlike bacteria, viruses aren't destroyed by antibiotics (see p.24). Instead, doctors can prescribe antiviral drugs, but they only prevent a viral infection from growing — only the body's immune system can destroy a virus for good.

DNA has given an insight into Genetic Conditions

1) Genes are the chemical 'instructions' that plan out human characteristics, like sex and hair colour. They are stored in cells as DNA. Your DNA is a mix of your parents' DNA.

2) The structure of DNA, a double helix (a kind of spiral) that can reproduce itself by splitting, was first described in 1953 by Francis Crick and James Watson.

3) Watson and Crick's discovery allowed other scientists to find the genes that cause genetic conditions — diseases that are passed on from one generation to another. These include cystic fibrosis, haemophilia and sickle-cell anaemia.

4) Knowledge of genetic conditions has improved diagnosis and treatment of them. Scientists can now produce a synthetic protein to replicate the work of a faulty gene and treat inherited conditions using techniques like gene therapy.

The structure of DNA is a double helix.

One of the biggest breakthroughs in genetic research was made in 2003 with the completion of the Human Genome Project — this identified all the genes in human DNA.

Lifestyle Factors can increase the Risk of some Diseases

A healthy diet, exercise and other lifestyle factors have long been suggested as ways to prevent illness, but it was only in the 20th century that lifestyle choices were linked to particular health conditions:

1) Smoking has been shown to cause lung cancer (see p.31).
2) Obesity increases the chance of getting heart disease or diabetes.
3) Drinking too much alcohol has been shown to cause liver disease.
4) Overexposure to ultraviolet radiation (e.g. from sunlight) can cause skin cancer.

Comment and Analysis

The advances in science and technology since 1900 have shown that there is not just one cause of disease. In addition to bacteria, we now know that disease can be caused by viral infections, genetic mutations and our lifestyle choices. This makes their treatment and prevention even more complex — with so many different causes, treatment needs to be more targeted to the specific disease.

Watson and Crick described DNA — they're gene-iuses...

Make a list of the causes of illness that people didn't know about in 1875 but did know about in 2000. For each one, write the name of a disease it is associated with.

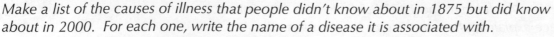

Developments in Diagnosis

New causes of disease demanded new ways of diagnosing them. These new methods were introduced rapidly in the 20th century, due to innovations in science and technology, from computers to X-rays.

Blood Tests allow doctors to Diagnose more illnesses

Blood tests were first introduced to test blood groups before blood transfusions (see p.26). Since then, blood tests have been used to test for a range of diseases.

1) Blood tests can be used to check a patient's cholesterol level. This can help diagnose their chance of suffering a heart attack or stroke.

2) Blood tests can be used to check a patient's DNA (see p.22). This can help diagnose a genetic condition, like haemophilia or cystic fibrosis.

3) Some blood tests can be used to show whether a patient has a certain type of cancer, including ovarian cancer, prostate cancer and breast cancer.

> Blood tests make diagnosis more accurate, providing doctors with clearer information of what is wrong. This means they can be more confident when deciding how best to treat their patients.

Doctors can see more of the body with Medical Scans

1) The use of medical scans began in 1895 when Wilhelm Röntgen discovered X-rays. They pass easily through soft flesh, but less well through bone. They also affect photographic film. These factors allowed simple X-ray images to be produced by directing X-rays at a body part in front of a photographic plate.

2) X-rays were used from the start of the First World War to find broken bones, but the equipment had glass tubes that were unreliable and often stopped working. The American scientist William Coolidge had invented a more reliable X-ray tube in 1913. The 'Coolidge tube' became widely used by the end of the war, and is still used today.

3) Advances in computers allowed doctors to use ultrasound scanning — this uses high frequency sound waves, which bounce off the patient's organs and other tissues to create an image of them on the computer.

4) Computed Tomography (CT or CAT) scans were invented in 1972 by Godfrey Hounsfield. They use X-rays and a computer to make detailed images of parts of the patient's body.

5) Magnetic Resonance Imaging (MRI) scans were initially invented in 1970s but became widely used in the 1980s. These use extremely powerful radio waves and magnetic fields to construct images.

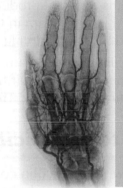

An X-ray image of a hand from 1904. Early medical scans used dyes so that blood vessels and organs showed up on the X-ray images. These were swallowed or injected into the patient.

Comment and Analysis

Improvements in technology, like medical scans, have given doctors a much more detailed picture of what's going on inside their patient's body. This has enabled them to intervene much earlier, before the disease has become too advanced. Early treatment is generally more effective and has a higher chance of success.

Patients can now Monitor their own bodies

Devices have been introduced to allow doctors and patients to monitor the body.

1) Blood pressure monitors were invented and developed in the 1880s and 1890s. They let doctors and patients see whether disease, lifestyle factors or medicines are causing high blood pressure, which can cause damage to the heart.

2) Blood sugar monitors were introduced in the mid 20th century. They allow those with diabetes to make sure their blood sugar is at the right level.

> An important change in the 20th century is the use of monitoring devices by people in their own homes — this has allowed individuals greater control over their own health.

I've taken an X-ray of my pet — I call it a cat scan...

In the exam, you only have a limited amount of time to answer each question. If you're spending too long on one question, write a conclusion then move on to the next question.

Penicillin

In the 1800s, Pasteur discovered that <u>bacteria</u> cause disease. But it wasn't until the 1900s that doctors were able to <u>treat</u> bacterial diseases. This was partly due to the discovery <u>penicillin</u>, the first <u>antibiotic</u>.

Fleming discovered Penicillin — the first Antibiotic

1) <u>Alexander Fleming</u> saw many soldiers die of septic wounds caused by <u>staphylococcal</u> bacteria when he was working in an army hospital during the <u>First World War</u>. Searching for a cure, he identified the <u>antiseptic</u> substance in tears, <u>lysozyme</u>, in 1922 — but this only worked on <u>some</u> germs.

2) One day in 1928, he came to clean up some old <u>culture dishes</u> on which he had been growing <u>staphylococci</u> for his experiments. By chance, a <u>fungal spore</u> had landed and grown on one of the dishes.

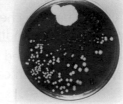

The original plate on which Fleming first observed the growth of Penicillium notatum.

3) What caught Fleming's eye was that the <u>colonies</u> of staphylococci around the <u>mould</u> had stopped growing. The <u>fungus</u> was identified as <u>Penicillium notatum</u>. It produced a substance that <u>killed</u> bacteria. This substance was given the name <u>penicillin</u>.

4) Fleming <u>published</u> his findings between 1929 and 1931. However, <u>nobody</u> would <u>fund</u> further research, so he <u>couldn't</u> take his work further. The industrial production of penicillin still needed to be developed.

Florey and Chain found a way to Purify Penicillin

1) Since it is a natural product, penicillin needs to be <u>purified</u>. A breakthrough was made by <u>Howard Florey's</u> team in Oxford between 1938 and 1940. <u>Ernst Chain</u>, a member of the team, devised the <u>freeze-drying</u> technique which was an important part of the purification process.

2) At first, Florey and Chain <u>didn't</u> have the <u>resources</u> to produce penicillin in large amounts. They made penicillin for their first <u>clinical trial</u> by growing <u>Penicillium notatum</u> in every container they could find in their lab. Their patient began to recover, only to die when the penicillin <u>ran out</u>.

Florey took penicillin to America for Mass Production

Florey knew that <u>penicillin</u> could be vital in treating the <u>wounds</u> of soldiers fighting in World War II. British <u>chemical firms</u> were too busy making <u>explosives</u> to start mass production — so he went to <u>America</u>.

1) US firms were also not keen to help — until America <u>joined the war</u> in 1941. In December 1941, the US government began to give <u>grants</u> to businesses that <u>manufactured</u> penicillin.

2) By 1943, British businesses had also started <u>mass-producing</u> penicillin. Mass production was sufficient for the needs of the <u>military medics</u> by 1944.

3) After the war, the <u>cost</u> of penicillin fell, making it more accessible for <u>general use</u>. Fleming, Florey and Chain were awarded the <u>Nobel Prize</u> in 1945.

> Today, penicillin is used to treat a <u>range</u> of <u>bacterial</u> infections. Other <u>antibiotics</u> were discovered after 1945, including treatments for lung infections, acne and bacterial meningitis.

Comment and Analysis

While <u>individuals</u> (like Florey, Chain and Fleming) were key in the discovery of penicillin, it was large institutions like <u>governments</u> that funded its mass production.

Antibiotic Resistance makes drugs like penicillin Less Effective

1) <u>Antibiotic resistance</u> is when a type of bacteria adapts so it <u>isn't affected</u> by antibiotics anymore. This resistance develops when doctors and patients <u>overuse</u> antibiotics.

2) Antibiotic resistance <u>stops</u> antibiotics from working properly, making it more difficult to treat some diseases. This has <u>increased</u> the <u>levels of disease</u> and the time taken for patients to recover.

Penicillin isn't just mould news — it's still used today...

How far do you agree that Alexander Fleming's discovery of penicillin was the most important moment in medicine since c.1900? Explain your answer. [16]

Modern Treatments

Scientists have found a range of other treatments for diseases, besides penicillin. These include magic bullets, which use chemical and synthetic substances to kill bacteria.

Paul Ehrlich discovered the first Magic Bullet — Salvarsan 606

Antibodies were identified as a natural defence mechanism of the body against germs. It was known that antibodies only attacked specific microbes — so they were nicknamed magic bullets. In 1889, Paul Ehrlich set out to find chemicals that could act as synthetic antibodies.

1) First, Ehrlich discovered dyes that could kill the malaria and sleeping sickness germs.

2) In 1905, the bacterium that causes the sexually transmitted disease syphilis was identified. Ehrlich and his team decided to search for an arsenic compound that was a magic bullet for syphilis. They hoped it would target the bacteria without poisoning the rest of the body. Over 600 compounds were tried, but none seemed to work.

3) In 1909, Sahachiro Hata joined the team. He rechecked the results and saw that compound number 606 actually appeared to work. It was first used on a human in 1911 under the trade name Salvarsan 606.

> **Comment and Analysis**
>
> Magic bullets showed that synthetic, targeted treatments were possible. Since Paul Ehrlich's first discovery, a huge pharmaceutical industry has grown, dedicated to researching and producing new treatments.

> After Ehrlich and Hata's discovery, more magic bullets were discovered. The second magic bullet, prontosil, was discovered by Gerhard Domagk in 1932. Prontosil was used to combat streptococcus, a type of bacteria that can cause blood poisoning.

The Pharmaceutical Industry has really taken off

For new treatments like magic bullets and antibiotics (like penicillin — see p.24) to make an impact, they needed to be made available to lots of people. This meant they had to be manufactured on a large scale.

1) In the late 19th and 20th centuries, the booming chemical industries in Britain, Germany, Switzerland and the United States were best placed to mass-produce these new drugs and medicines.

2) The success of their mass-produced drugs in the 1940s (particularly penicillin) helped the modern pharmaceutical industry take off.

3) Pharmaceutical companies have played an important role in researching and developing new medicines. They also mass produce these drugs to sell worldwide. These companies have been important in helping to cure new diseases and researching new forms of treatment:

> Chemotherapy is the treatment of cancer using drugs. It began to be developed during World War II when doctors found that nitrogen mustard (a chemical in mustard gas) could be used to reduce cancer tumours. Other drugs were later discovered, including a compound in folic acid that blocks the growth of cancer cells. Pharmaceutical companies have been producing cancer drugs since the 1960s.

Some people use Alternative Treatments

1) Mistrust of modern medicine and technology means some people use alternative therapies instead.
   - Acupuncture is the method of putting needles in specific points of the patient's skin to relieve pain.
   - Homeopathy is treatment using extremely weak solutions of natural substances.

2) Unlike mainstream treatments, alternative therapies aren't based on evidence gathered from scientific research. As a result, there is little scientific evidence that alternative treatments work effectively, and some doctors believe that they might do more harm than good.

3) However, some doctors are now working with alternative therapists to see if using a mix of alternative and mainstream medicine might result in benefits to the patient.

When it comes to magic bullets, Ehrlich hit the mark...

Write a paragraph describing the changes in treatment during the 20th century. Explain whether you think individuals or advances in technology were the most important factor.

Modern Surgery

Surgery improved rapidly during the 20th century. The discovery of <u>blood groups</u> made <u>blood transfusions</u> more successful, and even <u>heart transplants</u> are now possible. Nowadays the emphasis is on <u>precision</u>.

Blood Transfusions have solved the problem of Blood Loss

The idea of <u>blood transfusions</u> was known from the 17th century, but they were rarely successful because the blood of the recipient often <u>clotted</u>. Blood also clotted if it was stored <u>outside the body</u>.

1)   In 1900, <u>Karl Landsteiner</u> discovered <u>blood groups</u>. <u>Certain blood groups</u> can't be mixed as the blood will clot, <u>clogging</u> the blood vessels. He found that transfusions were <u>safe</u> as long as the patient's blood <u>matched</u> the blood donor's.

2)   In 1914, during World War I, doctors found that <u>sodium citrate</u> stopped blood clotting so it could be <u>stored</u> outside the body. In 1917, this discovery was vital when the first ever <u>blood bank</u> was set up at the Battle of Cambrai.

3)   In 1946, the <u>British National Blood Transfusion Service</u> was established.

> Patients always suffer some <u>blood loss</u> during <u>surgery</u>. If a lot of blood is lost, this can be <u>fatal</u>. Blood transfusions helped to <u>prevent</u> this cause of death by allowing surgeons to <u>replace</u> any blood lost during surgery.

Transplants have been made more Successful

1)   In 1905, the first successful <u>transplant</u> of the <u>cornea of the eye</u> was performed.

2)   During the First World War, surgeons developed <u>skin transplantation</u> techniques.

> <u>Harold Gillies</u> was interested in reconstructing <u>facial injuries</u> so that patients could have a <u>normal appearance</u>. He developed a skin graft technique called the <u>pedicle tube</u>, where <u>healthy skin</u> was used to cover scarring.

> The <u>First World War</u> (1914-1918) caused devastation in Europe, but it also had an impact on <u>surgery</u>. The soldiers' injuries gave surgeons the chance to find <u>new techniques</u> for carrying out <u>more complex operations</u>.

3)   The first complete organ to be successfully transplanted was the <u>kidney</u>. <u>Livers</u>, <u>lungs</u>, <u>pancreases</u> and <u>bone marrow</u> can now also be transplanted.

4)   The first successful <u>heart</u> transplant was carried out by the South African surgeon <u>Christiaan Barnard</u> in 1967. The patient only survived for <u>18 days</u> — he died of pneumonia.

5)   The problem for transplants is <u>rejection</u>. The <u>immune system</u> attacks the implant as if it were a virus.

> The success of early transplant operations was limited because doctors lacked effective <u>immunosuppressants</u> — drugs that <u>stop</u> the immune system attacking.

> Since the 1970s, researchers have developed <u>increasingly effective</u> immunosuppressants, making transplants <u>safer</u> and more likely to be <u>successful</u>.

New Types of Surgery increased Precision

1)   The development of <u>lasers</u> since the 1950s led to their widespread use in medicine in the 1980s. <u>Laser surgery</u> is used to correct <u>vision problems</u>, and lasers are also used in <u>cancer</u> treatment and <u>dentistry</u>.

2)   <u>Keyhole surgery</u> (developed in the 1980s) makes surgery <u>less invasive</u> — it leaves patients with smaller <u>scars</u> and allows them to <u>recover</u> more quickly.

3)   Keyhole surgery is useful for <u>investigating</u> the causes of pain or infertility. It's also used for vasectomies, removing cysts or the appendix, mending hernias and other minor operations.

> A type of surgical camera called an <u>endoscope</u> is put through a <u>small cut</u>, letting the surgeon <u>see inside</u> the body. Other surgical <u>instruments</u> are then introduced through even smaller cuts in the skin.

4)   <u>Robot-assisted surgery</u> has also improved precision.

> The first <u>surgical robot</u> was introduced in 1985, but robot-assisted surgery only became widely used after 2000 with the launch of the da Vinci system. Robot-assisted surgery allows surgeons to make <u>smaller</u> cuts. This means less <u>scarring</u>, less <u>infection</u> and <u>quicker healing</u> of wounds.

> These new types of surgery have made it <u>safer</u> for patients by limiting the possibility of <u>infection</u> and <u>blood loss</u>, as well as reducing the <u>shock</u> and <u>trauma</u> of surgery.

All you need to do is transplant these facts into your brain...

Explain why there were a lot of improvements in surgery between the end of 19th century and the end of the 20th century. [10]

EXAM QUESTION

The Liberal Reforms

In the 19th century, people believed government should have little involvement in public health. This all began to change after 1900, when the Liberal social reforms were introduced to deal with poverty.

Booth and Rowntree showed the effects of Poverty

1) Slums and other poor, overcrowded housing were still common in industrial towns in 1900. The poor worked long hours for low wages. Many people couldn't afford doctors or medicine — they could barely provide their children with three decent meals a day.

> There was no unemployment benefit, or pensions for the elderly. Workhouses were the only help — they provided basic food and lodging in exchange for working long hours in brutal conditions.

2) Two reports showed how widespread poverty was:

Booth's Report

Charles Booth's 1889 'Life and Labour of the People in London' showed that 30% of Londoners were living in severe poverty, and that it was sometimes impossible for people to find work, however hard they tried. He showed that some wages were so low they weren't enough to support a family.

Rowntree's Report

Seebohm Rowntree had a factory in York. He didn't believe the problem was as bad there as in London — so he did a survey of living conditions. His report, 'Poverty, a Study of Town Life' (published 1901), showed that 28% of people in York couldn't afford basic food and housing.

3) The lack of access to good healthcare meant that most people's health was pretty poor. When the Boer War broke out in 1899, army officers found that 40% of volunteers were physically unfit for military service — mostly due to poverty-related illnesses linked to poor diet and living conditions.

4) The government realised that it needed to improve basic healthcare in order to have an efficient army.

The Liberal Reforms improved health by tackling Poverty

Booth, Rowntree and the Boer War showed that there was a link between poverty and ill health. The newly-elected Liberal government and its Chancellor, David Lloyd George, realised it had to take action.

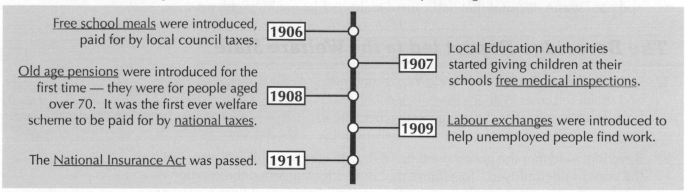

1906 — Free school meals were introduced, paid for by local council taxes.

1907 — Local Education Authorities started giving children at their schools free medical inspections.

1908 — Old age pensions were introduced for the first time — they were for people aged over 70. It was the first ever welfare scheme to be paid for by national taxes.

1909 — Labour exchanges were introduced to help unemployed people find work.

1911 — The National Insurance Act was passed.

The National Insurance Act introduced health insurance for workers — the worker, their employer and the government all contributed to a central fund that the workers could use for sick pay or to pay for a doctor.

Comment and Analysis

The Liberal reforms were the first real effort by the national government to improve people's living conditions as a way of improving their health. The reforms were a result of changing attitudes towards the role of government, and changed people's attitudes further.

'Doc, I feel poorly.' 'Try taking two shillings once a week...'

Create flashcards about the Liberal reforms — some with the dates and some with the names of the reforms. Match them up, then write a paragraph explaining why the reforms were important.

REVISION TASK

Public Health and the World Wars

After World War II, housing standards began to improve. The Beveridge Report argued that the state should provide support to people, resulting in the creation of the welfare state and the NHS.

The World Wars created Pressure for Social Change

The First World War (1914-1918) and the Second World War (1939-1945) broke down social distinctions and brought people together whose lives had been very separate.

1) Raising mass armies made government and military officials more aware of the health problems of the poor, because so many recruits were in poor health. Powerful people were more concerned with solving these health problems when at war, because of the need for a strong army to defend the country.

2) The evacuation of children during the Second World War increased awareness in richer rural communities of how disadvantaged many people were in other parts of the country.

3) After the Second World War, people looked for improvements in society. Such feelings led to the 1945 victory for the Labour Party, which promised healthcare for everyone and full employment.

Housing and Health Improved after the Second World War

1) Towards the end of the First World War, Prime Minister David Lloyd George promised to tackle poor-quality housing by building 'homes fit for heroes' to tackle bad housing. Some new council houses were built in the 1920s and 1930s, but many of them were too expensive for the poorest families, who still lived in slums.

2) During the Second World War, destruction from bombing and a lack of construction led to severe housing shortages, making the situation worse.

3) After the war, the Labour government built 800,000 homes between 1945-51. In 1946, it passed the New Towns Act — this created completely new towns near major cities. Governments in the 1950s and 1960s demolished over 900,000 old, cramped slums — around 2 million inhabitants were rehoused.

4) In 1961, a report called 'Homes for Today and Tomorrow' gave specific standards for new housing, including adequate heating, a flushing toilet and enough space inside and outside. This was the final step in tackling the issues of overcrowding, poor nutrition and poor waste disposal that had caused major public health problems.

The Beveridge Report led to the Welfare State

1) In 1942, during the Second World War, economist and social reformer William Beveridge published his famous report. The Beveridge Report became a bestseller — it was widely read and hugely popular.

> In his report, Beveridge called for the state provision of social security 'from the cradle to the grave.' Beveridge argued that all people should have the right to be free from want, disease, ignorance, squalor and idleness. He called these the five 'giants.'

2) Beveridge said that the government had a duty to care for all its citizens, not just the poor or unemployed. To achieve this, Beveridge suggested the creation of a welfare state — a system of grants and services available to all British citizens.

3) The 1945 Labour government was elected with the promise to implement Beveridge's proposals. One of their first acts was to pass a new National Insurance Act in 1946 to support anyone who couldn't work, whether as a result of sickness, pregnancy, unemployment or old age.

Comment and Analysis

The Labour Party's National Insurance Act went further than the one introduced by the Liberal government (see p.27) — anyone could apply for Labour's National Insurance without having to take a test to see if they were eligible.

Beveridge Report — nothing to do with your favourite drink...

Explain how significant the two world wars were for the improvement of housing and public health in Britain. [8]

EXAM QUESTION

The National Health Service

One of the most important changes in modern British medicine was the creation of the <u>NHS</u>.

The National Health Service was established in 1948

1) In 1948, the Labour government implemented Beveridge's last proposal — a <u>National Health Service</u>.

2) <u>Aneurin Bevan</u> was the Labour Minister for Health who, after a lot of negotiation, introduced the National Health Service (<u>NHS</u>). The government <u>nationalised hospitals</u> and put them under local authority control. Treatment was made <u>free for all patients</u>. There were arguments <u>for</u> and <u>against</u> the NHS:

For the NHS

- During World War Two the government took control of all hospitals, creating the <u>Emergency Medical Service</u>. Its <u>success</u> led many to support the creation of the NHS.
- The NHS would make medical care <u>free</u> so it was <u>accessible</u> to everyone.
- The NHS guaranteed that <u>hospitals</u> would receive <u>government money</u>, rather than having to rely on charities for money.

Against the NHS

- Many <u>Conservatives</u> opposed the NHS as they believed the <u>cost</u> would be huge.
- <u>Doctors</u> saw themselves as <u>independent</u> professionals — they <u>didn't</u> want to be <u>controlled</u> by the government. They also worried that they would <u>lose a lot of income</u>.
- Many doctors threatened to go on <u>strike</u> in protest against the NHS.

The government finally <u>convinced doctors</u> by offering them a <u>payment</u> for each patient and letting them continue treating <u>fee-paying patients</u>.

The NHS was Very Popular

1) Although many <u>Conservatives</u> were <u>opposed</u> to the creation of the NHS, they <u>couldn't abolish it</u> when they came back into power in 1951 — it was too <u>popular</u>.

2) The NHS <u>increased</u> the number of people with access to healthcare — the number of doctors <u>doubled</u> between 1948 and 1973 to keep up with demand.

3) Today, the NHS provides a range of health services, most of which are <u>free</u> and <u>accessible</u> to everyone. They include <u>accident and emergency</u> care, <u>maternity</u> care and major <u>surgery</u>, as well as <u>pharmacies</u>, <u>dentists</u>, <u>mental health</u> services, <u>sexual health</u> services and general practitioners (<u>GPs</u>).

In the long term, the NHS has contributed to a dramatic <u>improvement</u> in people's health and a rise in <u>life expectancy</u>. In 1951, men could expect to live to 66 and women to 72 — by 2011 this had risen to 79 for men and 83 for women.

Today the NHS faces several Challenges

1) The increase in <u>life expectancy</u> means there are many more <u>older people</u> in Britain today than there were in 1948, who are more likely to suffer from <u>long-term conditions</u> like diabetes and heart disease. They need <u>regular medical attention</u> and require a lot of NHS time and resources.

2) Many people's <u>lifestyle choices</u> are putting strain on the NHS. <u>Smoking</u>, <u>obesity</u> and <u>alcohol consumption</u> can all harm people's health and may require expensive treatment — for example, smoking can cause <u>lung cancer</u> and drinking too much alcohol can cause serious <u>liver disease</u>.

3) Many modern treatments, equipment and medicines are very <u>expensive</u>, and the NHS has had to face <u>rising expectations</u> of what it can and should offer.

4) As a result of all these factors, the <u>cost</u> of the NHS is rising rapidly — in 2015/16 the NHS budget was <u>£116 billion</u> overall. In order to stay within its budget, the NHS sometimes has to make difficult <u>choices</u> about which treatments it can and can't provide.

A 2015 poll suggested that around <u>60%</u> of British people are <u>satisfied</u> with the NHS, showing that it is still relatively <u>popular</u>.

Sadly the NHS doesn't offer an exam revision service...

Split your page in two. On one side, write down the successes of the NHS. On the other side, write down the problems and challenges it faces.

The Government's Role in Healthcare

Since 1900, the <u>government's role</u> in improving people's health has <u>grown and grown</u>.

Vaccination Campaigns have eradicated some Diseases

Since 1900, the government has launched several national <u>vaccination</u> programmes to <u>prevent</u> people from catching deadly diseases. These have been <u>successful</u> in reducing the number of deaths from such diseases.

<u>Diphtheria</u> is a contagious disease that is caused by bacteria in the <u>nose</u> and <u>throat</u>. It can eventually attack the heart muscles, causing <u>paralysis</u> or <u>heart failure</u>.

- Before the 1940s, diphtheria was a major killer disease — in 1940, there were over <u>60,000 cases</u> of the disease and over <u>3,000 deaths</u>.

- After fears that wartime conditions could lead to the spread of the disease, the government started a <u>vaccination campaign</u> in 1940.

- The government ran <u>publicity campaigns</u>, using posters, newspaper advertisements and radio broadcasts.

- The campaign was a success — by 1957, the number of diphtheria cases had dropped to just <u>38</u>, with only <u>six deaths</u>.

> In 1940, the easiest way to reach children was through <u>schools</u>, so <u>5-15 year olds</u> were vaccinated more than the youngest children who were most vulnerable. The establishment of the <u>NHS</u> in <u>1948</u> (see p.29) allowed the government to vaccinate <u>all</u> children by their <u>first birthday</u>.

<u>Polio</u> is an infection that can attack the digestive system, bloodstream and nervous system. The disease can cause <u>paralysis</u>, and particularly affects <u>children</u>.

- In the late 1940s and early 1950s, Britain suffered a series of polio <u>epidemics</u> — the disease made over 30,000 children disabled between 1947 and 1958.

- The first vaccine was introduced in Britain in 1956 alongside a <u>national campaign</u>, aiming to vaccinate every person <u>under the age of 40</u>.

- The campaign was successful, with the disease all but <u>eradicated</u> by the late 1970s. In the period 1985-2002, only <u>40 polio cases</u> were reported in Britain.

Lifestyle Campaigns aim to improve people's Health

In the 20th century, scientists showed a link between people's <u>lifestyle choices</u> and their <u>health</u> (see p.22). The government ran several <u>campaigns</u> to make people aware of the dangers and to <u>change</u> their <u>lifestyles</u>.

1) In 1952, a <u>Great Smog</u> caused by coal fires resulted in <u>4,000 deaths</u> in London. It showed the dangers of <u>air pollution</u>, which can cause breathing conditions like <u>asthma</u> and <u>bronchitis</u>. The government passed laws in the hope of limiting air pollution.

2) An increase in <u>less active lifestyles</u> has led to an increase in <u>obesity</u>. In 2009, the government launched the <u>Change4Life</u> campaign, with the aim of <u>improving diets</u> and <u>promoting daily exercise</u>.

3) Excessive <u>alcohol</u> intake has been linked to several diseases, most notably <u>liver cirrhosis</u>. Alcohol intake <u>rose</u> between 1950 and 2004, but has since <u>fallen</u>. This may be due to the government's <u>Drinkaware</u> campaign, launched in 2004. The Drinkaware logo appears on many alcohol advertisements.

Comment and Analysis

These campaigns mark a <u>big shift</u> in the government's approach from the foundation of the NHS, and an even bigger shift from the <u>laissez-faire attitudes</u> of the 19th century, when people thought government shouldn't intervene at all in public health. Not only is the government trying to <u>treat</u> and <u>vaccinate against</u> known diseases, it is now <u>intervening in people's lives</u> in order to stop them getting particular illnesses in the first place.

My free speech campaign is getting everybody talking...

Draw a mind map of all of the ways the government has tried to improve health and medicine in Britain since 1900. Include vaccinations, lifestyle campaigns and the NHS in your diagram.

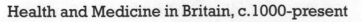

Lung Cancer

<u>Lung cancer</u> is a disease that was <u>much more common</u> after 1900 than before. The battle against lung cancer is an example of <u>science and technology</u> and <u>government campaigns</u> working side by side.

Lung Cancer can be caused by Smoking

1) Lung cancer was a rare disease in 1900, but became common by the 1940s. Today, around <u>20%</u> of all <u>cancer deaths</u> in the UK are due to lung cancer. Approximately <u>43,500</u> people are diagnosed <u>every year</u>.

2) Scientists have estimated that around 90% of lung cancer cases can be linked to <u>tobacco smoking</u>. The popularity of smoking increased during the <u>First World War</u>, particularly among soldiers. Smoking soon became popular among women too.

3) In 1950, the <u>link between smoking and lung cancer</u> was proven by Richard Doll and Austin Bradford Hill.

Lung cancer Diagnostics and Treatment have Improved

Advances in <u>science and technology</u> have made it easier to <u>diagnose</u> and <u>treat</u> lung cancer.

- <u>Chest X-rays</u> are the first means of diagnosing lung cancer. The X-rays can't show whether the patient definitely has cancer, but can show if there is anything on the lung that <u>shouldn't be there</u>.
- <u>CT scans</u> (see p.23) can be used to give a more <u>detailed</u> image of the lungs.
- Doctors can now use <u>bronchoscopy</u> to diagnose lung cancer. This involves putting a <u>thin tube</u> into the lungs to take a sample of the suspected cells. It requires a <u>local anaesthetic</u> to numb the throat.

- Lung cancer can be treated using <u>surgery</u>, for example by <u>removing</u> the affected lung.
- Modern treatments like <u>radiotherapy</u> and <u>chemotherapy</u> (see p.25) are also used to treat lung cancer. Radiotherapy involves directing <u>radiation</u> at the lungs. Lung cancer chemotherapy uses a <u>combination</u> of several drugs, which are normally injected directly into the <u>bloodstream</u>.

Government Campaigns have reduced smoking

When the link between <u>smoking</u> and lung cancer became clear, the government warned people of the risks.

1) In 1962, the <u>Royal College of Physicians</u> recommended a ban on tobacco advertising. Shortly afterwards, in 1965, <u>cigarette adverts were banned</u> from television. In 1971, tobacco companies were forced to put a <u>health warning</u> on cigarette packets.

2) In recent years, the government has put a <u>ban on smoking in public places</u> — this was introduced in Scotland in 2006, and in England and Wales in 2007.

3) Recent government campaigns have focused on helping people to <u>give up smoking</u> and on discouraging smoking in cars, homes and in front of children.

4) In March 2015, Parliament passed a law requiring all cigarette companies to use <u>plain packaging</u> on boxes of cigarettes.

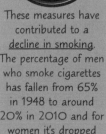

These measures have contributed to a <u>decline in smoking</u>. The percentage of men who smoke cigarettes has fallen from 65% in 1948 to around 20% in 2010 and for women it's dropped from 41% to 20% in the same period.

Comment and Analysis

Lung cancer prevention is a good example of an area of health where the government has been increasingly <u>active</u> — the large number of <u>television campaigns</u> and pieces of <u>legislation</u> show that the government is now taking health seriously, which is in contrast to its attitude before 1900.

Dreams of a healthy lifestyle went up in smoke...

'Lung cancer is more common now than it was in 1900. This shows that there has been little improvement in medicine in the 20th century.' Explain how far you agree with this statement. [16]

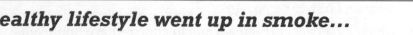

Revision Summary

Well, that was a healthy amount of information to revise. Now treat yourself to these revision questions.
* Try these questions and <u>tick off each one</u> when you <u>get it right</u>.
* When you've done <u>all the questions</u> for a topic and are <u>completely happy</u> with it, tick off the topic.

Medicine in Medieval England, c.1000-c.1500 (p.2-8) ☑

1) Give two supernatural causes of disease believed by people in medieval Britain. ☑
2) Briefly describe two natural explanations for disease believed by people in medieval Britain. ☑
3) Describe two medical discoveries made by Islamic doctors. ☑
4) Name six treatments for disease used by people in medieval Britain. ☑
5) List three types of people you might visit if you felt ill in medieval Britain. ☑
6) List two approaches to health in towns and two approaches to health in monasteries. ☑
7) Give three ways people tried to prevent the spread of the Black Death. ☑

The Medical Renaissance in England, c.1500-c.1700 (p.9-13) ☑

8) What was Vesalius' discovery and why did it help improve surgery? ☑
9) Explain why Thomas Sydenham was important in Renaissance medicine. ☑
10) What did Harvey discover and why did he have a limited impact on diagnosis and treatment? ☑
11) Describe how Paré found a better way to treat wounds. ☑
12) Describe the impact of the printing press on people's understanding of medicine. ☑
13) How did the Royal Society change perceptions of medicine? ☑
14) List five ways in which there was continuity between medieval and Renaissance medical treatments. ☑
15) List four treatments and four prevention methods people used against the Great Plague in 1665. ☑

Medicine in 18th and 19th Century Britain, c.1700-c.1900 (p.14-21) ☑

16) List three reactions by Parliament to Jenner's discovery of the smallpox vaccine. ☑
17) In what year did Louis Pasteur publish the Germ Theory? ☑
18) Explain how Florence Nightingale changed nursing. ☑
19) Name the year that chloroform was discovered and explain why it led to a higher death rate initially. ☑
20) What is the difference between antisepsis and asepsis? ☑
21) Describe John Snow's 1854 investigation and explain what he showed. ☑
22) Give three things that the 1875 Public Health Act forced local councils to do. ☑

Medicine in Modern Britain, c.1900-Present (p.22-31) ☑

23) Describe three causes of disease that have been discovered since Pasteur's Germ Theory. ☑
24) What did Watson and Crick discover in 1953 and how did it help medical diagnosis? ☑
25) When were X-rays discovered? How are they used in medical diagnosis? ☑
26) Explain how the following individuals or institutions contributed to the production of penicillin: Fleming, Florey and Chain, the United States government. ☑
27) Name the first two magic bullets, who discovered them and the dates they were discovered. ☑
28) State three ways in which housing and public health were improved as a result of World War II. ☑
29) Describe two government lifestyle campaigns. ☑
30) Give five ways in which lung cancer diagnosis and treatments have improved. ☑
31) List four ways that the government has tried to reduce smoking. ☑

North American Geography

Knowing a bit about the geography of America is really important to understanding this topic.

Many US citizens wanted to settle land in the West

North America can be divided into several different geographical regions. European settlers initially lived only on the east coast, leaving many regions of America unsettled.

Originally there were 13 British colonies along the east coast (p.34). Westward expansion began almost immediately.

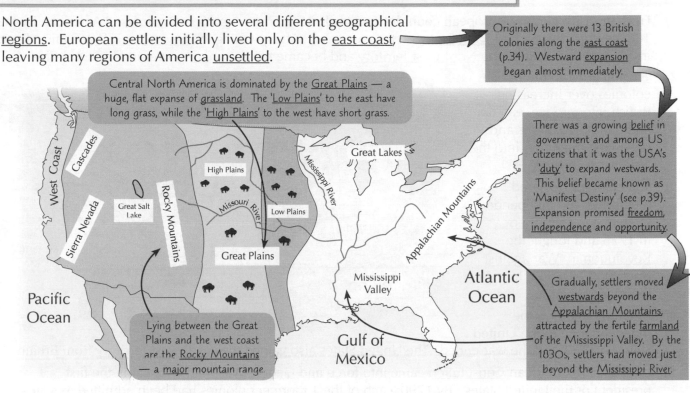

Central North America is dominated by the Great Plains — a huge, flat expanse of grassland. The 'Low Plains' to the east have long grass, while the 'High Plains' to the west have short grass.

There was a growing belief in government and among US citizens that it was the USA's 'duty' to expand westwards. This belief became known as 'Manifest Destiny' (see p.39). Expansion promised freedom, independence and opportunity.

Lying between the Great Plains and the west coast are the Rocky Mountains — a major mountain range.

Gradually, settlers moved westwards beyond the Appalachian Mountains, attracted by the fertile farmland of the Mississippi Valley. By the 1830s, settlers had moved just beyond the Mississippi River.

Geographical Obstacles separated the East from the West Coast

The west coast was attractive to settlers. The land is fertile and it has a temperate climate — temperatures don't vary hugely between summer and winter. But between would-be settlers and the west coast were the Great Plains and other geographical obstacles.

The Great Plains have a hostile climate...

- The Great Plains become drier and more desert-like the further south you go. US citizens didn't think they could live on the Great Plains — they called it the 'Great American Desert'.

- The mountains on either side of the Plains produce rain shadows (regions with little rain). You often get droughts in the summer and severe snow in the winter.

- Being so far from the sea means there's a huge difference in temperature between summer and winter.

There was a widespread view among the white settlers that the Great Plains were wild and harsh — many believed they were unsuitable for living and farming because of the extremes of weather, sparse rainfall and hard ground. However, attitudes towards the Plains would later change (see p.39 and p.50). Understanding these changing attitudes is important for understanding America's expansion.

The Rocky Mountains form a barrier across America...

- The slopes on either side of the Rockies are heavily wooded — especially in the South.

- At the centre of the Rockies is the Plateaux region. It's fairly flat but has areas of desert. Water can get trapped here, only escaping by evaporation. This has created the Great Salt Lake (see p.41).

You'd better learn the geography — or you're history...

Yep, you're still studying history, but geography was really important in the story of the expansion of the USA. So make sure you learn it to show you have a good grasp of the topic in the exam.

Early Territorial Expansion

When America gained independence from Britain in 1783, westward expansion began almost immediately.

Most of the American population used to live along the East Coast

1) From the 15th century, European countries such as Britain, France and Spain colonised America. By the 18th century, Britain had 13 colonies on the east coast. After winning the Seven Years' War against France in 1763, Britain gained the Northwest Territory and became the dominant power in North America.

2) Tension grew in the British colonies over increasing British interference, e.g. tax and trade regulations and outlawing migration into the Northwest Territory.

3) The colonies declared themselves the independent United States of America in 1776 and fought the Revolutionary War against Britain (1775-1783) to gain their independence.

4) Britain recognised the independence of the United States in 1783 and the war ended. The United States also gained the Northwest Territory from Britain.

5) In 1789, the American Constitution came into force and George Washington became the first president of the United States. By 1790, each of the 13 former colonies had been admitted as states.

The Northwest Ordinance of 1787 agreed that in time the Northwest Territory should be cut up into states and that these should be admitted to the Union (the United States of America).

Comment and Analysis

The Northwest Ordinance was important because it laid out plans for westward expansion into the Northwest Territory (Ohio was the first state to be created in the Territory). It also established a process for adding new states to the Union.

The Louisiana Purchase Doubled the size of America

1) In 1803, the US bought the Louisiana Territory from France — it covered over 800,000 square miles of land, but its boundaries weren't clear. It was a vast amount of land — all or part of 15 states would be formed from it.

The US claimed that the Louisiana Purchase included West Florida, which belonged to Spain — but Spain disagreed. In 1810, the people of West Florida revolted against Spanish rule — US soldiers occupied the area and President Madison declared it to be part of the US. Spain officially gave Florida to the US in the Adams-Onis Treaty of 1819.

2) The Louisiana Purchase encouraged westward migration. Settlers had already started to move westwards, but the Purchase provided even more land for people to settle on.

3) It gave the US control of the Mississippi River, which was important for trade, especially as the nation expanded westwards.

Comment and Analysis

The Louisiana Purchase helped the US establish itself as a nation. The Louisiana Territory was a huge amount of land, which increased the confidence of the USA and its power on the world stage.

4) President Thomas Jefferson commissioned the Lewis and Clark Expedition in 1803 to explore the Louisiana Territory and the land beyond. The group reached the west coast in 1805 and returned with their findings.

The expedition resulted in greater geographic and scientific knowledge of the West.

Justifies giving Independence Day another watch I reckon...

Try scribbling down a map of America without looking at the maps on pages 33-35.
Label the main regions and write a little about each one, using the information you can remember.

Early Territorial Expansion

A second war with Britain in 1812 made expansion <u>easier</u> for the US. Many US citizens <u>supported</u> expansion.

War Weakened Native American Resistance to western expansion

1) America <u>declared war</u> on Britain in <u>1812</u>. The government was angry that the British were <u>restricting</u> American trade, <u>forcing</u> American sailors to join the British Navy and <u>supporting</u> the Native American fight against western expansion.

> America <u>asserted</u> itself during the war — it was seen as a <u>second war of independence</u>.

2) The war ended in 1815. There was <u>no clear winner</u> and neither side <u>lost territory</u> — the <u>Treaty of Ghent</u> agreed to return things to how they were <u>before</u> the war.

3) However, <u>Native Americans</u> in the East were <u>badly affected</u> by the war:

- Native Americans felt <u>threatened</u> by westward expansion. Britain <u>supported</u> them in halting expansion, but at the end of the war Britain <u>withdrew</u> this support.
- The Shawnee war chief <u>Tecumseh</u> managed the difficult task of <u>uniting</u> different Indian tribes. But he <u>died</u> helping the British in the war and there was no-one to replace him.

Comment and Analysis

After the war, the Native Americans were <u>less able</u> to resist expansion — they were no longer united and had lost their external ally. Following Tecumseh's death, the USA made more than <u>200 treaties</u> with eastern tribes, which resulted in the tribes <u>losing</u> their <u>land</u>.

White Americans wanted to Expand Westwards

1) The US government and American people increasingly believed that it was America's <u>duty</u> to expand westwards. Thomas <u>Jefferson</u>, president from 1801-1809, believed that land ownership and farming would create a <u>healthy</u>, <u>virtuous</u> population. To American people, expansion promised <u>freedom</u>, <u>independence</u> and <u>opportunity</u>.

> The population of America was <u>growing</u> — people wanted <u>more</u> land to farm.

2) Better <u>transport links</u> were created which enabled western expansion.

- Construction of the 620 mile long <u>National Road</u> began in 1811, connecting the <u>east coast</u> to <u>Illinois</u>.
- The 353 mile long <u>Eerie canal</u> opened in 1825, connecting <u>New York</u> to the <u>Great Lakes</u>.

3) These transport links connected <u>farmers</u> who had moved westwards with <u>markets</u> in the <u>East</u>, creating profit-making opportunities for them.

> <u>Steamboats</u>, introduced in 1807, provided faster transportation along waterways.

4) <u>New technology</u> also made farming <u>profitable</u> and <u>attracted</u> settlers to move westwards, e.g. the <u>mechanical grain reaper</u> was invented in 1831, which allowed farmers to harvest crops more <u>efficiently</u>.

By 1838, <u>26 states</u> had been created from territory belonging to the United States.

Things were already going badly for the Native Americans...

Make a timeline of the important events from 1789 to 1838. If you're feeling adventurous, keep adding to it throughout this section all the way up to 1900 — you know you want to.

REVISION TASK

Cotton Plantations and Slavery

As cotton became more and more <u>profitable</u>, cotton plantations and slavery <u>expanded</u> in the South.

Cotton and slavery Weren't always Dominant in the South

1) <u>Plantations</u> were established in the South of America in the <u>17th century</u>. Plantations were large farms which harvested crops such as <u>sugar</u>, <u>tobacco</u> and <u>cotton</u> — these were <u>labour intensive</u> crops, so <u>large</u> numbers of workers were needed to harvest them.

2) At first, <u>indentured servants</u> were the main source of labour on these plantations, but they were gradually replaced by <u>African slaves</u>. Plantation owners got these slaves through the <u>Atlantic slave trade</u> — Africans were <u>forced</u> into slavery and <u>transported</u> to America on ships where they would be <u>bought</u> at market.

> Indentured servants agreed to work for a certain number of <u>years</u> in return for <u>passage</u> to America from <u>overseas</u>.

3) <u>Tobacco</u> was more profitable than cotton in the <u>18th century</u>. Cotton picking was a <u>time consuming</u> business — the cotton fibres had to be separated from the seeds <u>by hand</u>.

Technology increased the importance of Cotton and Slavery

1) Britain experienced an <u>industrial revolution</u> in the early 19th century. New <u>machines</u> were developed which allowed factories to <u>process</u> much <u>more</u> cotton. As a result, <u>demand</u> for cotton in Britain <u>increased</u> enormously, which meant US planters could <u>export</u> much larger quantities of cotton to Britain.

2) In the US, the <u>mechanical cotton gin</u> was invented by Eli Whitney in 1793. It removed the cotton fibre from the seeds <u>mechanically</u>.

> Cotton fuelled <u>westward expansion</u> because people wanted <u>more land</u> to farm cotton.

3) The cotton gin hugely increased the <u>speed</u> at which cotton on plantations could be processed. This allowed planters to <u>expand</u> their cotton production. They increased their labour force, which resulted in the <u>expansion</u> of <u>slavery</u>.

4) Cotton became the South's <u>most important crop</u> — the economy of the South came to <u>rely</u> upon cotton <u>exports</u> and the South became <u>dependent</u> on slavery.

> The end of the Atlantic <u>slave trade</u> in <u>1808</u> meant that the price of existing slaves in the US <u>increased</u>. (Although the slave trade ended, slavery and slave trading <u>continued</u> in the USA.)

5) Only a <u>small</u> number of <u>wealthier</u> southerners owned plantations and slaves, but many southerners saw slavery as part of their <u>way of life</u> — they called it their 'peculiar institution'.

Slaves were Treated Badly on plantations

1) Many white Americans saw black Africans as <u>inferior</u> to white people. African slaves were seen as <u>property</u> of the planters and had <u>no rights</u> or <u>freedom</u>.

2) <u>Cheap</u> labour was needed for plantations to be <u>profitable</u>, which meant that slaves had <u>poor living conditions</u>. They worked <u>long</u>, <u>hard hours</u>, were <u>not fed well</u> and lived in small, poorly built <u>cabins</u>.

3) Treatment of slaves on plantations <u>varied</u>, but was often <u>inhumane</u> and <u>cruel</u>. Owners tried to maintain <u>strict discipline</u> of slaves by <u>whipping</u> and <u>beating</u> them. <u>Sexual abuse</u> of female slaves was common.

> <u>Frederick Douglass</u> was a slave who was born on a plantation in 1818. He <u>taught himself</u> to read and write and managed to <u>escape</u> to the North where slavery was banned. His autobiography is a <u>useful source</u> for showing the <u>treatment</u> of slaves — he writes about his <u>separation</u> from his mother at an early age and the <u>brutal whippings</u> and <u>beatings</u> he suffered on one plantation.

Comment and Analysis

It's important to recognise slaves' efforts to <u>resist</u> this inhumane treatment. Some <u>ran away</u> and some even <u>rebelled</u>. Others worked <u>slowly</u>, <u>damaged</u> farm machinery and kept African <u>culture</u> alive through religion and music.

> Plantation owners tried to keep slaves like Douglass in <u>ignorance</u> by not allowing them to learn to <u>read</u> or <u>write</u>.

Cotton plantations and slavery went hand-in-hand...

It's important to understand the relationship between the expansion of cotton and the expansion of slavery. The success of cotton meant that slavery became a way of life in the South.

The Removal of Indigenous People from the East

A number of Native American tribes lived on land in the East which US citizens wanted to settle and farm on.

Washington aimed to 'Civilise' eastern Native American tribes

1) President George Washington pursued a policy of 'civilising' Native Americans living east of the Great Plains — many US citizens saw Native American society as inferior and savage and believed that they needed to be taught how to live like white settlers.

2) Washington claimed he wanted to respect the Native Americans' right to their homeland as long as they assimilated into society.

> This meant changing their lifestyle to fit in with that of white Americans.

3) Five tribes were considered 'civilised' as a result of this policy, because they took on aspects of white culture — the Cherokee, Chicksaw, Choctaw, Creek and Seminole.

Jackson Moved eastern tribes onto the Great Plains

1) Some of the land that settlers wanted to farm was occupied by Native American tribes. The five 'civilised' tribes lived on land in the South, which settlers wanted for growing cotton. Settlers harassed these Indian tribes and pressured the government to take their tribal land.

> The Cherokee lived in European-style houses and published their own newspaper, but people still didn't see them as equal.

2) In 1830, the Indian Removal Act was passed under President Andrew Jackson — this authorised the president to grant tribes land on the Great Plains in exchange for their land in the East. Jackson claimed that it would benefit the tribes to be moved away from settlers where they could live in peace.

3) The Removal Act was supposed to be voluntary, but when some tribes in the south-east resisted, the US government forced them to leave:

- The Cherokee resisted removal through legal means, but they were eventually forcefully marched by US soldiers to the Plains in 1838. It was winter and it's been estimated that 4000 Cherokee out of around 15,000 died on the march. This journey became known as the Trail of Tears.

- The Seminole fought a guerilla war against the US army from 1835-42. The war was costly for both sides, but the Seminole eventually surrendered and were moved onto the Plains.

4) By 1840, most of the eastern tribes had been moved onto the Plains — around 70,000-100,000 people in total.

5) The intention was that Native Americans would live on the Great Plains, while settlers farmed land in the East — the Plains would be like one large Indian reservation. The boundary between the two regions was known as the Permanent Indian Frontier.

6) At this point, white Americans viewed the Plains as 'The Great American Desert'. They believed that its harsh climate and lack of wood and water made it unsuitable for settling.

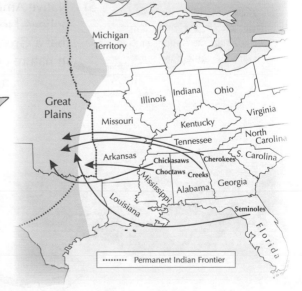

Comment and Analysis

The government gave the Native Americans the Great Plains, but only because white settlers didn't want the land themselves. Because they saw Native Americans as inferior, they felt it was acceptable to give them land they themselves didn't think was fit to live on.

'Here you are, you can have this lovely desert to live in...'

Use this page to understand how and why the Permanent Indian Frontier was created. It was actually a lot less permanent than the name suggests... more about this later.

EXAM TIP

The Plains Indians

Other Native American tribes already lived on the Great Plains — they're known as the <u>Plains Indians</u>.

The Plains Indians lived in different groups called Tribes

1) The Plains Indians weren't a single group with a single culture — there were many <u>different</u> tribes.

2) These tribes had things in <u>common</u>, but they were <u>diverse</u> in appearance, lifestyle and language.

> E.g. The <u>Cheyenne</u> led a <u>nomadic</u> lifestyle — they regularly moved from place to place, following the buffalo which they hunted for food. In contrast, the <u>Mandan</u> farmed and lived in <u>permanent</u> villages.

The Plains Indians led Very Different Lifestyles to white settlers

The <u>Lakota Sioux</u> are an example of a nomadic Plains Indian tribe who lived very <u>differently</u> to settlers. They had broadly <u>similar</u> beliefs and practices to other nomadic Plains Indian tribes.

1) The Lakota Sioux were the <u>largest</u> of the <u>three</u> Sioux-speaking tribes and were split into <u>seven bands</u>. Each band had a <u>chief</u> and a <u>council</u> of elders. The chief didn't have complete control, but he would have earned <u>loyalty</u> over the years by demonstrating <u>courage</u> and <u>generosity</u> — this gave him <u>influence</u> over the tribe.

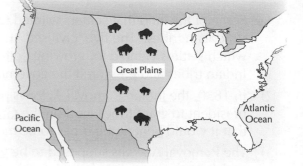

Great Plains

Pacific Ocean

Atlantic Ocean

2) Buffalo were <u>vital</u> for the Lakota Sioux. They used almost <u>every</u> part of the animal — <u>meat</u> for food, <u>skin</u> for clothing and tents, and <u>bones</u> for weapons and tools. Living in <u>tipis</u> (family tents) allowed the Lakotas to <u>quickly</u> follow buffalo herds — tipis are <u>easy</u> to take down and put back up.

3) <u>Tribal warfare</u> was common — it was a way for men to gain <u>prestige</u>. The aim wasn't necessarily to <u>kill</u> or <u>seize land</u>, but to perform acts of <u>bravery</u> such as <u>stealing horses</u> or <u>counting coup</u> (getting close enough to an enemy to touch him). The Lakota Sioux were <u>skilled</u> warriors. Their main enemies were the Crow and the Pawnee.

> Taking the <u>scalp</u> of an enemy was important to the Lakota Sioux for <u>religious</u> reasons. But scalping and killing were <u>less important</u> to them than counting coup.

4) The Lakota Sioux <u>didn't</u> see land as something that could be <u>bought</u> and <u>sold</u> — land belonged to <u>everyone</u>. Even other, more settled tribes believed agricultural land belonged to the tribe as a whole.

> The Lakota Sioux performed <u>rituals</u> such as the Vision Quest, Sweat Lodge Ceremony and Sun Dance to <u>contact</u> the spirits.

5) Native American religion was closely linked with <u>nature</u> — humans were believed to be <u>part of</u> nature, not masters over it. The Lakota Sioux believed that a <u>Great Spirit</u> called Wakan Tanka created the world, and that <u>everything</u> in nature contained <u>spirits</u> which they needed to keep on their side.

6) Women did most of the <u>work</u> in the village or camp, while the men <u>hunted</u> and <u>fought</u>. The Lakota Sioux were a <u>male-dominated</u> warrior society and men were the <u>heads</u> of their families, but women were <u>respected</u>. They owned the tipi and its contents, which gave them <u>status</u>.

> The Lakota Sioux practiced polygamy (having more than one wife) — the dangers of hunting and warfare meant there were often <u>more women</u> than men in tribes.

> Hunting became <u>easier</u> for the Lakota Sioux when they began to use <u>horses</u>, which were brought over by the Europeans in the <u>16th century</u>.

Comment and Analysis

Settlers <u>failed to understand</u> the culture of the Plains Indians because it was so <u>different</u> to their own. This led to <u>tension</u> and <u>conflict</u>.

I don't think they're going to get along, do you...?

Make a list summarising the different features of the Plains Indians' way of life. For each of the points you make, think about how it's different from the lifestyle and beliefs of the settlers.

REVISION TASK

Journeys of Early Migrants

Settlers made the journey to the <u>west coast</u> for a variety of <u>different reasons</u>.

People went to the west coast in Large Numbers from the 1840s

1) The first people to explore the West were <u>mountain men</u> who hunted animals in the <u>1820s</u> and <u>1830s</u> to sell their skins. They <u>didn't settle</u> in the West, but established westward <u>trails</u> that settlers would later use.

2) <u>Missionaries</u> were among the earliest settlers on the <u>west coast</u> in the 1830s. The aim was to <u>convert</u> the Native Americans there to <u>Christianity</u>.

3) Later, <u>larger</u> groups of people who wanted to make new lives for themselves went to the west coast. The first of these was the <u>Peoria Party</u> in 1839. Others followed in the 1840s — their routes became known as the <u>Oregon and California Trails</u>.

They had many Different Reasons for heading west

<u>The Great Migration</u> of <u>1843</u> saw a sudden <u>increase</u> in settlers — a party of around <u>1000</u> people moved to the west coast. This was because life in the East was <u>hard</u>, and there was promise of <u>better</u> things in the West.

Problems in the East

- <u>Economic</u> problems — <u>Recession</u> in 1837 caused banks to collapse and businesses to fail. <u>Wages</u> and <u>profits</u> fell and <u>unemployment</u> rose.

- <u>Overpopulation</u> — High levels of European immigration, particularly from Ireland and Germany from 1846-1854, led to <u>overcrowded</u> cities, <u>fewer jobs</u> and a lack of <u>land</u> for people to farm.

- <u>Disease</u> — Overcrowding and poor sanitary systems led to epidemics of <u>yellow fever</u> and <u>cholera</u>.

Comment and Analysis

Reasons why people went west can be split into <u>push and pull factors</u> — things that pushed them <u>out</u> of the <u>East</u> and things that pulled them <u>to</u> the <u>West</u>.

In 1841, Congress passed the <u>Distributive Preemption Act</u>, which allowed settlers to buy <u>160 acres</u> of land at a very low cost if they'd lived there for 14 months.

Attraction of the West

- <u>A new start</u> — Land was <u>fertile</u> and <u>cheap</u>.

- <u>Government encouragement</u> — The government passed <u>acts</u> which allowed settlers to <u>claim land</u> in Oregon — they wanted people to settle in the West to <u>strengthen</u> the USA's claim to the land there.

- <u>Gold</u> — Gold was found at John Sutter's sawmill in California in January <u>1848</u> (see p.42). In December, President Polk confirmed that there was gold in the area. In <u>1849</u> there was a <u>gold rush</u>, as tens of thousands of people made the journey to California, hoping to make their <u>fortune</u>.

Only about <u>8%</u> of early migrants to California during the Gold Rush were <u>women</u>. More followed later as their husbands and families settled in California.

Settlers also moved west because of a belief in '<u>Manifest Destiny</u>':

- Many <u>US citizens</u> believed that they were destined to <u>occupy</u> and <u>govern</u> all of North America. They saw it as their <u>god-given right</u>.

- They believed they were <u>superior</u> to Native Americans and that they should <u>civilise</u> the continent.

The term 'Manifest Destiny' was coined by John L. O'Sullivan in <u>1845</u>.

Paintings which created a <u>romantic</u>, idealised image of moving west <u>promoted</u> expansion and 'Manifest Destiny'. For many, the journey wouldn't have been as <u>pleasant</u> as this image suggests (see p.40).

Migrants crossing the plains towards the Rocky Mountains.

More facts you're destined to learn...

You should be able to explain the reasons why people went west. For example, there wasn't enough land in the East, but there was the promise of fertile land in the West.

EXAM TIP

Journeys of Early Migrants

Settlers faced many <u>challenges</u> on their journey to the west coast — it was a <u>long way</u> and it was <u>hard work</u>.

The journey to the west coast was Difficult

1) It took around <u>5 months</u> to complete the <u>2000 mile</u> overland journey to the west coast. The journey had to be completed <u>before</u> winter. People travelled in <u>wagons</u> and formed wagon trains with other settlers.

2) The journey was <u>dangerous</u> — as many as <u>10%</u> would die on the way.

- There were <u>mountains</u> and <u>rivers</u> to cross — this was difficult with <u>heavy</u> wagons.
- People suffered from <u>food</u> and <u>water</u> shortages, and <u>diseases</u> such as typhoid and cholera.
- <u>Accidents</u> were common, such as falling under wagon wheels and accidental shootings.

3) Travellers were <u>wary</u> of Native Americans — some killings did occur, but conflict was <u>rare</u>. Native Americans <u>traded</u> food with travellers and offered them <u>guiding</u> services, but they became more <u>hostile</u> with the rise in settlers in the <u>1850s</u> (see p.43). Travellers also had <u>disputes</u> among themselves.

4) Women did all of the <u>domestic chores</u> at this time, and this was made <u>harder</u> by trail life. Some women had to give birth on the journey, while children were vulnerable to <u>accidents</u>, e.g. falling off wagons.

> About <u>half</u> of the estimated <u>100,000</u> people who went to California during 1849 did so by <u>sea</u>. This journey also took around <u>5 months</u> and had its own <u>difficulties</u> — <u>crowded</u> conditions, <u>sickness</u> and <u>storms</u>.

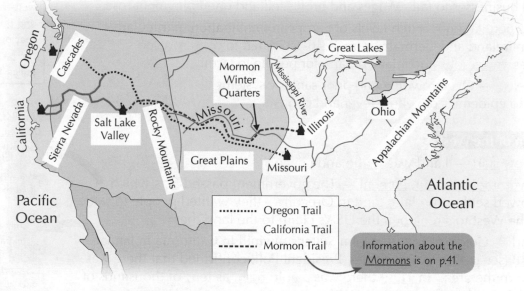

The Donner Party had a Disastrous journey

- In 1846 the Donner Party, heading for California, tried to take a <u>shortcut</u>, but they ended up <u>trapped</u> in deep snow in the <u>Sierra Nevada</u> mountains.
- They had to <u>camp</u> in the mountains over winter. Supplies were <u>low</u> and many of the party <u>starved</u> to death.
- Of the <u>87</u> migrants, less than <u>50</u> survived till the next spring — by <u>eating</u> those who had died.

> 'Still <u>snowing</u>; now about three feet deep; wind west; killed my last <u>oxen</u> today.'
>
> Extract from the diary of Patrick Breen, 27th November 1846.

> The Donner Party had to <u>kill</u> and eat the animals which pulled their wagons because they ran out of <u>food</u>.

Once settlers had reached the west coast, life was still <u>hard</u> — they had to create farms and homes by <u>hand</u> from <u>scratch</u>. However, the <u>fertile</u> land meant that a <u>good living</u> could be made.

For the settlers, heading west was a big risk...

Give a brief description of the difficulties settlers faced on their journey to the west coast. [4]

The Mormons

Another group of settlers were the Mormons — members of 'The Church of Jesus Christ of Latter Day Saints'.

The Mormons were Persecuted because of their beliefs

1) This religion was started by Joseph Smith, who published the Book of Mormon in 1830. It claimed that Jesus had visited America and that Native Americans were descended from the lost tribes of Israel.

   • Mormons separated themselves from American society and called non-Mormons 'gentiles'.

   • Some Mormons formed a militia called the Danites and there was violence against non-Mormons and dissenters (Mormons who questioned or abandoned the Mormon faith).

   • Mormons were against slavery and tried to convert Native Americans to Mormonism.

2) Many US citizens disliked the Mormons, and repeatedly drove them out of their homes. They didn't agree with the Mormon practice of polygamy (having more than one wife), feared the expansion of the Mormon faith and felt threatened by the Mormons' political and economic power.

> **Ohio, 1831**: The Mormons first settled in Kirtland, Ohio. They faced violence — Joseph Smith was tarred and feathered in 1832. The bank which Smith founded collapsed in 1837 — users of the bank were angry and drove the Mormons to Missouri.

> **Missouri, 1837**: The Mormons' anti-slavery stance annoyed slave-owners, and the Danites were suspected of plotting with Native Americans. Many leaders were arrested, so Brigham Young led the Mormons to Illinois.

> **Illinois, 1839**: The Mormons created their own city called Nauvoo, with its own army and laws. Joseph Smith declared his candidacy for President. Smith was eventually killed in jail by an angry mob and Brigham Young took over as leader.

They moved West and eventually settled in Salt Lake Valley

1) Brigham Young decided to move the Mormons further west. He wanted to create an independent Mormon state where they could live freely. He chose Salt Lake Valley — conditions there were dry and harsh, but he believed that nobody else wanted to live there and it was part of Mexico, not the US.

2) The Mormons planned to leave Illinois in the spring of 1846, but due to an increase in anti-Mormon violence they had to leave in February. This rushed departure meant that they left supplies behind and were disorganised. Conditions were hard — it was a cold winter and there was deep mud.

3) Their progress was very slow, which meant they couldn't complete the journey that year. They stayed in Winter Quarters by the Missouri River over winter (see map on p.40) — by the spring of 1847, around 400 Mormons had died from disease, the cold and lack of supplies.

> Although the journey was hard, the Mormons planted crops and built way stations along the trail to feed and help later travellers.

4) They set off again in April 1847 and organisation improved. They were divided into groups led by captains under the strict overall command of Young. They finally reached Salt Lake Valley in July.

5) The conditions in Salt Lake Valley were tough, but Young led the Mormons in solving their problems:

   • There was little rain or other water sources, so they dug irrigation ditches.

   • There were no trees for wood, so they built houses from bricks of earth.

   • They needed to become self-sufficient but there weren't enough of them, so Young encouraged Mormons from all over the world to move to Salt Lake.

> Tensions were high — later in 1857, 140 non-Mormon settlers were killed in the Mountain Meadows Massacre. Mormons blamed the Indians, but others suspected the Danites.

6) In 1848, Mexico gave Salt Lake City to the US — it became the territory of Utah and was subject to American laws. The Mormons ignored these laws and the Danites attacked US officials. In 1857, the US appointed a non-Mormon governor who arrived with 2500 US troops.

> The American government put pressure on the Mormons to abandon polygamy. The US only allowed Utah to become a state in 1896 after the Mormons had abandoned polygamy in 1890 — the Mormons successfully settled Salt Lake Valley, but they had to compromise their beliefs.

The Mormons had their own reasons for moving west...

Make sure you understand that different groups of people had different experiences. The Mormons went west to escape persecution — a very different motivation to other settlers.

Gold Miners

Migration to the west coast during the 1840s was gradual, with most people heading to Oregon. But the California Gold Rush changed this — in just a few years, huge numbers of travellers journeyed to California.

Gold was found in California in 1848

1) James Marshall found gold while working at John Sutter's sawmill in January 1848. News of this spread slowly to the east coast, until President Polk made a speech in December confirming that gold had been found. As a result, tens of thousands of people made the journey west during 1849.

2) People were excited at the prospect of making their fortune. Many hoped to find gold and then return home.

> James Carson, an army sergeant in California, abandoned his post to look for gold, writing later that he had 'a very violent attack of gold fever.'

3) People came to California from all over the world — e.g. China, Mexico and South America, as well as from other parts of North America.

A miner panning for gold.

The California Gold Rush presented many Challenges

1) Life as a miner was hard, even before reaching California. There were many deaths from cholera on the journey to California between 1849 and 1853.

> Some people ran service industries, e.g. stores and saloons. Unsuccessful miners often stayed on in California as farmers and merchants and started families.

2) Only a lucky few found gold in California. Surface gold (found using the simple method of panning) was limited and soon grew scarce. Some miners returned home, but others couldn't afford to.

3) Living and working conditions were poor. There was little hygiene, disease was common and nutrition among miners was poor. Miners who couldn't find gold worked for mining companies in dangerous conditions for low wages. When not working, people turned to drinking and gambling which often led to trouble in mining towns.

4) The rapid migration of mostly male gold seekers and the quick development of mining towns meant that society was unstructured — there were no stable families or communities. There were no laws at first — miners had to enforce the law themselves but their justice wasn't always fair (see p.54).

5) There was frequent racial conflict. White Americans considered themselves superior to foreign miners and more entitled to the gold, especially when it began to grow scarce.

> Native American tribes living in California suffered as a result of the Gold Rush. The Native American population in California dropped from around 150,000 to less than 30,000 during 1845-1870. This was the result of violent attacks, epidemics and being driven off their land.

California and the US as a whole felt the effects of the rush

1) Mining harmed California's environment. Timber for mine supports used up forests, chemicals such as mercury caused pollution, and the technique of hydraulic mining (the use of high powered jets of water to wash away hillsides and reach the gold beneath) destroyed the landscape.

2) But mining also kick-started California's development. The non-Native American population rose from around 14,000 to about 225,000 between 1848-1852. Mining towns such as Sacramento and Stockton expanded. San Francisco became the economic centre of California.

3) The Gold Rush accelerated the economic growth of the US. The wealth generated by gold mining gave America an important role in world trade. Settlement in California increased the need for better links between the east and west of the country, leading to improved mail services and a transcontinental railroad (see p.50).

Comment and Analysis

Mining had a negative impact on many individuals, especially the Native Americans, but it played an important role in the expansion of the US.

It's interesting how things panned out, isn't it...

Write a quick summary of all of the positive and negative impacts of the California Gold Rush.

REVISION TASK

The Clash of Cultures

As more settlers started to cross the Great Plains, tension grew between them and the Plains Indians.

There was a Lack of Understanding between settlers and Indians

1) To settlers, it seemed that the Plains Indians had no system of government, that their warfare was cowardly and their religion just superstition (see p.38).

2) They had different views on land ownership. Native Americans believed that the land was for everyone, but settlers wanted to own, farm and exploit land.

3) Settlers thought that the Plains Indians' nomadic lifestyle was uncivilised and that they wasted the land. Native Americans thought that the settlers ruined the land.

> Horace Greeley, a newspaper editor, wrote in 1859 that 'God has given this earth to those who will subdue and cultivate it.'

Native Americans and settlers Increasingly came into Contact

1) Significant numbers of settlers moved beyond the Permanent Indian Frontier (see p.37) and across the Plains to reach lands in the West from 1843. Many more came with the California Gold Rush of 1849.

2) The settlers disrupted buffalo herds which the Plains Indians relied on, and polluted water sources, bringing diseases such as cholera.

3) As a result, Plains Indians became more hostile. They sometimes attacked wagon trains, which increased the settlers' fear and distrust. The settlers also felt threatened by the Indians' inter-tribal conflict.

The Reservation System replaced the Permanent Indian Frontier

1) To reduce conflict on the Plains, the government pursued a policy of concentration — the Plains Indians would be concentrated onto specific areas of the Plains called reservations. The Indian Appropriations Act (1851) allocated funds to do this — it encouraged Native Americans to farm and build houses.

2) The Fort Laramie Treaty (1851) was the government's first attempt to concentrate the Plains Indians in certain areas. It defined the territory of each tribe to try to minimise inter-tribal conflict.

3) Tribes agreed to remain in their territory, allow settlers to cross the Plains, and allow the government to build roads and forts along the trails. In return, the government promised the tribes that they would have permanent rights to their lands, and that tribes would receive $50,000 of goods a year for 50 years.

4) Neither side kept to the treaty. Not all tribes agreed with it and many didn't even know it existed. The US government didn't keep its side of the deal either — it couldn't ensure settlers kept to the agreement, and in 1852 it reduced the yearly payments from 50 years to 10.

> The government never allowed existing treaties to prevent settlement it was in favour of — it simply negotiated new ones. For example, thousands of people encroached on Cheyenne land in Colorado during the Pike's Peak Gold Rush (1858-1861). The government then negotiated the Fort Wise Treaty, reducing Cheyenne land to make room for white settlers, and moving the Cheyenne to poor quality land on the Sand Creek Reservation. Some Cheyenne later claimed that they didn't understand the terms of the treaty when they signed it.

5) The treaty had a large impact:

- Settlement increased in California and Oregon.
- Restricting Native Americans to reservations threatened their way of life, as did the building of roads and forts in their territory.
- Broken promises increased Native American resentment towards government and settlers.

Comment and Analysis

The Fort Laramie Treaty is significant because it marked the end of the Permanent Indian Frontier — the Native Americans could no longer live freely on the Plains. It paved the way for further treaties in the 1850s and 1860s which resulted in tribes losing land, e.g. in 1853 treaties were made with tribes in Kansas and Nebraska to make room for settlers in those areas — these tribes lost nearly 17 million acres.

> Native Americans had been given the Great Plains when they were considered uninhabitable. This changed when settlers decided that they wanted the land.

'Well, when we said you could have all this lovely desert'...

Explain why the Fort Laramie Treaty was important. [8]

The Causes of the Civil War

The North and the South developed in <u>different</u> ways and had different attitudes towards slavery.

The North and South had Different Economies

1) In the early 19th century, the <u>South's economy</u> was heavily based on <u>cotton</u> <u>exports</u>. Cotton was produced <u>cheaply</u> using slave labour on <u>plantations</u> (p.36).

2) Slavery wasn't as important in the <u>North</u> — it had a more <u>diverse economy</u> that was based on lots of <u>different industries</u> and <u>agricultural crops</u>.

3) By <u>1804</u>, all of the <u>northern</u> states had <u>abolished slavery</u> (banned it). This created a <u>division</u> between southern 'slave states' and northern '<u>free states</u>'.

4) As time went on, the North became even <u>more industrialised</u>, while the South <u>relied</u> more and more on <u>cotton cultivation</u>. By the <u>1860s</u>, the <u>North</u> had <u>six times</u> as many <u>factories</u> as the South.

5) The North was <u>more wealthy</u> than the South as a result of its <u>diverse</u> and <u>industrialised</u> economy.

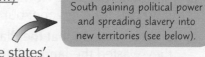

The North didn't necessarily want <u>racial equality</u>. They were more worried about the South gaining political power and spreading slavery into new territories (see below).

Comment and Analysis

Some historians point out that the <u>South</u> didn't <u>need</u> to <u>industrialise</u>, because they made lots of money out of <u>plantation agriculture</u>. This might have been true, but it was a bad idea to <u>rely</u> on <u>one industry</u> (cotton) to keep the economy going.

Not <u>all</u> southerners were slave owners — in <u>1860</u>, only about <u>5%</u> of southerners <u>owned</u> slaves. <u>Less than 1%</u> of these slaveholders had <u>large slave plantations</u> with 200 or more slaves. However, because the southern <u>economy</u> was based on slave labour, southerners saw it as part of their <u>way of life</u>.

The North had a Bigger Population than the South

1) The <u>North's</u> population was <u>bigger</u> than the South's. A <u>big proportion</u> of the <u>South's population</u> were <u>slaves</u> — by <u>1860</u>, there were almost <u>4 million slaves</u> in the <u>South</u> compared to <u>8 million</u> free white Americans.

2) The North's population gave it more <u>political power</u>, as states with a bigger population could have <u>more representatives</u> in the <u>lower house</u> of Congress.

3) The <u>South</u> still had lots of <u>political power</u>, though. Each state had <u>two</u> representatives in the <u>Senate</u> (the upper house of Congress). Each <u>new state</u> that applied to join the Union had to <u>decide</u> whether to allow or ban slavery. As long as the number of <u>free</u> and <u>slave</u> states in Congress was <u>balanced</u>, the <u>South</u> could use its votes in the <u>Senate</u> to <u>protect slavery</u>.

Slaves were counted as <u>three-fifths of a person</u>. This gave southerners <u>more power</u> than they would've had if only <u>free people</u> were counted.

Westward expansion Increased the Tension over Slavery

1) <u>Slavery</u> became so important in the <u>South</u> that many southerners believed there would be <u>economic</u> and <u>social chaos</u> if it was abolished. They were keen to <u>protect</u> their way of life.

2) As <u>westward expansion</u> continued, <u>northern senators</u> tried to stop <u>new states</u> becoming slave states. They wanted to use <u>land</u> in the West for their <u>own economic development</u>.

3) This caused <u>tension</u> between the North and the South, which came to the surface when <u>new states</u> asked to join the Union.

The <u>southern states</u> feared that admitting more free states would give the North enough <u>power</u> to pass a law abolishing slavery in <u>all</u> states. The <u>northern states</u> worried that they would be <u>outvoted</u> in the Senate if <u>too many</u> slave states were admitted. Both sides wanted the <u>balance</u> to tip in their <u>own favour</u>.

In <u>1820</u>, the <u>Missouri Compromise</u> was created to try and <u>reduce tension</u> over slavery. An <u>imaginary line</u> was drawn from the southern border of Missouri to the western edge of US territory. All <u>future states</u> that formed <u>north</u> of the <u>Missouri Line</u> were to be <u>banned</u> from becoming <u>slave states</u>.

Comment and Analysis

The North and the South were <u>suspicious</u> of each other. They both feared that the other's way of life would be <u>forced</u> upon them.

4) The <u>Missouri Compromise</u> worked well for about <u>twenty years</u> and Congress stayed balanced. However, the debate started up again in <u>1846</u> after the USA gained <u>more territory</u> in the West.

And I thought the UK had a North/South divide...

Describe the differences in economics, population and political power between North and South.

The Causes of the Civil War

Tensions continued to build, and Lincoln's election as President was the final straw for the South.

Free State Abolitionists wanted Slavery to End

Some people in northern free states campaigned for slaves to be freed — they were called abolitionists. At first, abolitionists wanted slavery to be ended slowly and for owners to be compensated for losing their slaves.

1) Opposition became more radical in the 1830s — abolitionists began to call slavery a moral evil which should end immediately. They became more organised, forming the American Anti-Slavery Association in 1833.

2) Abolition gained some support in the North. However, many northerners didn't support abolition — they worried about the impact of freed slaves coming to the North in big numbers. Southerners felt that their way of life was being attacked, so there was little support for the movement in the South.

3) In 1851, abolitionist Harriet Beecher Stowe wrote a novel attacking slavery called 'Uncle Tom's Cabin'. It sparked support for abolition by making many in the North more aware of the immorality of slavery.

Comment and Analysis

Attitudes to slavery varied in the North — not everyone was opposed to it. But this didn't make the South feel any less threatened — they believed that the North was united against them to end slavery.

The Missouri Compromise was Broken in 1854

1) The Kansas-Nebraska Act of 1854 ended the Missouri Compromise. Under the Compromise, slavery had been outlawed in the Kansas-Nebraska territory — but when the Act admitted Kansas and Nebraska to the Union, it allowed settlers to vote on whether they were to become free or slave states.

2) Many northerners were angry with the Act. The Republican Party was formed as a result of this discontent — it aimed to stop the spread of slavery. By 1856, the Republicans had gained much support in the North, but the Democrats stayed popular in the South. This created more tension.

The Act was designed to reduce tension, but it actually made things worse. Many in the North saw it as giving in to the South.

Lincoln's Election as President in 1860 triggered Secession

1) In 1860, Republican Abraham Lincoln won the presidential election. He thought slavery was immoral and opposed its spread into new territories, but said he didn't want to interfere with it in areas where it already existed.

Lincoln was a minority president — he only got 40% of the overall vote and he didn't get any votes in 10 of the southern states.

2) Many Southerners felt that they didn't owe any loyalty to a man who threatened their way of life. His election triggered the secession (withdrawal) of seven states, and in February 1861 these states formed the Confederate States of America with Jefferson Davis as their president.

3) When Lincoln was sworn in as Union president in March 1861, he said that he wouldn't accept secession. Davis thought that states had the right to secede — he didn't want the Union to break up, but he also believed in the South's freedom to own slaves.

4) Lincoln refused to withdraw US government troops at Fort Sumter in South Carolina — the Confederates saw this as a lack of respect for their independence. Lincoln sent more supplies to the fort, but said that he would only attack if the South did so first. In April 1861, Confederate troops attacked the fort.

5) This triggered a Civil War between the Union and the Confederates. By August 1861, 11 southern states had seceded from the Union. Lincoln declared that the Confederate states were in rebellion.

Lincoln insisted that the aim of the war was to preserve the Union rather than abolish slavery — he knew that many northerners and citizens in the remaining loyal southern states wouldn't support abolition as a war aim.

- The aim of the war changed with Lincoln's Emancipation Proclamation in 1863 — all slaves in rebellious states were to be emancipated (freed). This made ending slavery an aim of the war (in addition to preserving the Union).
- Emancipation made military sense because it would strengthen the northern army. It also tied in with the moral beliefs of Lincoln, who was facing increasing pressure from fellow Republicans to make the war about slavery.

Lots of tasty marks up for grabs here...

Do you agree that Lincoln's election was the main cause of the Civil War? Explain your answer. [18] (Use the information from page 44 in your answer too).

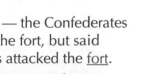

America, 1789-1900

The Impact of the Civil War

The Civil War had a big impact on the lives of civilians — things were especially tough for southerners.

The War had a Negative Impact on the South's Economy

1) In 1861, the South introduced a ban on cotton exports to force Europe to side with them in the war. Europe had more cotton than they needed, so the ban failed and the South lost valuable income.

2) Southerners were cut off from northern markets during the war and the blockade made it hard to import food. Also, lots of farmland was destroyed by fighting. Things got worse in 1864 when the North started to target southern transport and civilian property to deliberately cause economic hardship.

> Lincoln knew the value of cotton exports, so he ordered a blockade of ships to be put in place. By July 1861, all Confederate ports were surrounded by Union ships. Even after the South ended their ban, they struggled to export cotton because of the blockade.

3) Food shortages led to inflation (when prices go up and money loses value) — black markets formed and made inflation worse. In 1863, the Confederacy introduced new ways of collecting tax to help cover the costs of the war effort.

4) The Confederate government issued paper money in 1861. Once it became obvious that the South was losing the war and had printed too many notes, the value of the notes fell quickly and inflation increased.

Comment and Analysis

Some historians criticise Davis's government for taking over the economy and then failing to protect it — its handling of paper currency and interference in the cotton industry made things worse.

The Economy in the North actually Benefited from the War

1) The North suffered from inflation too, but its economy was in a stronger position to deal with it. During the war, northern agricultural and industrial production increased, as the army needed a good supply of food and weapons. This created job opportunities and increasing prosperity for northerners.

2) Northerners were also taxed, but only those with incomes above a certain amount had to pay. The government borrowed a lot of money from richer northern citizens to fund the war.

The Social Impact of the War was Serious

> Around 260,000 Confederate soldiers and 360,000 Union soldiers died during the war. Historians reckon that about 50,000 southern civilians died because of the war too, though no one knows the full death toll.

1) Most of the fighting happened in the South — some areas were occupied by Union soldiers. Lots of property was destroyed, so many southerners became refugees. There was guerilla warfare too, where armed civilians fought against Union soldiers, raided their bases and cut their lines of communication. However, some guerilla groups also robbed and attacked other civilians.

2) People who weren't close to the fighting still knew quite a lot about what was going on — soldiers wrote letters to their families and newspapers ran stories about the war.

3) Civilians in both the North and South lost civil liberties during the war.

> Conscription (forcing civilians into the army) was introduced in the South by Davis in 1862 and in the North by Lincoln in 1863.

> Both sides suspended the right to a trial and introduced martial law (where a military commander takes control).

4) As men were fighting in the South, jobs were created for women and freed slaves in the North. This caused social tension — some felt that freed slaves were taking 'white jobs'.

5) In 1863, there were riots against conscription in New York. A lot of anger was directed at black citizens.

> During the 1864 election, a northern Democrat stirred up fears of mixed-race marriage as part of a racist campaign that played on this social tension.

An engraving from the Illustrated London News, August 1863. A black man is hanged by rioters during the New York Draft Riots in July 1863.

The war was bad news for the South...

If you're writing about the impact of the war, think about how the differences between the North and the South might have influenced the way that civilians experienced the war.

EXAM TIP

African American Experiences of the Civil War

The Civil War was fought from 1861 to 1865. The North won — seceded states returned to the Union and slavery was abolished. The Civil War had a huge impact on the lives of African Americans.

Many African Americans wanted to Serve in the Union Army

1) Many African Americans tried to join the army (enlist) at the outbreak of war, but they were rejected. Those who tried to enlist included freemen in the North and slaves who escaped from the South after the war started.

> Lincoln was worried he would lose the support of the remaining loyal southern states if he allowed African Americans to join the Union Army.

2) African Americans were eventually accepted into the Union Army with the Emancipation Proclamation of 1863 (see p.45). Thousands enlisted and formed all-black units. One of the first of these was the 54th Massachusetts Infantry Regiment.

3) Around 180,000 African American soldiers had joined the Union Army by the war's end.

4) African Americans also helped the war effort in other ways, e.g as blacksmiths, nurses and cooks. Some served as guides and spies for the Union Army in the South.

> **Comment and Analysis**
>
> After the Emancipation Proclamation, the aim of the war became about ending slavery as well as preserving the Union — African Americans now had a chance to fight for their own freedom.

They faced Prejudice from northerners

1) Although there was opposition to slavery in the North, many northerners didn't see African Americans as equal. Black people faced racism and discrimination in the Union Army:

- They fought in segregated regiments led by white officers.
- Many people didn't believe that black men were as skilled or brave as white men — they were often given menial jobs.
- Black soldiers were paid $10 a month — $3 less than white soldiers.
- African Americans were given poorer supplies and worse rations.

The assault on Fort Wagner.

> But black troops proved their bravery, e.g. the 54th Massachusetts Infantry Regiment's 1863 assault on Fort Wagner in which half the troops were killed.

2) Black soldiers faced more danger than white soldiers if they were captured by the South in battle — the Confederates threatened to enslave them.

> There was racial tension in the North. When conscription was introduced in 1863, many northerners were angry — they didn't want to be forced to fight to free slaves. This led to riots in New York in which African Americans were killed.

Many African Americans Unwillingly helped the South

1) As white men left to fight in the Confederate Army, discipline on some plantations was relaxed. Many slaves began to resist by working at a slower pace, refusing to obey orders and breaking rules.

2) Many slaves and free African Americans were forced to support the Confederate war effort. They were made to build fortifications, work in factories or work as nurses and cooks.

3) Some free African Americans in the South did volunteer to help the Confederates — usually as skilled or manual labourers — but they were in the minority.

4) Confederates were unwilling to arm slaves because of fears of slave rebellion. Slaves were only accepted as troops in 1865, when the South was coming close to losing the war.

The Civil War changed the lives of African Americans...

Make sure you understand the effect of the Civil War on African Americans. Many fought for their own freedom. But many faced prejudice — their next battle would be one for equality.

EXAM TIP

The Reconstruction Era

After the Civil War, efforts were made to <u>rebuild</u> the United States — this is known as the <u>Reconstruction Era</u>.

Slavery was Formally Abolished after the War

After the <u>Union</u> won the war in <u>1865</u>, over <u>four million slaves</u> were <u>freed</u> and the South's <u>plantation economy</u> was <u>destroyed</u>. Politicians started to <u>rebuild</u> the South and help <u>freed slaves</u> to become part of <u>free society</u>.

1) Securing <u>freedom</u> for <u>African Americans</u> was a key part of Reconstruction. Many slaves in the South had already been freed by the <u>Emancipation Proclamation</u> in <u>1863</u>, but slavery still existed in the <u>border states</u> (the slave states of Delaware, Kentucky, Maryland and Missouri which remained <u>loyal</u> to the Union).

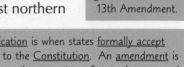

Lincoln was <u>assassinated</u> in <u>April 1865</u>, but it was his government that laid the <u>groundwork</u> for the 13th Amendment.

2) The <u>13th Amendment</u> to the US Constitution was introduced by <u>Lincoln</u> when he was <u>re-elected</u> in <u>1864</u> — it <u>abolished slavery</u> in all states. It was <u>ratified</u> by most northern and border states, and some southern states in December <u>1865</u>.

The 13th Amendment freed slaves, but it <u>didn't</u> give them <u>equal rights</u>. There was a debate over how far African Americans should be given <u>civil rights</u> during the Reconstruction Era.

<u>Ratification</u> is when states <u>formally accept</u> changes to the <u>Constitution</u>. An <u>amendment</u> is <u>ratified</u> once <u>three-quarters</u> of states have agreed.

3) The <u>Freedmen's Bureau</u> was set up in <u>March 1865</u> to help <u>freed slaves</u> and <u>poor southerners</u> to <u>rebuild</u> their lives. It provided <u>food</u> and <u>shelter</u>, and <u>legal</u> and <u>medical aid</u>. It also helped communities to establish new <u>schools</u>. But it was <u>poorly funded</u> and limited by <u>political issues</u> — it closed in <u>1872</u>.

Andrew Johnson began Presidential Reconstruction in 1865

1) <u>Andrew Johnson</u> took over as President in <u>April 1865</u> after Lincoln was <u>assassinated</u>. He took a <u>lenient</u> approach to the South.

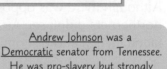

<u>Andrew Johnson</u> was a <u>Democratic</u> senator from Tennessee. He was <u>pro-slavery</u> but strongly disagreed with southern <u>secession</u>.

- He <u>pardoned</u> all white southerners except Confederate <u>leaders</u> and <u>wealthy planters</u>, but many later received <u>individual pardons</u>.
- Property was <u>returned</u> to its original owners instead of being <u>redistributed</u>. Many African Americans <u>rented</u> land from white people (<u>sharecropping</u>) — sometimes they rented from their <u>former masters</u>.
- Some of the southern <u>elite</u> regained <u>power</u> — many had been in the Confederate <u>government</u> and <u>army</u>.
- Some southern states created the <u>Black Codes</u>, which limited the <u>freedom</u> of African Americans. For example, South Carolina made <u>black people</u> pay a <u>tax</u> if they were not <u>farmers</u> or <u>servants</u>.

2) Johnson <u>didn't support equal rights</u> for African Americans, so he did <u>nothing</u> to stop the <u>Black Codes</u>.

3) In <u>1866</u>, he tried to <u>veto</u> (reject) the Civil Rights Act. However, his veto was <u>overturned</u> (see below), and the Civil Rights Act became <u>law</u> in 1866.

The <u>Civil Rights Act</u> gave <u>citizenship</u> and <u>equal rights</u> to <u>all</u> who were <u>born in the US</u> — it excluded <u>Native Americans</u> and people who were under the control of a <u>foreign power</u>. The Act was designed to <u>protect</u> the rights of <u>African Americans</u>.

Some Republicans disagreed with Johnson's Approach

1) Some <u>radical Republicans</u> wanted <u>racial equality</u> and greater <u>punishment</u> of Confederate leaders.

2) <u>Moderate Republicans</u> didn't agree with Johnson's <u>veto</u> of the <u>Civil Rights Act</u>. They created an <u>alliance</u> with the radicals and <u>overturned</u> his veto to ensure that the Act became law.

3) Congress passed the <u>14th Amendment</u> in 1868 — Johnson <u>opposed</u> it and the southern states <u>refused</u> to ratify it. Many in the North began to think that a <u>tougher</u> approach was needed in the South.

The <u>14th Amendment</u> had a 'Citzenship Clause', which guaranteed <u>citizenship</u> to all males born in the US regardless of race. It also had an 'Equal Protection Clause', which gave black people the same rights as white people to <u>state protection</u>.

If only you could abolish exams...

The North and the South had different attitudes to slavery. In the exam, consider how these different views could have influenced their positions on the Reconstruction of the South.

EXAM TIP

The Reconstruction Era

Radicals won the 1866 elections — they decided Congress should control Reconstruction, not the President.

Radical Republicans took over Reconstruction in 1867

1) The First and Second Reconstruction Acts were passed by Congress in March 1867. These acts placed the South under military rule. Before rebel states could rejoin the Union, they were forced to ratify the 14th Amendment (p.48) and rewrite their state constitutions to allow black people to vote.

2) Congress's approach to the South was more forceful than Johnson's — they sent troops to the South to keep the peace and protect freed slaves and their right to vote. Leading rebels were removed from office.

3) Johnson tried to obstruct Radical Reconstruction — he vetoed both Reconstruction Acts, so radicals impeached him (put him on trial). He wasn't convicted, but he lost power and Ulysses Grant was elected President in 1869.

4) The 15th Amendment was passed in 1869 and ratified in 1870 — it ruled that citizens of the USA could not be denied the right to vote based on their 'race, colour, or previous condition of servitude'.

> Northerners who went to carry out the government's Reconstruction policies in the South were called 'carpetbaggers' by southerners. They were accused of being corrupt and exploiting the South.

5) By 1870, all states had been re-admitted to the Union. The southern states had Republican governments made up of white southerners who supported Reconstruction, northerners, and African Americans.

6) Three Enforcement Acts were passed between 1870 and 1871. They made it illegal to use terror, force or bribery to stop black people from voting, and they gave the government powers to quickly suppress the Ku Klux Klan.

> The Ku Klux Klan was a white supremacist group that formed in 1865. They murdered, lynched, beat and threatened African Americans, white Republicans and their supporters. They also burned churches, homes and schools. Many Klan members were arrested and put on trial under the Enforcement Acts.

Comment and Analysis

Radical Reconstruction was a period of hope and idealism for many, in spite of southern grievances. Radicals believed that equality could be achieved.

The Reconstruction Era ended in 1877

> In 1876, the Supreme Court ruled that only states, not the federal government, could prosecute people under the Enforcement Acts — this resulted in many violent crimes going unpunished in the South.

1) By 1873, political support for Reconstruction had weakened in the North. Economic depression in 1874 caused high unemployment, so northerners lost interest in the South.

2) Supreme Court decisions also weakened the power of the 14th Amendment to protect black civil rights.

3) The depression, and corruption and scandal under President Grant, meant that Republicans lost support. The Democrats won control of the lower house of Congress in 1874 for first time since the Civil War.

4) Republican Rutherford B. Hayes was elected President in 1876, but the election results were disputed. In return for recognition of his election, he accepted the Democrats' control of the South and ended federal military involvement there. The Reconstruction Era was over.

The Reconstruction Era improved rights for African Americans, but many issues were unresolved by 1876:

- More than 700,000 black people were registered to vote and over 1500 were elected to state and national offices. However, while they had representation, it wasn't in proportion to their population.
- Some southerners ignored laws like 15th Amendment — they tried to stop black people from voting using literacy tests and poll taxes.
- Many Ku Klux Klan members were fined and let off with a warning. Other violent groups emerged, like the Rifle Clubs and the Red Shirts, who carried on murdering and threatening southern Republicans.

Comment and Analysis

A key barrier to the success of Reconstruction was that the attitude of many white southerners didn't change. African Americans had more independence than under slavery, but in many ways, their rights were still limited.

Some southerners found ways to get around the law...

Write down a description of what these acts or amendments did to protect African Americans — the First and Second Reconstruction Acts, the 15th Amendment and the Enforcement Acts.

Development of the Plains, c.1861-c.1877

Homesteaders and the Railways

After the Civil War, large numbers of settlers began to move on to the Great Plains — an area once seen as unsuitable for living. The US government did a lot to encourage homesteaders and the building of the railways.

Different Groups of people moved to the Plains

Many settlers had previously viewed the Plains as a 'desert' (see p.33). More began to move there from the 1840s (see p.43), but after 1865, thousands followed — this was a big change in attitude. This included:

1) Migrants from eastern states who moved because of growing population and high land prices.

2) Immigrants who'd come to America to escape poverty and religious and political persecution.

3) Slaves who had been freed after the Civil War and ex-Civil War soldiers who wanted a new start.

> After the end of the Reconstruction Era in 1877 (see p.48-49), African Americans faced growing oppression in the South. As a result, thousands moved west — e.g. approximately 20,000 black migrants known as 'Exodusters' moved to Kansas in 1879.

The Government encouraged people to Settle on the Plains

1) The government encouraged people to move west and settle on the Plains by promoting the idea of 'Manifest Destiny' (see p.39). They moved Indians onto reservations, which freed up land for settlement (see p.43).

> Before the US Civil War, southerners in Congress opposed acts which encouraged non-slave-owning settlers to move into new areas — southerners were worried that this would result in these areas eventually becoming free states (see p.44). When the South seceded, the North was able to pass these acts.

2) In 1862, they passed the Homestead Act, which gave each settler 160 acres of free land if they farmed it for five years. This opened up 2.5 million acres for settlement and was open to everyone, including immigrants, freed slaves and single women. Between 1862 and 1900, around 600,000 people claimed land under the Act.

3) The condition of farming the land for five years was meant to discourage speculators — those aiming to make a short-term profit on rising land prices rather than settling and living on the land. However, the Act was still affected by speculators and corruption.

Comment and Analysis

The Act was important because it opened up land ownership to ordinary people. Although there were problems, it helped to establish settlement on the Plains.

Railway Companies also encouraged homesteading

1) The Pacific Railroad Act of 1862 approved the construction of the First Transcontinental Railroad — a railway which ran across the US from east to west. The government believed it would make migration into unsettled land easier and create national unity by connecting the West and the East. The railway was completed in 1869.

2) Railway companies were granted huge areas of land on the Plains by the government — they sold this land cheaply to settlers to help fund their railway building.

3) These companies produced advertising posters which made exaggerated claims about the 'good life' on the Plains. They knew that settlers would become customers for their railways.

> 'The Location is Central, along the 41st parallel, the favorite latitude of America. Equally well adapted to corn or wheat; free from the long, cold winters of the Northern, and the hot, unhealthy influences of the Southern states...
> The Soil is a dark loam, slightly impregnated with lime, free from stone and gravel, and eminently adapted to grass, grain and root crops...
> The Climate is mild and healthful; the atmosphere dry and pure. Epidemic diseases never prevail; Fever and Ague are unknown...
> Timber is found on the streams and grows rapidly.'

Extract from a Union Pacific Railroad advertisement for farming lands in Nebraska, 1870.

Comment and Analysis

After these acts were passed, economic development was made easier because the West was now linked with markets in the East. People could also be transported more easily, as well as supplies which aided settlement, such as building materials and machinery.

The role of the Great Plains was far from settled...

The Homestead Act and the Pacific Railroad Act were both important developments in the settlement of the Great Plains. Make sure you're able to explain why they were so significant.

Living and Farming on the Plains

The government was <u>encouraging</u> people to settle on the Plains, but homesteading was a <u>tough</u> life. As <u>more people</u> faced the difficulties of living and farming on the Plains, they found ways to <u>survive</u>.

Life on the Plains was Hard for homesteaders...

1) The soil was <u>fertile</u>, but the thick top layer of earth (known as <u>sod</u>) was too <u>hard</u> for light ploughs.
2) There was little or no <u>wood</u> for building or fuel.
3) Lack of <u>water</u> meant crops like maize <u>failed</u> and deep <u>wells</u> had to be dug.
4) <u>Wind</u>, extremes of <u>weather</u>, <u>grasshopper</u> plagues and prairie <u>fires</u> often <u>destroyed</u> crops.

Technology and Government Acts helped settlers farm the Plains

1) Conditions on the Plains made farming (and life generally) <u>difficult</u> (see p.40).
   But new developments in <u>technology</u> and <u>crops</u> helped:

   - John Deere developed a stronger <u>steel plough</u> in the 1830s which could break through the tough soil. This was improved on by <u>James Oliver</u> who invented a <u>lower cost</u> iron plough called the 'sodbuster' in 1868.
   - <u>Windpumps</u> increased the supply of <u>water</u> by pumping underground water to the surface.
   - The introduction of <u>barbed wire</u> in 1874 meant that farmers could <u>cheaply</u> fence off their land to keep animals off their crops.
   - <u>Turkey Red Wheat</u> was a hardy crop brought over from Russia in around 1874 which was <u>well-suited</u> to growing on the Plains. People also learned which crops were most <u>suitable</u> for growing on different types of land, e.g. people in Kansas and Nebraska realised that their land was more suited to growing <u>wheat</u> than <u>corn</u>.

2) The government helped people living in <u>less fertile</u> areas who struggled to make a living from the 160 acres given to them by the Homestead Act (see p.50). For example, the <u>Timber Culture Act</u> of <u>1873</u> gave these settlers another 160 acres for free — as long as they planted <u>trees</u> on one quarter of the land. This meant that <u>wood</u> eventually became more widely available on the Plains.

> **Comment and Analysis**
> Farming was still <u>hard</u>. Not all settlers could <u>afford</u> new farming equipment.

Settlers had to Adapt to survive everyday life on the Plains

1) Because of the lack of wood, people originally had to make houses out of <u>sod</u>. But these became <u>infested</u> with insects and were <u>unhygienic</u>. Settlers <u>whitewashed</u> the walls to try and stop insects coming into the house through the walls.

2) <u>Women</u> were responsible for housework and their children's <u>education</u>. They had to collect buffalo dung for <u>fuel</u> and made a lot of what they needed, such as <u>clothes</u> and <u>soap</u>. They also <u>nursed</u> the sick and helped each other in childbirth.

> There weren't many <u>doctors</u> on the Plains.

3) <u>Isolation</u> was a constant problem for early settlers, as towns and neighbours were often far away. Women formed <u>church groups</u> and other <u>social networks</u> to combat the loneliness.

4) As more settlers arrived, <u>communities</u> formed. This eventually led to the building of <u>schools</u> and <u>shops</u>.

Settlers with their sod house in Nebraska.

© The Art Archive / Granger Collection

Life on the Plains was... well... plain difficult...

Make two columns. In the first, make a list of the hardships faced by settlers on the Plains and in the second write down how people tried to overcome them.

REVISION TASK

Cattling and Cowboys

The popularity of beef in the 1850s led to the 'Beef Bonanza' — when the beef trade became very profitable. This was when ranchers started to drive their cattle along cattle trails to reach lucrative markets further north.

The Beef Bonanza began in Texas

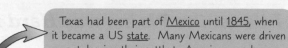

Texas had been part of Mexico until 1845, when it became a US state. Many Mexicans were driven out, leaving their cattle to American ranchers.

1) The famous Texas Longhorn cattle was the result of interbreeding between Mexican cattle and cattle brought to the USA by Anglo-American settlers.

2) Numbers of Texas Longhorn grew massively during the Civil War. Many Texans left their ranches to fight, and while they were away, their cattle continued to breed. E.g. Charles Goodnight (who would become a key figure in cattle ranching) left behind 180 cattle, but returned in 1865 to find he owned 5000.

3) Beef grew in popularity in the 1850s — there was a large demand for it in northern markets. So ranchers drove their cattle to the railroads, which then transported them to these markets.

Comment and Analysis

Railroads were very important in the growth of the cattle industry — they connected ranchers with lucrative markets. Railroads had become established by the end of the Civil War and continued to expand afterwards (see p.50).

The great Cattle Trails linked supply with demand

1) The four main cattle trails were the Goodnight-Loving Trail, the Western Trail, the Chisholm Trail and the Shawnee Trail. Trails were between 1200 and 1500 miles long and progress of 15 miles was considered a good day's drive.

1871 was the peak year for the cattle drives — 600,000 cattle were driven north.

2) Early cattle drives followed the Shawnee Trail, and cattle would then be taken east by rail to Chicago.

3) However, Oliver Loving and his partner Charles Goodnight decided to target western markets. They established the Goodnight-Loving Trail in 1866, making it possible to drive cattle from Texas to Wyoming. They sold their beef in New Mexico to the army, to growing numbers of settlers and to the US government to feed Indians on reservations. They then drove the cattle up to Colorado to sell to miners.

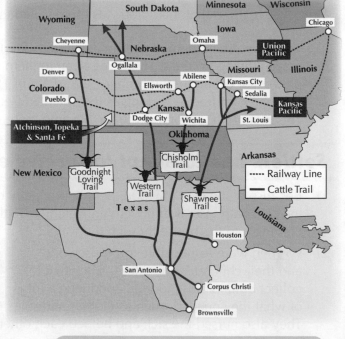

Some Indian tribes were being put on reservations in the 1860s (see p.55). Goodnight and Loving supplied beef to the Apache and Navajo Indian reservation at Fort Sumter in New Mexico.

4) Instead of driving their herds all the way north from ranches in Texas, some cattlemen decided that it would be more efficient to set up ranches on the Plains.

Open ranching meant there were no fences — cattle were free to graze where they liked.

5) The first man to do this was John Iliff, who set up open-range ranching in Wyoming in 1867. In 1868, Goodnight drove cattle up to Iliff in Wyoming, which Iliff sold on to the transcontinental railroad construction gangs. Iliff also won a government contract in 1868 to supply beef to the Sioux reservation.

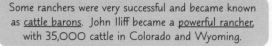

Some ranchers were very successful and became known as cattle barons. John Iliff became a powerful rancher, with 35,000 cattle in Colorado and Wyoming.

I think that 'Cow Cornucopia' sounds better...

Make sure you know the key players and how they contributed to the growth of the cattle industry. You won't get marks for getting your Goodnights and Lovings mixed up with your Iliffs.

Cattling and Cowboys

The cattle industry continued to develop and thrive with the emergence of cow towns. But it wasn't all plain sailing — cowboys had a tough job, and there was rivalry between ranchers and homesteaders.

The Cattle Trails led to the Cow Towns

> The development of refrigerated rail carriages from 1878 meant that cattle could be slaughtered before transportation.

1) The Shawnee Trail (see p.52) was threatened when homesteaders in Kansas and Missouri objected to ranchers' cattle crossing their land.

2) Joseph McCoy, a livestock trader and entrepreneur, saw the potential of moving beef cattle by rail to the eastern cities and Indian reservations. He decided to create a cow town away from homesteaders' land where cattle could be driven. He chose Abilene to be his cow town — the Kansas Pacific railway had pushed westward to run past Abilene and it was away from settled areas.

3) In sixty days in 1867, McCoy built Abilene up to a fully equipped cow town, with a stockyard, hotel, and bank. It was soon connected to Texas via the Chisholm Trail — McCoy persuaded ranchers to drive their cattle to Abilene, where they would be sold and transported to northern markets.

4) In a few years, about 3 million cattle had passed through Abilene. Soon, other cow towns such as Wichita, Ellsworth and Dodge City emerged, as the railway continued to advance westwards.

The Cowboys' job was Very Tough and Badly Paid

1) The men who drove the cattle on the trails were called cowboys. Cowboys had a tough job — they had to contend with storms, river floods and, worst of all, stampedes on the trail.

2) Boredom and discomfort were also part of the job. Winters were spent watching the cattle from line camps on the edges of the ranch. Trail life mostly involved breathing dust and staring at cows.

> Many cowboys were Mexican or African Americans. Some were ex-soldiers from the Civil War, some were outlaws. Most cowboys were young and single with little time for a family life.

3) Longhorn cattle are big and aggressive, so rounding them up by 'cutting out' the correct cattle from mixed herds on the open range took skill.

4) Cowboys sometimes came into conflict with other people on the Plains. Native Americans and other rustlers could steal or stampede cattle. Diplomacy would help deal with some situations, but others ended in violence, so cowboys had to know how to use a gun.

5) Cowboys had to work as a team on the trail to succeed. They were highly disciplined and were kept in line as much by each other as by their bosses.

> The hardships of the trail led to many cowboys letting off steam and misbehaving once a cattle drive was over (see p.54).

6) Cowboys' pay was low but tended to come in one lump at the end of a drive.

> The work of the cowboy changed as ranches became increasingly established on the Plains in the 1870s. It reduced the distance that cowboys had to drive cattle — the journey from Texas to the railroads could take up to two months, but from ranches on the Plains it could be done in around 35 days.

There was Rivalry between Ranchers and Homesteaders

1) Homesteaders living on the Plains weren't always delighted to see ranchers' cattle heading for their homes. The lack of wood on the Plains for fences meant that homesteaders' crops could be destroyed by the cattlemen's herds as they passed. Homesteaders' cattle sometimes died — the cattlemen's Longhorn herds carried a disease called Texas fever which they were immune to but homesteaders' cattle weren't.

2) Homesteaders used barbed wire as a cheap way to fence off their land from 1874, but this reduced cattlemen's access to water and made cattle drives much harder.

3) As ranches moved onto the Plains there were clashes with homesteaders over land ownership. This would lead to violent confrontations later on, such as the Johnson County War (see p.59).

Beef up your knowledge by making some mind maps...

Create a mind map of how the cattle industry developed. Make sure you have each of the main factors and then add detail to explain each one. You'll need to use the information from p.52 too.

Law and Order Problems

Law and order became a big problem as more people settled more areas of the West.

Settled areas became Territories, which then became States

1) As the USA expanded, it brought more land and people under the control of its government.

2) The USA has a federal system of government — there's a national government in Washington, and then each state also has a government of its own, which is responsible for things such as law and order.

3) As the West developed, it was carved up roughly into territories. The federal government controlled these, and took responsibility for law and order by sending a governor, a marshal and three judges into each territory. As the population increased, people could elect some of the lawmen, such as sheriffs.

> Marshals sent in by the government looked after whole territories. They had deputy marshals to help them. Territories were split into counties and towns — sheriffs were in charge of counties and some towns elected town marshals.

4) Territories became states when the population reached 60,000. On becoming a state, law and order decisions could be made locally, instead of relying on the federal government a long way away.

Many Factors led to Crime on the Plains

1) **Gold** — Gold was discovered in Montana and Nevada in the 1860s and 70s. These areas had the same problems as California during the 1849 Gold Rush (see p.42). The areas grew quickly, and criminals were attracted by the potential riches, but it took time to establish systems of law and order.

2) **Cow towns** — Cowboys would go to cow towns such as Abilene and Dodge City at the end of long cattle drives. These places grew to provide lots of temptations for cowboys who wanted to relax after their hard work on the trail. There was drunkenness, gambling and gun fights.

3) **Homesteaders and cattlemen** — There was conflict as homesteaders and cattlemen clashed with each other (see p.53). They struggled to live side-by-side on the Plains.

> Many people carried guns — this created a culture of violence. Poverty and lack of stable communities to promote good behaviour in new settlements also contributed to lawlessness.

4) **Gangs** — Outlaws formed gangs, which robbed trains and banks, and often committed murders. In the late 1860s, many of these men were ex-Confederate soldiers who turned to crime after the Civil War, e.g. the famous outlaw Jesse James.

5) **Racial tensions** — Different groups of people including African Americans, Chinese, Europeans and Mexicans, created the potential for conflict.

Policing these areas was Difficult

1) The West was a huge area of land, and transport was slow — it could take a long time for marshals to reach remote areas.

> **Comment and Analysis**
> The geography of America was an important cause of law and order problems.

> Plummer was caught and hung by vigilantes. Vigilante groups could do some good, but their justice was violent, quick and not always fair.

2) Law officers such as sheriffs and marshals were sometimes criminals themselves. For example, Henry Plummer was elected Sheriff of the gold mining town of Bannack in Montana in 1863 while he was still the leader of a gang of robbers.

3) For lawmen such as sheriffs, the work was dangerous and they were poorly paid — this made it difficult to attract new recruits. There was also a shortage of money to train anyone who wanted to do the job.

4) This lack of formal law enforcement meant that vigilante groups often sprang up. These were made up of ordinary citizens who tried to keep law and order — often brutally.

5) The army also tried to police the West. 'Buffalo soldiers' were black soldiers whose job it was to keep order among settlers and fight Native Americans who raided white settlements.

These guys had worse problems than stolen wheelie bins...

Make a bullet point list of law and order problems on the Plains. Then write down the attempted solutions to these and how successful you think they were. Use evidence to back up your opinion.

The Indian Wars

The Plains Indians grew increasingly <u>threatened</u> as more people settled on the Plains — this led to <u>conflict</u>.

Railroads, Ranching and Gold angered the Plains Indians

1) <u>Railroad companies</u> often clashed with the Plains Indians. They encouraged the <u>settling</u> of the Plains as they expanded their networks and they frequently built railroads <u>through</u> Native American lands, even if it <u>violated</u> treaties.

2) Railroad companies also encouraged the <u>hunting</u> of buffalo — both to <u>feed</u> the railway construction gangs, and to make money by <u>transporting</u> hunters.

Buffalo hunting became a popular sport (see p.61).

3) Buffalo were a hugely important <u>resource</u> for Native Americans (see p.38). Some tribes <u>derailed</u> trains and <u>ambushed</u> workmen. In response, the military built <u>forts</u> to safeguard the railroad.

Sioux raiding a train on the Great Plains.

© The Art Archive / Granger Collection

4) <u>Ranchers</u> clashed with the Plains Indians when their <u>cattle drives</u> went through Indian land and when they built <u>ranches</u> on Indian territories. Again, this disrupted buffalo herds, leading to Indian <u>attacks</u> on ranchers and the cattle drives. <u>Oliver Loving</u> (see p.52) died in 1867 after a fight with <u>Comanches</u>.

5) When gold was discovered in <u>Montana</u> in <u>1862</u>, miners arrived in the area and prospected on Indian <u>reservation</u> land, breaking the treaties which had <u>promised</u> this land to the Native Americans.

Many Plains Indians were Unhappy with the Reservation Policy

1) More Indians were moved onto <u>reservations</u> as more settlers came to live on the Plains.

Many Plains tribes were still <u>able</u> to hunt <u>buffalo</u>, but only within <u>certain areas</u>.

2) Life on reservations <u>varied</u>. The <u>Navajos</u> achieved <u>peace</u> and <u>prosperity</u> after 1868 when a treaty with the US allowed them <u>sufficient</u> reservation area in their <u>homeland</u>.

3) Other tribes were moved off their <u>homeland</u> and onto <u>unfamiliar</u> territory. They were encouraged to <u>farm</u> the land, which went against their <u>culture</u> and <u>nomadic</u> lifestyle.

4) Often reservation lands were <u>insufficient</u> and <u>unsuitable</u> for farming — some tribes faced <u>starvation</u>.

5) If the lands were <u>good</u>, they were often <u>grabbed</u> by settlers, despite the <u>promises</u> in the government treaties. Many chiefs also lacked the <u>authority</u> to make their tribes keep to the agreements.

Many tribes wanted <u>peace</u>, but the situation had become <u>intolerable</u>. They were forced into <u>conflict</u> during the 1860s in a series of <u>Indian Wars</u>.

Comment and Analysis

It isn't <u>surprising</u> the Native Americans went to war. The government had given them the Great Plains (see p.37), but the government repeatedly <u>broke</u> their promises and <u>forced</u> tribes onto <u>ever-smaller</u> areas of land.

Little Crow's War was an uprising in Minnesota — 1862

1) The first major Indian War was Little Crow's War. Little Crow was the chief of the Santee Sioux, also known as the <u>Dakota</u>, who lived on a reservation in Minnesota.

2) They were peaceful and <u>accepted</u> reservation life. But they nearly <u>starved</u> as a result of Civil War <u>shortages</u>, a <u>delay</u> in their payment from the government, <u>cheating</u> by traders and a <u>poor</u> harvest.

3) In August 1862, four Dakota returning from an unsuccessful hunt <u>murdered</u> five settlers for a dare. Fearing <u>retaliation</u> on the entire tribe, Little Crow reluctantly led his warriors in an <u>uprising</u>. Hundreds of settlers and about 100 soldiers were killed, and the town of <u>New Ulm</u> was burned.

4) The uprising was ended when the Dakota were defeated at <u>Wood Lake</u> in September. 38 Dakota prisoners were <u>hanged</u> and most of the Dakota were <u>expelled</u> from what was left of their land.

Railroads didn't have a positive impact on everybody...

Give two consequences of the building of the railroads for the Plains Indians and explain them. [8]

The Indian Wars

More Indian Wars followed during the 1860s. This led the US government to try a more peaceful approach.

The Cheyenne Uprising and the Sand Creek Massacre — 1864

1) In 1863, the Cheyenne faced starvation because they couldn't grow enough food on their infertile reservation land at Sand Creek (see p.43) or find any buffalo. They decided to raid settlers' wagon trains for food. There was further violence between Indians and the army during 1864.

2) Chief Black Kettle, who wanted peace, moved his band to a camp where he believed they would be safe. But in November 1864, Colonel John Chivington attacked the camp while most of the band's men were out hunting. Of the 500 people left in the camp, at least 163 were killed — mostly women and children.

3) The Cheyenne, Arapaho and Sioux retaliated by attacking ranches and other settlements, and killing those inside, including women and children. The central Plains erupted into war.

Red Cloud's War and the Bozeman Trail — 1866-1868

1) The Bozeman Trail was established to link the gold fields in Montana with the Oregon Trail. However, this trail passed through the hunting grounds of the Sioux, which had been guaranteed to them by the Fort Laramie Treaty of 1851.

2) The Sioux attacked travellers who used the trail, so the army wanted to build forts to protect them. Talks were held with Red Cloud, a Sioux chief, to negotiate the building of these forts, but they were abandoned when the Sioux saw soldiers marching out to begin building before any deal had been made.

3) The Sioux began to attack the army. In a major incident known as Fetterman's Trap, the Sioux ambushed Captain W.J. Fetterman and his troops — Fetterman and all 80 of his men were killed.

Red Cloud.

4) As a result, the US army surrendered and abandoned the forts. This was a major defeat for the army.

- Red Cloud eventually signed the 1868 Fort Laramie Treaty, which created a large Sioux reservation on an area that included the sacred Black Hills of Dakota. The government also agreed not to rebuild their forts on the Bozeman Trail.

- Red Cloud promised never again to make war on the settlers — and kept his promise. But not all of the Sioux bands agreed with the treaty. Sioux chiefs Crazy Horse and Sitting Bull would be involved in future conflict (see p.60).

Policies of Separation and Assimilation were tried

> Many settlers and army officers such as General Sherman thought the Native Americans should be destroyed. Many politicians took a more humane view.

1) The Indian Wars made it clear to the government that their Indian policy wasn't working. The government wanted to move away from aggressive military actions.

2) In 1867, the Indian Peace Commission tried to establish peace by negotiating the Medicine Lodge Treaty — this treaty moved southern Plains Indian tribes onto smaller reservations away from settlers.

3) Following on from this, President Grant established his 'Peace Policy' in 1868 — the aim was to assimilate the Indians peacefully into white society. But it was agreed that those who resisted the policy would face military action.

4) The policy failed — the Native Americans didn't want to give up their lifestyle and Grant didn't stop settlers encroaching on Indian land when gold was found on the Black Hills of Dakota in 1874. More conflict would follow (see p.60).

Comment and Analysis

Although the 'Peace Policy' had humane intentions, it still aimed to deny the Native Americans their way of life — many didn't want to be assimilated.

The Indian Wars soured relations ever further...

'Settlers and the Plains Indians were equally to blame for the conflict on the Plains in the period 1849-1870'. Explain whether you find this interpretation convincing or not. [8]

Changes in the Cattle Industry

The <u>1860s</u> to the <u>1880s</u> were the ranchers' <u>heyday</u> (see p.52-53) — but the Beef Bonanza didn't last <u>forever</u>.

Changing Tastes and Hard Winters ended the Beef Bonanza

1) Eastern markets eventually began to demand a <u>higher quality</u> of meat than the Longhorn could provide. This led ranchers like Iliff and Goodnight to start <u>crossbreeding</u> Longhorns with Herefords — the meat from these cattle was better quality, but the cattle were <u>less resistant</u> to harsh conditions.

2) States passed <u>quarantine</u> laws because settlers were concerned about diseases carried by the ranchers' cattle (see p.53) — from <u>1885</u> Kansas <u>shut its borders</u> to Texas cattle between March and November.

3) Ranchers <u>overstocked</u> their cattle and after 1885 there was <u>less demand</u> for beef — herds grew very <u>large</u> and <u>prices fell</u>. The herds became too large for the grazing area and the <u>drought</u> of 1886 meant there wasn't enough <u>grass</u> to feed the cattle.

> Ranchers had become <u>greedy</u> — they wanted to take <u>advantage</u> of the high demand for beef, but they allowed their herds to grow too <u>large</u>.

Comment and Analysis

> The winter of 1886-1887 was the <u>catalyst</u> for change on the ranches.

4) The <u>over-grazed range</u> meant that underfed cattle entered the terrible winter of <u>1886-1887</u> in weakened condition. <u>Thousands</u> of cattle died. Homesteaders' <u>fences</u> became death traps as cattle piled against them during <u>blizzards</u>. Average losses were perhaps 30%. Many cowboys also died.

The end of the Beef Bonanza Transformed cattle Ranching

1) Ranchers had to <u>adapt</u> when the cattle boom ended.

2) Businesses which survived the 1880s <u>economised</u> by raising better-quality animals on smaller areas of land, shifting towards a <u>more managed</u> environment.

3) More intensive ranching also favoured <u>smaller scale</u> operations — these were more likely to be <u>family-owned</u> than corporate.

> The bad winter of 1886-1887 had shown ranchers the importance of <u>caring</u> for their cattle in harsh weather, including being able to <u>feed</u> and <u>shelter</u> them.

4) Ranching now depended on the ability to <u>feed</u> livestock in <u>winter</u>. Ranchers grew crops such as <u>hay</u> so that they could feed their cattle and this meant that dependence on <u>irrigation</u> increased.

> <u>Windpumps</u> made it <u>easier</u> for ranchers to fence off their land. Previously, cattle had <u>moved</u> around to find water sources, but this invention allowed water to be pumped from <u>underground</u>.

5) Ranchers, like homesteaders, began to use <u>barbed wire</u> enclosures to fence off their land — this allowed them to <u>control</u> their herds and look after them. Cattle could no longer roam <u>freely</u> — it was the <u>end</u> of the open range.

The end of the open range had a large Impact on the Cowboy

1) The change from the <u>open range</u> to <u>fenced pastures</u> changed the <u>role</u> of the cowboy.

2) The expansion of the <u>railroads</u> made long drives <u>unnecessary</u>. <u>Round-ups</u> (herding cattle together) occurred <u>less often</u> and involved much <u>smaller</u> herds of cattle. This meant that <u>fewer</u> cowboys were needed and those who remained spent less time <u>roaming</u> the Plains on their horses.

Comment and Analysis

> The end of <u>cowboy culture</u> and the <u>cattle trails</u> helped bring some <u>order</u> to the Plains.

3) Cowboys became <u>domesticated</u> ranch hands with more <u>mundane</u> jobs, such as mending <u>fences</u>. As ranchers were growing more <u>crops</u>, cowboys became more involved in <u>farming</u>.

> The <u>romantic</u> image of the cowboy has remained <u>strong</u> in popular culture — it's a symbol of a <u>wild</u> and <u>free</u> existence.

4) As a whole, their lives became more <u>settled</u> — their living conditions on ranches were more <u>comfortable</u> than life on the trail, they had to follow <u>ranch rules</u> and their hours were more <u>regular</u>.

The 'Cow Cornucopia' was good while it lasted...

Make a list of the factors which resulted in the decline of the cattle industry and explain each one. Decide which you think is the most important factor and write a paragraph explaining why.

Changes in Farming

Living and farming on the Great Plains was still <u>hard</u>, but the area was eventually <u>successfully</u> settled.

People continued to Settle on the Plains...

> People had started to move onto even <u>drier</u> areas of the Plains by 1880.

1) Different groups of people were still helping to settle the West:

- There were <u>10 million immigrants</u> to America during <u>1865-90</u> — many of these helped settle the West, such as the <u>Scandinavians</u> on the <u>Dakotas</u>. By 1900 there were 500,000 farms on the Plains.
- At the end of the Reconstruction Era in 1877, <u>African Americans</u> faced growing oppression in the South. As a result, thousands moved West (see p.63). This mass migration is known as the <u>Exoduster movement</u>.

> The effects of the <u>Civil War</u> were still being felt.

2) <u>Government</u> actions also helped:

- **The Desert Land Act 1877** — Farmers who lived on <u>drier</u> land could buy up to <u>640 acres</u> at a low cost as long as they <u>irrigated</u> the land within three years.
- **The Oklahoma Land Rush of 1889** — The government opened up <u>two million acres</u> of land in Oklahoma to settlers in 1889 — this had previously been <u>Indian</u> territory (see p.37). Thousands of people rushed into the territory to claim their land.

> In <u>1893</u> another <u>6 million acres</u> was opened up. This land was known as the '<u>Cherokee Strip</u>' and had been promised to the <u>Cherokees</u> 60 years previously on their <u>removal</u> to the Plains.

3) By 1890, <u>six</u> railroads crossed the US from east to west. This helped to make the Plains a <u>less isolated</u> place and linked farmers on the Plains with wider <u>markets</u>.

4) People continued to <u>adapt</u> to life on the Plains. <u>Towns</u> developed and <u>communities</u> grew, as more people settled the Plains. Life was made more <u>comfortable</u> by luxury goods brought by railroads from the East.

5) There were still <u>hardships</u> though, and the <u>failure</u> rate for new farms was high. There were severe <u>droughts</u> in the <u>1870s</u> and <u>1880s</u>, and problems caused by <u>overgrazing</u>. Some people got into debt and <u>lost</u> their farms, while others gave up and moved on.

... and Farming continued to Develop

1) Farmers began to learn techniques to cope with the low rainfall and retain the moisture in the soil, e.g. '<u>dry farming</u>' involved turning the soil after rain.

2) Machinery — such as reapers, binders and harvesters — was <u>developed</u> and <u>improved</u> to harvest grain <u>faster</u>.

> Farmers who could afford to were using <u>steam-powered tractors</u> by the <u>1890s</u>.

3) Initially only farmers making good profits could afford to buy new machinery, but it eventually became more <u>widespread</u> as it became more <u>affordable</u>. The <u>railroads</u> gave farmers greater access to machinery by transporting it to the Plains from the <u>East</u>.

Steam-powered wheat thresher, 1878.

> This image shows the <u>productivity</u> of the Plains and the growing use of <u>new</u> machinery.

4) <u>Bonanza farms</u> were established. These were large farms which grew and harvested wheat on a <u>large scale</u>.

5) The Great Plains helped the US become a major world <u>wheat</u> producer. In <u>1895</u>, the US grew around <u>three times</u> as much wheat and corn as it did in <u>1860</u>.

Comment and Analysis

By the 1890s, farming was becoming increasingly <u>mechanized</u> — farm work took <u>less time</u>, required <u>less labour</u> and became <u>more productive</u>.

Settle down at the back — there's a lot to plough through...

A lot of the problems faced by homesteaders had been solved by the 1890s. Make sure you can give specific examples in the exam of the technology and farming methods which helped settlers.

Wild West

It was known as the <u>Wild West</u> for a reason. <u>Lawlessness</u> was still a big issue.

Conflicts over Land and Power led to Violence and Lawlessness

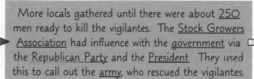

The violence in the late 1800s in the American West was partly due to changes in <u>society</u>. Cattle barons, railroads and other <u>corporations</u> — using the power and influence that their size gave them — were <u>taking over</u> from the homesteaders, small ranchers and prospectors. Some historians call the violence it sparked the '<u>Western Civil War of Incorporation</u>'.

1) There were conflicts called the <u>Range Wars</u> — the <u>Lincoln County War</u> and the <u>Johnson County War</u>.

2) The <u>Lincoln County War</u> of <u>1878</u> resulted in the murder of a <u>cattle baron</u> called <u>John Tunstall</u>. A gang of <u>outlaws</u> called the <u>Regulators</u> took the law into their own hands and got revenge on Tunstall's killers. One of the Regulators, <u>Billy the Kid</u>, escaped justice and later became a famous figure of the Wild West.

3) The <u>Johnson County War</u> took place in <u>1892</u>. Homesteaders in <u>Johnson County</u>, Wyoming, felt that the <u>cattle barons</u> were stealing their <u>land</u>. Cattle barons felt that homesteaders were blocking their use of the <u>open range</u> and accused them of <u>rustling</u> (stealing) their cattle.

In <u>1892</u>, the <u>Wyoming Stock Growers Association</u> (who represented the cattle barons) mounted a vigilante raid into <u>Johnson County</u>. They killed two alleged rustlers, but locals came out of <u>Buffalo</u> and laid siege to the vigilantes.	More locals gathered until there were about <u>250</u> men ready to kill the vigilantes. The <u>Stock Growers Association</u> had influence with the <u>government</u> via the <u>Republican Party</u> and the <u>President</u>. They used this to call out the <u>army</u>, who rescued the vigilantes.	There were <u>no prosecutions</u>, but the cattle barons lost their <u>power</u> and <u>influence</u> and the war marked the <u>end</u> of the open range in Wyoming.

Lawmen fought the Outlaws

1) A career as a lawman in the Wild West was open to <u>all sorts</u> of people. <u>Wyatt Earp</u> was a natural recruit for the forces of <u>incorporation</u> (corporations and big businesses) as he was a keen <u>entrepreneur</u> and an effective <u>gunman</u>.

> Earp had been <u>arrested</u> in 1871 for <u>stealing</u> horses in Missouri. He <u>fled</u> the state and the federal system did nothing to <u>prevent</u> his later career as a lawman.

2) Earp, his <u>brothers</u> and <u>Doc Holliday</u> killed three men who were accused of cattle rustling and other crimes at the <u>OK Corral</u> in Arizona in <u>1881</u>. The dead men were <u>typical</u> of the small ranchers/outlaws who opposed the growth of big business in the West.

3) Some people believed that the violence <u>wasn't justified</u> — the Earps and Holliday were charged with <u>murder</u>, but this was later <u>dropped</u>. A bloody <u>feud</u> followed the shootout. When Wyatt's brother Morgan was killed, Wyatt got his <u>revenge</u> by killing the men he believed responsible.

4) Other lawmen had successes in hunting down outlaws. <u>Pat Garrett</u>, who became sheriff of Lincoln County in 1880, hunted down and shot <u>Billy the Kid</u> after he escaped from jail in <u>1881</u>.

> Some lawmen, such as <u>Bill Tilghman</u>, gained reputations for being <u>respectable</u> and <u>honest</u>. Unlike other lawmen, he wasn't quick to resort to <u>violence</u>. He became Deputy US Marshal in <u>Oklahoma</u> in 1892 and played a <u>major</u> part in stopping outlaw activity there.

Law and order in the West gradually Improved

1) The expansion of the <u>railroads</u> and improved <u>communication</u> (e.g. the telegraph) helped law enforcement — <u>news</u> travelled faster and lawmen could more <u>easily</u> reach areas where there was trouble.

2) More <u>homesteaders</u> arrived who wanted to make a successful life — they demanded <u>better</u> law and order.

3) As towns developed, <u>living conditions</u> improved — towns and roads were planned, with better <u>buildings</u> and <u>sanitation</u> systems. This created a more <u>civilised</u> atmosphere and encouraged <u>better</u> behaviour.

4) More <u>states</u> were created, so more areas were becoming <u>responsible</u> for their own law and order rather than <u>relying</u> on a distant federal government. <u>Seven</u> more territories became states between <u>1876</u> and <u>1890</u>, bringing the number of states up to <u>44</u>.

Learn it or lose marks — it's Earp to you...

The lines between who was right and wrong in the Wild West aren't that clear. When answering exam questions, remember that lawmen such as Wyatt Earp weren't squeaky clean.

EXAM TIP

War on the Plains

The government attempted a more 'peaceful' approach to Native Americans, but it only led to more conflict.

Fighting occurred at the battle of Little Bighorn

1) In 1874, troops under Lt. Col. George Custer confirmed the presence of gold in the Black Hills of Dakota and a gold rush began. The US government tried to buy the Black Hills from the Sioux, but they refused — the hills were sacred and belonged to them under the 1868 Fort Laramie Treaty.

2) Despite the Sioux's refusal to sell the Black Hills, miners arrived to search for gold. In protest, many of the Sioux left the reservation and gathered in Montana in the Bighorn Valley. The government ordered the Sioux back to their reservation, but they refused. By the start of 1876, Sitting Bull and Crazy Horse had raised the largest Native American force ever seen (several thousand men).

3) The US government sent soldiers to oppose the uprising. The Sioux launched a successful attack on the soldiers while they were resting, killing 28 of them. This became known as the Battle of the Rosebud.

4) Army commanders Sheridan and Terry planned an attack on the Sioux village at Little Bighorn, but Custer and his men arrived first and decided to attack alone.

5) Custer split his men into three groups — the other two were led by Reno and Benteen. When Custer approached the village with around 220 soldiers, they were surrounded by Indians — he and all of his men were killed. This was the greatest Native American victory in battle against the US army.

Different Factors explain the Defeat of the US army

1) **Custer** He was ambitious and after personal glory. He marched his men through the night and arrived at Little Bighorn a day early, so his men were tired. He ignored orders to wait for the rest of the army and warnings from his Indian scouts that the Sioux village was too large for them to fight alone. He also turned down the offer of extra men and guns, and weakened his force by splitting it into three.

2) **Custer's commanders** Terry and Sheridan didn't try to find out how many Indians were in the village.

3) **Reno and Benteen** Custer ordered them to come to his support but they didn't. They were under attack themselves and later argued that this was why they were unable to help Custer.

4) **Bad luck** Quicksand stopped Custer from crossing the river to attack the village — he and his men were forced onto higher ground, where they were seen by the Sioux.

5) **Native Americans** The Sioux were determined to save their territory. Instead of fleeing, which was their usual tactic, they stood and fought — Custer wasn't expecting this. He also wasn't expecting the Indians to have superior weaponry — many had repeating Winchester rifles, while Custer's soldiers had single shot Springfields. Sioux leaders such as Crazy Horse were experienced warriors, and they joined forces with their traditional enemies, the Cheyenne and Arapaho, to greatly outnumber the US army.

The Indians Won at Little Bighorn but it made things even Worse

- In 1876-1877, the army launched a winter campaign known as the Great Sioux War. Facing hunger and the loss of their horses, the Sioux surrendered and were forced onto reservations. Crazy Horse surrendered in May 1877 and was later killed by a US soldier while resisting arrest.

- Sioux reservations were put under military control and, in 1877, the Black Hills were opened to white settlement.

- Sitting Bull retreated to Canada, but returned and surrendered in 1881.

Comment and Analysis

Little Bighorn was only a short-term victory for the Native Americans. It wasn't enough to turn their fortunes around and the US army's determination to defeat them increased following the battle.

I don't get it — was it a little or a big horn?

Was Custer's ambition or the Indians' determination the more important reason for the US army's defeat at Little Bighorn? Explain your answer, referring to both reasons. [12]

A Way of Life Destroyed

It seems as though the Indians had always been fighting a losing battle against land-hungry settlers.

Buffalo Slaughter forced Native Americans to accept Reservations

1) <u>Millions</u> of buffalo had once roamed the Plains. They were <u>vital</u> to the Native Americans' survival (see p.38) and were <u>sacred</u> to them.

2) Buffalo were <u>slaughtered</u> in large numbers by white settlers (see p.55). They were killed to <u>feed</u> soldiers and railroad construction workers. People also killed them for their <u>skins</u> — there was a demand for buffalo <u>robes</u> in the East from the 1850s, and from 1871 a process was developed to make buffalo hides into <u>leather</u>. Others just killed them for <u>sport</u> — men would shoot the animals from the windows of trains.

3) As a result of this, buffalo numbers <u>decreased</u> rapidly — it has been estimated that there were <u>13 million</u> buffalo on the Plains in <u>1865</u>, but by the <u>end</u> of the century they were almost <u>extinct</u>.

A buffalo skinner. Buffalo skins were much in demand. The rest of the animal would be left to decay on the Plains.

4) The effect on the Plains Indians was <u>devastating</u> — their main source of <u>food</u> was gone, as well as a major part of their <u>culture</u>. This caused many Indians to accept life on the <u>reservations</u> — they feared <u>starvation</u>.

5) It's not <u>clear</u> whether there was an official <u>policy</u> to exterminate the buffalo, but many people recognised that destroying them would help <u>defeat</u> the Indians.

> General Sheridan is quoted as saying, 'let them kill, skin and sell until the buffalo is <u>exterminated</u> as it is the only way to bring lasting <u>peace</u> and allow <u>civilisation</u> to advance'.

Reservations destroyed their Culture

1) Many Plains Indians were <u>nomadic</u>. Confined to smaller areas, they could no longer feed or clothe themselves without government aid. Living on <u>hand-outs</u>, they became demoralised. There were high rates of <u>alcoholism</u>.

2) Many tribes were moved off their culturally significant <u>ancestral lands</u> and onto reservations elsewhere. The influence of <u>chiefs</u> declined because reservations were run by Indian agents, <u>undermining</u> tribal structure. <u>Hostile</u> tribes were sometimes put on reservations in close <u>proximity</u>.

3) Many children were taken away to be <u>educated</u>, for example at the Carlisle Indian School in Pennsylvania (founded in 1879). <u>Polygamy</u> (having more than one wife) and <u>religious practices</u> such as the Sun Dance, were banned. The threat of <u>withholding rations</u> was used to enforce cooperation.

Comment and Analysis

The government had always wanted the Indians to <u>assimilate</u>. As Indians living on the reservations were now <u>dependent</u> on the state, there was a way to force them to abandon their own <u>culture</u>.

Native Americans were Unable to fight back Successfully

It's <u>debatable</u> whether the Plains Indians could ever have <u>protected</u> their traditional way of life. There were many <u>factors</u> at work against them:

1) The US army usually had better <u>weapons</u> than the Native Americans — repeating rifles, machine guns and cannons.

2) The system of <u>forts</u> gave the US army control on the Plains. The <u>railroads</u> and <u>telegraph</u> system provided fast transport and communication.

3) <u>Divisions</u> between Native American nations meant that they had no <u>organised</u> resistance. Reservation life also made it more <u>difficult</u> for them to resist.

Comment and Analysis

It seems that <u>nothing</u> could halt the tide of white settlers — and <u>broken</u> government promises failed to <u>protect</u> the Indians from it.

Not a particularly proud moment in American history...

Give an account that analyses how the Native American way of life was destroyed. [8]

EXAM QUESTION

Assimilation of the Native Americans

America's population was growing — increasing the pressure on reservation land.

The Dawes Act (1887) Parcelled Out tribal lands

1) The aim of the Dawes Act was to convert tribesmen into independent farmers. It was hoped this would help destroy tribal bonds and lead to the assimilation of Native Americans into white society.

> Some reformers supported the Act because they wanted to stop Indian suffering on reservations. Some believed that reservation life encouraged idleness and reliance on government hand-outs. Others just wanted to open up reservation lands to settlers.

2) The Dawes Act broke reservations up into allotments. Each head of family was assigned 160 acres, each single adult 80 acres, and each child 40 acres. US citizenship was also part of the deal.

3) When all the inhabitants of a reservation had been assigned their holdings, the remaining land was thrown open to white settlement. Indian schools were established from the sale of this surplus land.

4) The Act was a disaster for the Native Americans:

*   Their tribal communities were broken up and their culture almost destroyed — the idea of land ownership went against Native American tradition.

> Men found it difficult to adapt to farming — this had traditionally been seen as a woman's role. In Indian schools, children had to dress like white Americans and weren't allowed to speak tribal languages.

*   The creation of allotments led to Indians losing their land — down from 138 million acres in 1887 to 78 million acres in 1900. They also lost land granted to them under the Act (nearly two thirds of it between 1887 and 1934) as a result of being cheated by land speculators.

Comment and Analysis

While many reformers may have believed they had good intentions, their actions were based on their prejudiced belief that Native Americans needed to be introduced to Christianity and western civilisation to improve themselves.

*   Lands belonging to the five eastern tribes that had been moved on to the Plains in the 1830s (see p.37) were exempt from the Dawes Act, yet through forced sales they too were eventually lost.

*   In 1934, the government repealed the Dawes Act and encouraged tribal identities. But by that time, Native Americans had lost over 60 per cent of their original reservation lands and were suffering from high rates of poverty, alcoholism, illiteracy and suicide.

The Wounded Knee Massacre was the End of Indian resistance

The Wounded Knee Massacre (also known as the Battle of Wounded Knee) was the last confrontation between Native Americans and the US army.

> Some ghost dancers believed that special shirts would protect them from bullets. The sight of the shirts pierced by bullets after the battle destroyed their faith in a magical restoration of the old way of life. The reservation was reluctantly accepted as home.

*   Native American spiritual leader Wovoka said that a special Ghost Dance could raise the dead and bring a world free from settlers. He was against violence, but ghost dances built the dancers up into a frenzy. This unsettled white Americans, who feared that the dance would lead to rebellion.

*   Tensions peaked at the Pine Ridge Reservation in Wounded Knee Creek, South Dakota. Fighting broke out between a band of Sioux and the US army — 150 Sioux and 25 soldiers died.

Americans became aware of the End of the Frontier

1) In 1890, census results revealed that, unlike in 1880, there was no longer a definable western frontier of settlement. The frontier was declared officially closed.

> The Native Americans were no longer a barrier to settlement — they'd been subdued and were in the process of being assimilated into white society.

2) This didn't mean that there was no more land available for settlers, but what remained was in isolated pockets and the best areas had been taken.

The frontier closed — and the West is history...

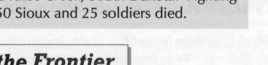

To sum up — settlers in, Indians out. It's all very well knowing all the little facts about this period of American history, but to write a good answer you've got to know how they fit together too.

Changes to the Lives of African Americans

After 1877, African Americans <u>lost</u> many of the <u>gains</u> they had made during <u>Reconstruction</u> (see p.48-49).

African Americans lost their Civil Rights

African Americans had an <u>inferior</u> status in society as a result of <u>segregation</u>. This meant that they were <u>separated</u> from white people, for example in schools, shops, hotels, theatres and on public transport.

1) Southern states passed '<u>Jim Crow</u>' laws which <u>legalised</u> segregation. <u>Intermarriage</u> also became illegal.

2) In 1883, the <u>Supreme Court</u> ruled that the 1875 <u>Civil Rights Act</u>, which had outlawed <u>discrimination</u> in public places, was <u>unconstitutional</u> (against the constitution).

3) The Supreme Court also <u>supported segregation</u>. In the <u>Plessy v. Ferguson</u> case of 1896, it ruled that a Louisiana law requiring <u>separate railway coaches</u> for African Americans was <u>constitutional</u>.

> There was an increase in <u>violence</u> against African Americans in the 1890s. <u>Lynchings</u> became more common — lynchings are killings <u>without trial</u>, often by <u>hanging</u>.

They faced Economic Repression

Many African Americans lived in <u>poverty</u> and were <u>prevented</u> from making money.

1) Many worked as <u>sharecroppers</u>, harvesting cotton and tobacco, or in <u>low paid</u> jobs in the coal and iron industries. Sharecroppers were often <u>exploited</u> by landowners and became <u>trapped</u> in a cycle of poverty and debt.

2) They had few chances to <u>improve</u> their lives — legal restrictions and violence often <u>prevented</u> them from working in <u>skilled</u> professions. <u>Education</u> for African Americans was <u>poor</u> — African American schools were given <u>less funding</u> than white schools by state governments.

> White southerners felt <u>threatened</u> by African Americans and wanted to maintain <u>white superiority</u>. Many in the South were still <u>bitter</u> about the outcome of the <u>Civil War</u>.

3) States passed laws which punished <u>small</u> crimes with <u>harsh</u> sentences, e.g. the <u>Pig Laws</u>, which punished people for stealing farm animals, and <u>vagrancy statutes</u>, which made it a crime to be unemployed. These laws targeted African Americans as they were <u>more likely</u> to be <u>poor</u> and <u>unemployed</u>.

They were Denied their Political Rights

Democrats regained control of the South in <u>1877</u>. They tried to <u>remove</u> African American <u>voting rights</u> — rights which they had been guaranteed under the <u>15th Amendment</u> (see p.49).

1) States passed new state <u>constitutions</u> which introduced voting <u>restrictions</u>, such as <u>poll taxes</u> and <u>literacy tests</u>. This mostly affected African Americans because they were more likely to be <u>poor</u> or <u>unable</u> to read and write — the voting restrictions made it <u>difficult</u> or <u>impossible</u> for many of them to vote.

> People who couldn't vote weren't able to run for <u>office</u> or serve on <u>juries</u> — <u>reducing</u> African American <u>participation</u> in politics even further.

2) The <u>Supreme Court</u> upheld these new constitutions. It ruled that Mississippi's 1890 constitution <u>wasn't</u> discriminatory and other southern states adopted <u>similar</u> constitutions between 1890 and 1908.

Many African Americans Moved out of the South

1) Many African Americans moved to the <u>West</u>. For example, around 20,000 'Exodusters' moved to Kansas in 1879, creating all-black communities such as <u>Nicodemus</u>. Others moved to the <u>North</u>.

2) Even though there were no discriminatory laws in these areas, African Americans still faced <u>racism</u>. '<u>Sundown towns</u>' were white communities which <u>excluded</u> African Americans — these towns existed all across America. In the North, African Americans and white people lived <u>separately</u>, and African Americans experienced racism from <u>European immigrants</u> who they competed with for housing and jobs.

Sadly, the battle for equality wasn't over...

Summarise the ways the lives of African Americans changed after 1877.
Explain how these changes went against acts passed during Reconstruction.

Big Business, Cities and Mass Migration

The USA underwent huge economic growth between 1870 and 1900 — a few people became very wealthy. But this period is known as the 'Gilded Age' — beneath the appearance of wealth, there were problems.

America Industrialised and Big Business emerged

1) The period between 1870 and 1914 is known as the Second Industrial Revolution. It was a time of rapid industrial growth and technological change. America's economy changed from being mainly agricultural to industrial.

2) Industries were developed such as steel and oil. New technologies like electricity emerged. Factories multiplied — they began to use machinery and production increased.

3) Successful businesses were created in these industries. Big businesses appeared when several businesses were merged to form one large corporation — these corporations forced out competition and took control of the market. The businessmen who owned these corporations became very wealthy.

> The nature of industry changed from small businesses employing skilled craftsmen to big businesses using mass production techniques and employing unskilled workers.

> John Rockefeller founded the Standard Oil Company. He introduced new techniques which transformed the oil industry. He was the first American billionaire.

> Andrew Carnegie created the Carnegie Steel Company. He used improved technology and methods to quickly and efficiently mass produce steel.

> These figures were seen as contributing to the prosperity of America. They were also philanthropists — they gave away much of their wealth to good causes such as schools and libraries.

Industrialisation and mass Migration led to the Growth of Cities

1) Industrialisation was centred on the cities where factories were built. Growing numbers of factories created a demand for labour, attracting people to move to cities for jobs — migrants from rural areas in America and immigrants from Europe. Nearly 11 million immigrants arrived between 1870 and 1900.

2) The US population nearly doubled between 1870 and 1900. It has been estimated that in 1870 25.7% of the population lived in cities, but this increased to almost 40% by 1900.

> Initially, most immigrants came from north-west Europe, but after 1890, most came from southern and eastern Europe, e.g. Italy and Russia.

3) Cities like New York and Chicago grew and developed as more people moved to them. America began to build its first skyscraper in Chicago in 1884 — the first tall building to use steel in its frame.

> New electric transport was introduced, such as electric streetcars (trams). This resulted in the growth of suburbs — people could now travel into cities quickly, which meant that those who could afford to didn't have to live in the cities themselves.

There was Corruption, Poverty and Inequality

1) While some businessmen grew very wealthy, many other people struggled in poverty. Some people called the wealthy 'robber barons' — accusing them of using unfair methods to gain their wealth.
   - They put smaller competitors out of business, could control markets and had political influence.
   - Workers were paid low wages and worked long hours, often in dangerous conditions.

2) The rich showed off their wealth while many others struggled with life in crowded and unsanitary cities — crime was common and there was a lot of racial conflict.

> Men at the Carnegie steelworks worked 12 hours a day, seven days a week with only one day off a year. Accidents and deaths were common.

3) Discontent among workers led to the rise of trade unions — organisations formed by workers which aim to improve their rights. Workers also went on strike.

> Many of the elite believed in survival of the fittest — that people with the right skills would be successful in life. As a result, they didn't support measures to help the poor, such as improving working conditions.

Comment and Analysis

> While the wealth of the country increased, there was a growing gap between the wealthy and the poor.

From a few farms to a powerful industrial nation...

Name one of the main industries which developed during the 'Gilded Age'. [1]

EXAM QUESTION

Revision Summary

Now you've absorbed all of that lovely knowledge, here are some revision questions to get your teeth into.
- Try these questions and <u>tick off each one</u> when you <u>get it right</u>.
- When you've done <u>all the questions</u> for a topic and are <u>completely happy</u> with it, tick off the topic.

America's Expansion, 1789-c.1830 (p.33-36) ☑

1) Explain why many people viewed the Plains as the 'Great American Desert' before the 1860s. ☑
2) Give two reasons why the Louisiana Purchase was important for the expansion of the USA. ☑
3) How did the War of 1812 affect the Native Americans? ☑
4) Which part of the USA became reliant on slavery? ☑

The West, c.1830-c.1861 (p.37-43) ☑

5) What was the Permanent Indian Frontier? What was its purpose? ☑
6) Why were the buffalo important to the Plains Indians? ☑
7) Give a brief description of 'Manifest Destiny'. ☑
8) What difficulties did the Mormons face on their journey to Salt Lake Valley? ☑
9) How did the expectations of miners compare with the reality of life in California? ☑
10) Give three examples of settler activity on the Plains which caused tension with the Plains Indians. ☑

Civil War and Reconstruction, c.1861-c.1877 (p.44-49) ☑

11) Explain why westward expansion increased tension over slavery. ☑
12) What was the impact of Abraham Lincoln's election as President in 1860? ☑
13) Give two reasons why the South's economy suffered during the Civil War. ☑
14) How and why did African Americans help the Union war effort? ☑
15) Give two examples of Andrew Johnson's lenient approach to the South during Reconstruction. ☑
16) What were the Enforcement Acts? ☑

Development of the Plains, c.1861-c.1877 (p.50-56) ☑

17) What was the Homestead Act? ☑
18) List three things which helped settlers live and farm on the Plains. ☑
19) Why did the cattle trails develop? ☑
20) Explain why there was rivalry between ranchers and homesteaders. ☑
21) Why was there a lot of crime on the Plains? ☑
22) Why did many Native Americans dislike life on the reservations? ☑
23) Describe the events in 1863-1864 that led to war between settlers and Native Americans. ☑

Conflict and Conquest, c.1877-1900 (p.57-64) ☑

24) Why did ranchers begin to fence off their land? ☑
25) What role did Wyatt Earp play in enforcing law and order? ☑
26) Explain five factors which led to the defeat of the US army at Little Bighorn. ☑
27) What impact did the destruction of the buffalo have on the Native Americans? ☑
28) What was the aim of the Dawes Act? ☑
29) Explain three ways that African Americans lost their rights after 1877. ☑
30) What was the Exoduster movement? ☑
31) Why did cities grow between 1870 and 1900? ☑

America, 1789-1900

Elizabeth's Background and Image

Elizabeth I became queen in <u>1558</u>. She reigned for <u>almost 45 years</u>, until her death in <u>1603</u>.

Elizabeth I was Cautious, Intelligent and Powerful...

1) Elizabeth was <u>Henry VIII's</u> second child, the daughter of his second wife, <u>Anne Boleyn</u>. As a child, she was <u>third</u> in line to the throne, so <u>no-one</u> really <u>expected</u> her to become queen.

2) Elizabeth was <u>very cautious</u> and only trusted a few <u>close advisers</u>. She could also be <u>indecisive</u> — she was reluctant to make decisions without carefully considering their possible <u>consequences</u>.

3) She was <u>intelligent</u>, <u>confident</u> and very <u>well educated</u>. Despite having had little training in how to govern, she became a <u>powerful and effective</u> leader.

But some people didn't want her to rule...

- When Henry VIII's marriage to Anne Boleyn was <u>dissolved</u> and Anne was <u>executed</u> in 1536, Henry declared Elizabeth <u>illegitimate</u>. Although Henry later <u>changed his mind</u> about this, some <u>Protestants</u> still questioned Elizabeth's <u>legitimacy</u>.

- Most people believed the <u>monarch</u> should be a <u>man</u>. They thought that rule by a <u>woman</u> was <u>unnatural</u>, and expected Elizabeth to be a <u>figurehead</u>, without any real power. They thought she should let her <u>male counsellors</u> take control or find a <u>husband</u> to govern for her (see p.67). Elizabeth was <u>determined to rule</u> in her own right and <u>refused</u> to let her counsellors take over.

Elizabeth used Propaganda to maintain Public Support

<u>Public support</u> helped to make Elizabeth's position more <u>stable</u>, especially as some people doubted her. She and her councillors used <u>propaganda</u> to ensure she had a <u>positive</u> public image.

1) <u>Portraits</u> were commissioned showing Elizabeth as a <u>powerful</u> queen who was <u>pure</u> and <u>chaste</u> (a virgin) — they suggested she was married to her <u>people</u> and was concerned with their <u>welfare</u> above <u>all</u> else.

2) <u>Plays</u> which emphasised Elizabeth's <u>wealth</u> and <u>power</u> were performed at court (see p.69). These helped to <u>combat</u> courtiers' fears that an unmarried woman was <u>too weak</u> to rule England properly.

3) Elizabeth was careful to make ordinary people feel <u>recognised</u> by the state. She often went on 'royal progresses' — she journeyed across <u>different parts</u> of England, allowing the public to <u>see</u> and <u>praise</u> her. Their public displays of <u>affection</u> helped her seem <u>popular</u> and <u>loved</u> by her subjects.

Patronage helped to ensure Loyalty

1) <u>Patronage</u> involved handing out <u>titles</u> and <u>offices</u> which gave men a source of <u>income</u>. Elizabeth had <u>lots</u> of these to give away, including high positions in the Church. Patronage was distributed at <u>court</u>.

2) Elizabeth's use of <u>patronage</u> helped to ensure <u>loyalty</u>. Those who received patronage became <u>dependent</u> on Elizabeth for some or all of their <u>income</u> and <u>status</u>, so they were likely to be <u>loyal</u> to her.

Comment and Analysis

Traditionally, the <u>elite</u> was <u>dominated</u> by <u>noble families</u>. Their power mainly came from <u>land</u> that they <u>inherited</u>. By promoting men who <u>relied</u> on her for their wealth and influence, Elizabeth <u>limited</u> the power of the traditional <u>noble families</u> and made the new elite <u>more loyal</u> to her.

3) Elizabeth <u>distributed</u> patronage very <u>widely</u>. This helped to ensure political <u>stability</u> — all members of the elite felt they had a chance to be <u>rewarded</u> by the Queen, so they were <u>unlikely</u> to <u>rebel</u> against her.

Elizabeth's popularity overcame her doubters...

Write a few sentences summarising why some people didn't want Elizabeth to rule.

Marriage and Succession

One of Elizabeth's biggest headaches as queen was the issue of marriage and the succession. She faced constant pressure to marry or name her successor, but was very reluctant to do so.

Elizabeth was expected to Marry and produce an Heir

1) Because people believed that women couldn't rule effectively (see p.66), there was pressure for Elizabeth to find a husband who could rule for her.

2) There were also concerns about the succession. If Elizabeth died without an heir, there would be a risk of civil war, with different groups competing for the throne. To prevent this, Elizabeth was expected to marry and produce an heir as quickly as possible.

3) The Privy Council (see p.70) and Parliament were deeply concerned about the succession. They repeatedly asked the Queen to marry or name her heir, but she always refused. When they asked Elizabeth to find a husband in 1563, she refused to even discuss the matter.

It was Difficult to find a Suitable Husband

1) If Elizabeth married a European prince or king, this could give a foreign country too much influence over England. In the past, Queen Mary I's marriage to King Philip II of Spain had forced England to become involved in an expensive war with France.

2) If Elizabeth chose a member of the English nobility, this would create anger and resentment among those who weren't chosen.

3) The religious settlement had made England a Protestant country (see p.80), so it was difficult for Elizabeth to marry a Catholic. Growing anti-Catholic feeling in England would have made a Catholic husband unpopular and might have undermined support for Elizabeth's rule.

4) Elizabeth was reluctant to marry anyone — women were expected to obey their husbands, so she would lose much of her power and freedom if she married.

Elizabeth Considered many Suitors, but she Rejected them All

1) Early in her reign, Elizabeth received proposals from foreign rulers, including King Philip II of Spain, Archduke Charles of Austria and King Eric of Sweden. She and her Privy Council seriously considered King Eric's proposal, but in the end all these early suitors were rejected.

2) Elizabeth seems to have been in love with her 'favourite', Robert Dudley, and seriously considered marrying him. However, members of the Privy Council and the nobility, including William Cecil (see p.70), were strongly opposed to this match and it did not go ahead.

3) In the 1570s, Elizabeth was courted by Duke Francis of Anjou, brother of the King of France. Although there was some support for the match, there was also strong opposition to the idea of Elizabeth marrying a French Catholic, and in the end the marriage negotiations were abandoned.

Comment and Analysis

Marriage negotiations could be a useful tool in foreign policy. Anglo-Spanish relations were breaking down in the 1570s (see p.87), and England needed a new European ally. The proposed marriage to Duke Francis played an important role in efforts to create an alliance with France.

By the late 1570s, Elizabeth was in her mid-forties and it was clear that she would never have children. The issue of the succession still needed to be resolved, but Elizabeth refused to name a successor. She was concerned that a successor might become the focus of plots to overthrow her. Towards the end of her reign, her advisors began secret negotiations to make James VI of Scotland (son of Mary, Queen of Scots) heir to the throne. When Elizabeth died in 1603, James became king of England.

Elizabeth couldn't find a suitor who suited her...

Scribble down a spider diagram showing all the reasons why it was difficult for Elizabeth to find a husband. Name two suitors Elizabeth considered and explain why she didn't marry them.

REVISION TASK

Problems at the Start of Elizabeth's Reign

Elizabeth also faced <u>other problems</u> — the <u>economy</u> was <u>weak</u> and there was a threat of a <u>French invasion</u>.

Elizabeth's reign began with a French Threat in Scotland

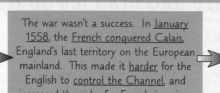

In 1557, <u>Mary I</u> (see p.80) took England to <u>war with France</u>. She did this to support her husband, Philip II of Spain, who was already fighting the French.

The war wasn't a success. In <u>January 1558</u>, the <u>French conquered Calais</u>, England's last territory on the European mainland. This made it <u>harder</u> for the English to <u>control the Channel</u>, and increased the risk of a <u>French invasion</u>.

When Elizabeth became queen in November 1558, she wanted to <u>end the war</u> with France as quickly as possible. <u>Peace</u> was agreed in <u>1559</u>.

Elizabeth tried to <u>avoid foreign wars</u> — a policy partly influenced by England's <u>financial weakness</u>. She feared that <u>raising taxes</u> to fund a war would be <u>unpopular</u> and might fuel <u>opposition</u> to her rule.

1) Elizabeth had <u>quickly ended</u> the war with France, but there was still a <u>French threat</u> in <u>Scotland</u>. When she became queen, <u>Scotland</u> was controlled by <u>France's Catholic royal family</u> and there were many <u>French troops</u> in the country. However, French rule was unpopular with many Scots.

2) In 1558 <u>Mary, Queen of Scots</u> (p.82) married the <u>heir to the French throne</u>. As Catholics, the French royal family disliked Elizabeth (a Protestant), and wanted England to be ruled by a <u>Catholic</u>. Mary's marriage <u>increased</u> the risk that the French might <u>invade</u> from Scotland to try and put her on the English throne.

3) In the late 1550s, <u>Scottish Protestants</u>, led by the preacher John Knox, <u>rebelled</u> against French rule. They asked England for support, and in <u>1560</u> English troops and ships were sent to help them.

4) The <u>French</u> were <u>defeated</u> and forced to <u>leave Scotland</u>. The departure of the French, combined with the death of Mary's French husband in 1560, greatly <u>reduced</u> the <u>threat of invasion</u>.

Comment and Analysis

There were many <u>Catholics</u> in England who wanted to be ruled by a <u>Catholic monarch</u>. There was a risk that they'd <u>betray</u> Elizabeth and <u>support the French</u> if they invaded.

The English Economy was Weak

1) Under <u>King Edward VI</u>, huge sums of money had been spent on <u>wars in Scotland</u>. Queen Mary I had also spent too much money. As a result, Elizabeth inherited <u>enormous debts</u> when she became queen.

2) Mary I had <u>sold off</u> lots of <u>land</u> owned by the Crown to cover her debts. This had raised money in the short term, but it also <u>reduced</u> the monarch's <u>income from rent</u>.

3) The tax system was <u>old-fashioned</u> and <u>ineffective</u>. Ordinary people paid <u>high taxes</u>, but it had become common for the <u>nobility</u> and <u>gentry</u> to pay <u>less</u> tax than they owed.

4) England was suffering high levels of <u>inflation</u> (when <u>prices rise</u> and wages don't). The <u>poor</u> (see p.73) and those living in <u>urban areas</u> were hit hardest by inflation.

Elizabeth was <u>reluctant</u> to reform the tax system and raise taxes because she feared it would <u>upset</u> the nobility and gentry who <u>supported</u> her.

There were Social and Economic Divisions

1) England's <u>population</u> had been <u>rising</u> steadily since around 1500. Most people lived and worked in <u>rural areas</u>, but <u>towns and cities</u> were <u>growing</u> rapidly. <u>London</u> was by far the <u>largest</u> and most important city.

2) The economy was dominated by <u>agriculture</u>, but farming was <u>changing</u> (p.73). The export of <u>woollen cloth</u> to <u>Europe</u> was a key part of the economy, but merchants were also starting to trade with the <u>Americas</u> and <u>Asia</u> (p.78-79).

3) Elizabethan society was dominated by a small, <u>land-owning aristocracy</u> of nobility and gentry (see p.74). There was also a growing number of wealthy men who made a living as <u>lawyers</u> or <u>merchants</u>.

4) There was great <u>inequality</u>, and the divide between rich and poor was growing. <u>Poverty</u> became a <u>major problem</u> in Elizabethan England (see p.73).

Foreign wars — a luxury Elizabeth couldn't afford...

Include plenty of specific information in your answers. For example, don't just say that Elizabeth faced lots of problems when she became queen — explain the different challenges she faced.

EXAM TIP

Political Power and Government

Elizabeth's court was the heart of social and political life — but local government had a lot of power, too.

The Court was the Centre of Elizabethan Social Life

1) The royal <u>court</u> was a large group of people who <u>surrounded</u> the monarch at all times. More than <u>1000 people</u> attended the court, including Elizabeth's personal servants, members of the Privy Council (see p.70), members of the nobility, ambassadors and other foreign visitors, and Elizabeth's 'favourites'.

> Some courtiers became Elizabeth's '<u>favourites</u>'. Early in her reign, Elizabeth was very close to <u>Robert Dudley</u>. She made him <u>Earl of Leicester</u> in 1564 and may have considered <u>marrying</u> him (see p.67). <u>Christopher Hatton</u> was another of her 'favourites'. In <u>1587</u>, she made him <u>Lord Chancellor</u>, even though he had <u>little relevant experience</u>. <u>Sir Walter Raleigh</u> came to Elizabeth's court in 1581. Elizabeth gave him many <u>valuable gifts</u>, including the right to colonise the <u>New World</u> (see p.79).

2) Courtiers were expected to <u>flatter</u> Elizabeth, shower her with <u>gifts</u> and pretend to be in <u>love</u> with her.

3) Courtly <u>pastimes</u> included plays, concerts, hunting, jousting and tennis. There were also balls and grand meals.

4) Members of the court <u>travelled</u> with Elizabeth when she moved between her <u>palaces</u>, and when <u>great processions</u> were held. They also went with her when she went on her '<u>royal progresses</u>' (see p.66).

Comment and Analysis

The <u>entertainments</u> and <u>fashionable clothes</u> on show at court were a way for Elizabeth to <u>impress</u> her subjects and foreign visitors by <u>displaying</u> her <u>wealth</u> and <u>power</u>.

Political Power relied on Access to the Queen

1) The Queen was the <u>centre</u> of <u>government</u>, and political power revolved around her. This meant that those <u>closest</u> to Elizabeth had the <u>greatest influence</u> and power.

2) The <u>court</u> was the centre of <u>political life</u>. Anyone who wanted to <u>get ahead</u> and increase their political power had to have a place at <u>court</u>.

3) Courtiers didn't necessarily hold government positions — they became <u>powerful</u> through their <u>close relationship</u> with the Queen.

> Courtiers had to <u>compete</u> with one another for the Queen's <u>attention</u> and <u>favour</u>. Towards the end of Elizabeth's reign, this <u>competition</u> led to growing <u>conflict</u> at court (p.72).

Local Government enforced National Laws

1) The role of local government was to <u>supervise</u> the running of each <u>county</u> and enforce the <u>law</u> there.

2) Most local government positions were <u>unpaid</u>. Members of the <u>nobility</u> and <u>gentry</u> (see p.74) often <u>volunteered</u> for them because being a part of the local government was a symbol of <u>status</u> and <u>power</u>.

3) An important local government position was <u>Justice of the Peace</u>. They were in charge of administering national policies like <u>poor laws</u> (see p.73) and <u>taxation</u> in their counties, and enforcing <u>law</u> and <u>order</u>. They also looked after local issues like maintaining <u>sewers</u>, <u>roads</u> and <u>bridges</u>.

4) Most counties had a <u>Lord Lieutenant</u>, appointed by the Queen. Lord Lieutenants were in charge of the Justices of the Peace, and had an important <u>military</u> role. For example, they maintained <u>defences</u> and managed the training of the <u>militia</u> (ordinary people called to fight alongside the army in an emergency).

5) Towards the end of the 16th century, the <u>number</u> of Justices of the Peace and Lord Lieutenants <u>increased</u>.

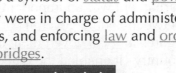

Comment and Analysis

After England went to war with Spain in 1585 (p.87), there was a <u>higher demand</u> for Lord Lieutenants, as <u>military preparations</u> in each county became more important. Elizabeth also needed more Justices of the Peace to collect <u>extra taxes</u> to fund the war.

The court was the place to be in Elizabethan England...

Jot down a quick description of Elizabeth's court, including the names of some of her favourite courtiers. Write a few sentences to explain the role of local government in Elizabethan England.

REVISION TASK

Political Power and Government

The <u>Queen</u> was the <u>head of government</u>. She was <u>advised</u> by her <u>Privy Council</u>, which included her <u>key ministers</u>. <u>Parliament</u> could be involved in granting <u>taxes</u>, passing <u>laws</u> and giving <u>advice</u>.

The Privy Council was Central to Elizabethan Government

1) The Privy Council had <u>two</u> main <u>roles</u>. It gave <u>advice</u> to the Queen and managed the <u>administration of government</u>.

> This involved making sure that Elizabeth's <u>policies</u> were <u>enforced</u>. The council <u>oversaw</u> many different areas of <u>government</u>, including <u>religion</u>, the <u>economy</u>, the <u>military</u>, <u>foreign policy</u> and the Queen's <u>security</u>.

2) The Council was made up of around <u>twenty</u> men, all <u>chosen</u> by Elizabeth. Members of the Privy Council were the Queen's <u>closest</u> and <u>most trusted</u> advisors. Some <u>key ministers</u> served on the Council for <u>many years</u>.

3) The Queen <u>didn't</u> have to follow the <u>advice</u> of the Privy Council. Councillors were expected to carry out her <u>instructions</u>, even when doing so went <u>against their advice</u>.

William Cecil was Elizabeth's Closest Advisor

1) When she became queen in 1558, Elizabeth made <u>William Cecil</u> her <u>Principal Secretary</u>. He became her <u>closest advisor</u>, leading the Privy Council and making sure the government ran smoothly.

2) In <u>1571</u>, Elizabeth gave Cecil the title <u>Lord Burghley</u>. The next year she made him <u>Lord High Treasurer</u>, giving him greater <u>control</u> over <u>royal finances</u>. Cecil continued to serve Elizabeth until his death in <u>1598</u>.

3) Elizabeth's other <u>key ministers</u> included <u>Nicholas Bacon</u>, who was <u>Lord Chancellor</u> from 1559 to 1579, and <u>Francis Walsingham</u>, who became <u>Principal Secretary</u> in 1573.

Comment and Analysis

Cecil was a <u>highly skilled</u> politician and administrator. Some historians argue that <u>Elizabeth's success</u> as queen was as much due to <u>Cecil's remarkable skills</u> as it was to Elizabeth's own talents.

There were Two Chambers of Parliament

1) The <u>House of Lords</u> was <u>not elected</u> — it was made up of members of the <u>nobility</u> and senior <u>churchmen</u>.

2) The <u>House of Commons</u> was <u>elected</u>, but only <u>men</u> who owned <u>property</u> over a certain value were allowed to <u>vote</u>. Elections <u>weren't free</u> — the <u>Crown</u> controlled who got elected in some areas, and in others <u>powerful local figures</u> controlled who was chosen.

Parliament's main functions were Advice, Taxation and Legislation

Advice

Parliament was an important point of <u>contact</u> between <u>central government</u> and the leading figures in <u>local government</u> throughout the country. It enabled the Queen and her councillors to gauge the <u>mood</u> of the country and levels of <u>support</u> for their <u>policies</u>.

Taxation

When the Queen needed <u>extra revenue</u>, she had to ask <u>Parliament's permission</u> to raise <u>taxes</u>.

Legislation

The Queen needed <u>Parliament's approval</u> to pass <u>new laws</u>. However, she could <u>bypass</u> this function by issuing <u>royal proclamations</u> instead.

Comment and Analysis

Elizabeth took <u>little interest</u> in the <u>advice</u> of Members of Parliament (<u>MPs</u>), and she could <u>bypass</u> Parliament's role in passing <u>new laws</u>. For Elizabeth, Parliament's <u>main purpose</u> was to grant her <u>taxes</u>.

Elizabeth was very powerful, but she didn't rule alone...

To really ace the exam, you need to understand the key features of Elizabethan government. Make sure you know the role of the Queen, the Privy Council, key ministers and Parliament.

Political Power and Government

Unlike today, in the 16th century Parliament was only a secondary part of government. Its sessions were temporary and occasional, and its powers were limited.

Parliament's Powers were Limited

1) Elizabeth had the power to summon and dismiss Parliament. She disliked working with Parliament and tried to use it as little as possible — she only called 13 sessions of Parliament during her 44-year reign.

2) Parliament was not free to decide what topics it debated. It had to have permission from the Queen to discuss matters of state (e.g. religion, the succession, foreign policy). As a result, most parliamentary business focused on local matters and social or economic issues, which it could discuss without royal permission.

Elizabeth I in Parliament.

Comment and Analysis

Elizabeth believed in Divine Right — that rulers were sent by God to govern their country. She believed that this gave her a royal prerogative — the right to decide about matters of state without interference from Parliament.

The Privy Council helped Elizabeth to Manage Parliament

1) The Privy Council managed relations between Elizabeth and Parliament very effectively. In particular, Cecil (see p.70) was highly skilled at convincing MPs to support the Queen's policies.

2) Some members of the Privy Council sat in Parliament. They acted as royal spokesmen and helped to steer debates in favour of royal policies.

3) The Speaker, who kept order in the House of Commons, was chosen by the Queen and closely monitored by members of the Privy Council. This helped the Queen's councillors to control Parliament and convince MPs to support royal policy.

4) Elizabeth was a strong public speaker. She made a number of powerful speeches in Parliament which helped to persuade MPs to obey her wishes.

There were some Disagreements, but Elizabeth stayed In Control

During Elizabeth's reign, Parliament didn't always agree with her policies:

- Throughout her reign, MPs were concerned about who would rule England after Elizabeth's death — they repeatedly tried to persuade her to marry or name an heir (see p.67).

- Some Puritan MPs challenged the religious settlement (see p.81) and tried to make England more Protestant.

- MPs were worried about the threat from Mary, Queen of Scots, and the Catholic plots surrounding her (see p.82). They tried to convince Elizabeth to take action against Mary.

Occasionally, MPs tried to force the Queen to change her mind by threatening to refuse taxation. Elizabeth never gave in to this kind of parliamentary pressure. Effective management by the Privy Council, combined with Elizabeth's powers to dismiss Parliament and select the topics it debated, meant that she remained firmly in control.

Parliament was no match for Elizabeth and her ministers...

Why was Parliament an important feature of Elizabeth's reign? Explain your answer. [8]

The End of Elizabeth's Reign

The last 15 years or so of Elizabeth's rule were so different to her early years that they're sometimes called her 'second reign'. One of the main differences was the growth of competing groups at court.

Elizabeth's Court split into Rival Groups in the 1590s

1) The make-up of Elizabeth's Privy Council changed towards the end of her reign. Several of her key ministers, including Christopher Hatton and Francis Walsingham, died around 1590. William Cecil died in 1598 and was succeeded by his son, Robert Cecil.

2) In 1593, Elizabeth made Robert Devereux, Earl of Essex, a member of the Privy Council. Essex's rise led to the growth of two conflicting groups at court, one around the Earl of Essex and the other around William and Robert Cecil.

3) The two groups were constantly competing for royal patronage and influence. They also disagreed over important matters, especially strategy in the war with Spain (see p.87). Elizabeth's inability to control this conflict undermined her authority.

> Essex was the stepson of Elizabeth's earlier 'favourite', Robert Dudley. He came to court in 1584 and quickly became a 'favourite' himself. He was extremely ambitious for military success and could be arrogant and disrespectful, even towards the Queen.

Essex launched a Rebellion in 1601

1) In 1599, Elizabeth sent Essex to Ireland at the head of a huge army. His task was to crush Tyrone's Rebellion (also known as the Nine Years' War), which had been going on since 1594.

2) Essex made some limited attempts to fight the rebels, but when these were unsuccessful, he made a truce with them. He then abandoned his post and returned to England without the Queen's permission.

3) As a punishment, Elizabeth put Essex under house arrest for a time, banished him from court and took away most of his public offices. In November 1600, she also took away Essex's role as the sole distributor of sweet wines, his main source of income.

4) The loss of his political power and his income drove Essex to revolt. On 8th February 1601, he launched a rebellion in London. Essex aimed to seize the Queen and force her to replace her closest advisers, especially Cecil, with himself and his followers.

5) Essex's rebellion failed within just a few hours. He received no support from ordinary Londoners, and most of his own supporters quickly abandoned him too. Essex was arrested, tried for treason and executed on 25th February 1601.

> **Comment and Analysis**
>
> In her later years, Elizabeth rarely appointed new men to the Privy Council, which created resentment among some courtiers. These men became frustrated at Elizabeth's refusal to promote them to government posts, and so they encouraged Essex's rebellion.

The Conflict at court Undermined Elizabeth's Authority

1) The lack of popular support for Essex's rebellion shows that it wasn't a serious threat to Elizabeth's rule. She was still a popular and respected queen, and there was no desire to overthrow her or her government.

2) However, the rebellion does suggest that Elizabeth's authority over her court became weaker towards the end of her reign. By the 1590s, she was no longer using patronage as effectively as she had in the past.

3) Instead of balancing the different groups at court, she let the Cecils become too powerful, while failing to promote many others. This led to a build-up of anger and resentment, which risked fuelling challenges to her authority — like Essex's revolt.

4) The conflict at court in the 1590s also made Elizabeth's government less effective. Constant competition and in-fighting between groups made it more difficult to make decisions and get things done.

Get to grips with the facts about the court factions...

Give an account of the reasons for Essex's rebellion in 1601. [8]

EXAM QUESTION

The Elizabethans, 1558-1603

Poverty

The growing number of people living in <u>poverty</u> was a major problem in Elizabethan society.

Poverty Increased during Elizabeth's Reign

Poverty had <u>several</u> different causes, and not all of them were under Elizabeth's <u>control</u>.

1) In the past, monasteries had provided support for many <u>poor</u>, <u>ill</u> and <u>disabled</u> people. However, between 1536 and 1541, Henry VIII had closed down England's <u>monasteries</u> and sold off most of their land.

2) In the 16th century, landowners began <u>changing</u> their <u>farming techniques</u> to try and make <u>more money</u> from their land. Instead of sharing open fields among many farmers, they <u>enclosed</u> these fields to create a <u>few large farms</u>. These new farms needed <u>fewer labourers</u>, so farmers who rented land were <u>evicted</u>, leaving them <u>unemployed</u> and <u>homeless</u>. Many were forced to <u>migrate</u> to towns to find <u>work</u>.

3) In the 16th century, England's birth rate <u>increased</u> and the death rate <u>fell</u>:

   - Food production couldn't <u>keep pace</u> with the growth in population. As a result, <u>food prices</u> rose.
   - Prices rose much <u>more quickly</u> than <u>wages</u>. Standards of living <u>fell</u> as ordinary people struggled to afford the necessities — many were forced into <u>poverty</u>.
   - There was also growing competition for <u>land</u>, and so <u>rents</u> increased.

People believed the Poor could be split into Three Categories

The Helpless Poor

Those who were <u>unable</u> to support themselves — including young <u>orphans</u> and the <u>elderly</u>, <u>sick</u> or <u>disabled</u>.

The Deserving Poor

People who <u>wanted to work</u>, but weren't able to find a job in their home town or village.

The Undeserving Poor

<u>Beggars</u>, <u>criminals</u> and people who <u>refused to work</u>. Also <u>migrant workers</u> ('<u>vagabonds</u>') who left their homes and travelled around looking for work.

The Government became More Involved in Poor Relief

1) <u>Support</u> for the poor normally came from <u>charity</u> — rich people made donations to hospitals, monasteries and other organisations that helped the poor. However, <u>poverty</u> became <u>so bad</u> that this was <u>no longer enough</u>.

2) People realised that <u>society</u> had to take <u>responsibility</u> for the poor, so the <u>government</u> began to take <u>action</u>. In <u>1563</u>, they passed a Poor Law which introduced a <u>local tax</u> to raise money for the poor (known as the '<u>poor rate</u>').

3) Poverty reached a <u>crisis point</u> in the <u>1590s</u>. In response, the government passed further Poor Laws in <u>1597</u> and <u>1601</u>. Under the laws, the poor rate became a <u>national</u> system of <u>compulsory taxation</u>.

> **Comment and Analysis**
>
> As poverty levels rose, <u>crime rates</u> <u>increased</u> and there were <u>food riots</u> in some places. The government feared that the poor might <u>rise up</u> in <u>rebellion</u> if the problem of poverty wasn't tackled.

4) Poor rates were used to provide <u>hospitals</u> and <u>housing</u> for the elderly, sick and disabled. Poor children were given <u>apprenticeships</u>, and local authorities had to provide <u>financial support</u> or <u>work</u> for the <u>deserving poor</u>. Poor people could be <u>imprisoned</u> if they <u>refused</u> to work.

5) Although the Elizabethans <u>tried to help</u> the <u>helpless</u> and <u>deserving poor</u>, they had <u>little</u> <u>sympathy</u> for the <u>undeserving poor</u>. Under the Poor Laws, they could be <u>publicly whipped</u> and then forced to return to their <u>home parish</u>. Repeat offenders could be sent to <u>prison</u>.

> The <u>undeserving poor</u> were treated so <u>harshly</u> because they were seen as a serious <u>threat</u> to <u>society</u>. Many people believed that poor <u>criminals</u> and <u>vagabonds</u> had encouraged the <u>Northern Rebellion</u> in 1569 (see p.83). In <u>response</u> to the Rebellion, the government introduced particularly <u>harsh punishments</u> for the undeserving poor in <u>1572</u>.

The Poor Laws helped some, but punished others...

Why was poverty a growing problem in Elizabethan England? Explain your answer. [12]

A 'Golden Age'

Despite the very high levels of poverty, Elizabeth's reign is often seen as a 'Golden Age'. The growing prosperity of the elite contributed to a flourishing in architecture, the arts and education.

The Gentry became Richer during Elizabeth's reign

1) Population growth and changes in farming practices (see p.73) were good for landowners, especially members of the gentry.

2) The enclosures meant that land was farmed more efficiently. At the same time, rents were increasing and prices of agricultural products like grain were rising, so landowners were earning a lot more money from their land.

3) As a result, the land-owning gentry became much wealthier during Elizabeth's reign, and members of the nobility also saw their incomes increase.

4) The growth of towns and the development of national and international trade allowed some merchants to become very rich. They often used their money to buy land and become part of the gentry.

> The gentry were part of the social elite in Elizabethan England, below the level of the nobility. Members of the gentry were people who owned land and lived off the income it provided. They didn't have to do other work to survive.

Some members of the Elite built New Houses

1) From the 1570s, many members of the gentry and nobility improved their homes or built new ones. This is sometimes called the 'Great Rebuilding'.

2) These building projects enabled members of the elite to show off their wealth. New houses often had many large windows — glass was very expensive, so using a lot of it was a sign of prosperity. Large landscaped gardens were also a popular way to display wealth.

3) The 'Great Rebuilding' improved living standards for the wealthy, because the new houses were much more comfortable. The large windows made them lighter, and bigger chimneys and fireplaces meant they were better heated.

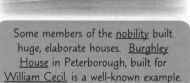

> Some members of the nobility built huge, elaborate houses. Burghley House in Peterborough, built for William Cecil, is a well-known example.

Art, Literature and Education were all highly Fashionable

1) The nobility and gentry had money to spend on elaborate decorations for their homes. Portraits, miniatures (very small portraits), tapestries and embroidery were all popular.

2) It was also fashionable to take an interest in literature — some people collected large libraries, and members of the elite supported the work of poets and playwrights. Elite support for playwrights and acting companies contributed to the flourishing of Elizabethan theatre (see p.77).

3) More people could afford to give their children an education (see p.76).

A miniature of Queen Elizabeth's 'favourite', Robert Dudley, painted by Nicholas Hilliard.

> Members of the elite wore elaborate clothing to show off their wealth and status. Their clothes were often made of expensive fabrics like silk, satin, velvet and lace, and were decorated with detailed embroidery. Women's dresses had very full sleeves and a large skirt, supported by a hoop-skirt, which gave it shape (see the portrait of Elizabeth on p.66). Both men and women wore wide, ruffled collars, called ruffs.

Comment and Analysis

Many elite fashions started at the royal court. For example Nicholas Hilliard was employed as Queen Elizabeth's miniaturist in the 1570s and painted many miniatures of Elizabeth and her courtiers. This encouraged the growing popularity of miniatures among the nobility and gentry.

Miniatures were huge in Elizabethan England...

Write a sentence or two to explain why the gentry got richer during Elizabeth's reign. Then make a quick spider diagram showing some things that members of the elite spent their wealth on.

Family Life

Families were at the <u>heart</u> of Elizabethan society, and were usually <u>positive</u> and <u>loving</u> environments. Family life taught children important <u>morals</u> and reinforced Elizabethan <u>social structures</u>.

Families played an Important Role in Elizabethan Society

1) Elizabethan families were usually <u>loving</u>, and <u>close relationships</u> with family members were <u>encouraged</u>.

2) Elizabethan family life was <u>hierarchical</u> — some members of the family had <u>more authority</u> than others. The father was the <u>head</u> of the family. The mother <u>assisted</u> him, and the children <u>obeyed</u> their parents.

3) <u>Wider kinship</u> (extended family) was also important. <u>Kin</u> formed part of a family's <u>social life</u> and could be called upon to provide <u>financial</u> help.

> **Comment and Analysis**
>
> This hierarchical structure <u>reflected</u> the structure of larger organisations in society like the <u>Church</u> and the <u>state</u>. Elizabethans believed that families were essential for <u>maintaining</u> the idea of hierarchy, which helped to <u>strengthen</u> and <u>stabilise</u> the country.

4) Having important or rich ancestors was a source of <u>pride</u> and <u>status</u>. Noble families would often hang <u>portraits</u> or <u>miniatures</u> (very small portraits) of their kin or ancestors in their homes.

5) Kin also provided useful <u>political</u> and <u>social</u> connections, particularly in wealthy families, e.g. children's education in other households (see below) was sometimes arranged using <u>wider family connections</u>.

People got Married for Different Reasons

1) In Elizabethan England, marriage could be a way of increasing a family's <u>wealth</u> or <u>social standing</u>. Husbands usually owned all of their wife's <u>money</u> and <u>property</u> once they were married.

2) For members of the <u>nobility</u> and <u>gentry</u>, the right marriage could <u>advance</u> a man's career at <u>court</u> or in <u>government</u>. But marriage wasn't always about money or status — many Elizabethans married for <u>love</u>.

3) A husband was the <u>head</u> of the household, and was responsible for providing an <u>income</u> for his family. He was expected to <u>care</u> for his wife and children.

4) A wife's main role was to run the <u>household</u> and look after her <u>children</u> and <u>husband</u>.

> If their husbands went away, women were often left <u>in charge</u> of all household staff and servants. In some poor families, wives had to <u>work</u>. Women could help their husbands with <u>farm work</u> and sometimes even took on <u>separate jobs</u>, e.g. as midwives or shop assistants.

Children often Left Home to learn New Skills

1) Childbirth was extremely <u>dangerous</u> in Elizabethan times. Many women died giving birth, and infant mortality rates (the number of children who died) were <u>high</u>, especially amongst the <u>poor</u>.

2) The Elizabethans expected parents to <u>love</u> and <u>take care</u> of their children. Parents were also responsible for teaching children <u>morals</u> and <u>social expectations</u>.

3) <u>Richer</u> Elizabethan children were often <u>sent away</u> from the family home. Some went to <u>school</u>, but many became <u>skilled apprentices</u>. Children of the nobility were often sent to <u>noble households</u> to train for <u>knighthoods</u>.

> **Comment and Analysis**
>
> The <u>affection</u> between parents and children was demonstrated by the regular practice of giving a '<u>parental blessing</u>'. Every morning and evening children would <u>kneel</u> before their parents, who would reach out, place their hands on them and <u>bless</u> them.

4) Most <u>poor</u> and <u>middle-class</u> children stayed at home to work, but some were servants in other <u>households</u> or did an <u>apprenticeship</u>.

5) In poorer families, life was often a <u>struggle</u> for both parents, who had to work hard to <u>feed</u> and <u>clothe</u> their children.

The Elizabethans tried to create loving families...

If you had to investigate another aspect of Elizabethan family life, what would you research? Explain how this would help historians understand more about daily life in the Elizabethan era. [5]

Education

During Elizabeth's reign, people increasingly began to recognise the <u>importance</u> of <u>education</u>. Many <u>new schools</u> were set up and <u>more</u> people than ever learned how to <u>read</u> and <u>write</u>.

Children received a Basic Education at Home

1) Children received their early education <u>at home</u>. Most parents probably taught their children how to <u>behave correctly</u> and gave them a basic <u>religious education</u>. From the age of six, all children had to go to <u>Sunday school</u>, where they learnt things like the <u>Lord's Prayer</u>, the <u>10 Commandments</u> and the <u>Creed</u> (a basic statement of the Christian faith).

2) From a young age, boys were trained in simple <u>work skills</u>, while girls helped their mothers with <u>household activities</u>.

3) Some children from <u>noble</u> households were taught at home by a <u>private tutor</u>. Others were sent to live with another noble family and educated there.

> This kind of education was intended to teach children how to <u>behave</u> in <u>noble society</u> and give them the <u>skills</u> to be <u>successful</u> at <u>court</u>.

Petty Schools taught Reading, Writing and Maths

1) Petty schools were <u>small</u>, <u>local schools</u> that provided a <u>basic education</u>. Many petty schools were run by the local <u>parish priest</u>. Others were attached to <u>grammar schools</u>, or were set up by <u>private individuals</u>.

2) The schools taught basic <u>reading</u> and <u>writing</u>, and sometimes a little <u>maths</u>. There <u>wasn't</u> a set curriculum, although lessons usually had a strong <u>religious focus</u>. The schools <u>didn't</u> usually have any books — instead the main teaching aid was the <u>hornbook</u>, a wooden board showing the <u>alphabet</u> and the <u>Lord's Prayer</u>.

3) <u>Most</u> pupils were <u>boys</u>, although some petty schools admitted a few girls. There was <u>no fixed age</u> for pupils to start school, but they usually started at about six and stayed until they could read and write.

> Only a <u>small minority</u> of children in Elizabethan England went to <u>school</u>, but the number was <u>growing</u>. Education was increasingly <u>important</u> for many <u>careers</u>, including trade and government administration.

There was a Big Increase in the number of Grammar Schools

1) <u>Grammar schools</u> had existed for centuries, but there was a <u>big expansion</u> during Elizabeth's reign, with the foundation of around <u>100 new grammar schools</u>.

2) It was <u>very rare</u> for <u>girls</u> to go to grammar school — most pupils were <u>boys</u> from the <u>upper and middle classes</u>. Some schools offered <u>free</u> places to bright boys from <u>poorer backgrounds</u>, but <u>few</u> poor boys were able to attend because their parents needed them to <u>work</u> at home.

> There was <u>no state education system</u> at this time. Instead, most schools were set up by <u>wealthy individuals</u>.

3) Children usually started grammar school around the age of <u>seven</u>. Lessons focused mainly on <u>Latin</u> and <u>classical literature</u> (literature from Ancient Greece and Rome), and a few schools also taught <u>Greek</u>.

The number of University Students was Increasing

1) When they left grammar school, some boys went on to study at one of the two English universities, <u>Oxford</u> and <u>Cambridge</u>. The growing <u>prosperity</u> of the upper and middle classes meant that the number of university students <u>increased</u> during Elizabeth's reign.

2) University courses were conducted almost entirely in <u>Latin</u>. Students studied advanced written and spoken Latin, before moving on to study arithmetic, music, Greek, astronomy, geometry and philosophy. After completing an undergraduate degree, students might specialise in <u>law</u>, <u>theology</u> or <u>medicine</u>.

Comment and Analysis

The <u>printing press</u> had been introduced to England in the late 15th century. As printing spread, it encouraged <u>increased literacy levels</u> because it made books much <u>cheaper</u> and more <u>widely available</u>.

Those Elizabethans really loved their Latin...

Write down these headings: Home, Petty School, Grammar School, University. Under each heading, jot down the main things pupils were taught in that place.

Popular Culture

Some Elizabethan pastimes, including <u>tennis</u>, <u>fencing</u>, <u>football</u> and the <u>theatre</u>, are still popular today.

Hunting and Sports were an Important part of Court Life

1) Elizabeth and her <u>courtiers</u> often <u>hunted</u> deer and other wild animals. As well as being a form of <u>entertainment</u>, hunting was an important source of <u>food</u> for the court. The Queen was skilled at <u>hawking</u>, spending many hours with her trained <u>falcons</u> as they <u>hunted</u>. Only the <u>rich</u> could <u>afford</u> to train falcons.

2) Elizabeth's courtiers and other nobles practised <u>fencing</u> from a young age. <u>Tennis</u> and <u>bowls</u> were also becoming more <u>popular</u>. These sports needed <u>expensive equipment</u>, so they were only played by the <u>rich</u>.

3) Most ordinary people <u>worked</u> six days a week and went to <u>church</u> on Sundays, so they had <u>little leisure time</u>. However, there were several <u>festival days</u> in the calendar, including Midsummer's day and Ascension day. On these days, people were free to enjoy <u>sports</u>, <u>feasting</u> and other <u>pastimes</u>.

4) <u>Football</u> was a popular sport, often played between two villages. An unlimited number of players could take part, and there were <u>few rules</u> — games often descended into long and violent <u>fights</u>.

5) <u>Blood sports</u> like <u>cockfighting</u> and <u>bull- or bear-baiting</u> were also very popular.

The Theatre became Very Popular later in Elizabeth's reign

A performance at London's Globe Theatre, which was built in 1599.

1) There were <u>no permanent theatres</u> in England at the start of Elizabeth's reign. Instead, actors <u>travelled</u> around, performing in <u>village squares</u> or <u>inn courtyards</u>.

2) The first theatres were built in <u>London</u> in the <u>1570s</u>. They included <u>The Theatre</u> and <u>The Curtain</u>. They were usually round, <u>open-air buildings</u> with a raised stage that stretched out into the audience.

3) The theatre appealed to both <u>rich and poor</u>. Poorer audience members, known as <u>groundlings</u>, <u>stood</u> around the stage, while <u>richer</u> people sat under cover around the theatre's walls.

4) <u>Elizabeth</u> enjoyed plays and often had them performed at <u>court</u>. She supported her favourite performers and even set up an <u>acting company</u>, The Queen's Men. Members of the <u>elite</u> (including some Privy Councillors) also supported theatre companies.

> **Comment and Analysis**
>
> The <u>London authorities</u> and the <u>Puritans</u> opposed the theatre because they saw it as a source of <u>crime</u> and <u>immorality</u>. As a result, many theatres were built just <u>outside</u> the City of London in <u>Southwark</u>.

> Lots of <u>plays</u> were written in the Elizabethan era. Famous Elizabethan playwrights include <u>William Shakespeare</u>, <u>Christopher Marlowe</u> and <u>Ben Johnson</u>.

Elizabethans became More Hostile towards Witches

1) Elizabeth banned <u>Catholic rituals</u> like charms, blessings or <u>exorcisms</u>, which were used to cleanse someone of the Devil or evil spirits. This made some Elizabethans feel more <u>vulnerable</u>.

> People believed that witches acted on the <u>Devil's orders</u> and wanted to cause <u>harm</u> to others.

2) In <u>1562</u>, Elizabeth passed the Witchcraft Act, which made all acts of witchcraft a <u>crime</u>. Accused witches were given a <u>trial</u> in a court. Witches found guilty of <u>causing death</u> would be <u>hanged</u>. Less serious offences, like providing herbal remedies, carried a <u>prison sentence</u> of one year.

3) Those accused of witchcraft were usually older <u>women</u> who didn't <u>fit</u> in to society. These included mothers with <u>illegitimate</u> children, <u>spinsters</u> (unmarried women) and women who were <u>rude</u> or <u>outspoken</u>.

I'm not sure I like the sound of Elizabethan football...

Remember that there were social distinctions in leisure activities — the rich and the poor mostly enjoyed different pastimes and even at the theatre the two groups didn't mix.

Elizabethan Sailors

The Portuguese and Spanish were the first to explore beyond Europe and establish colonies in the New World (the Americas). It was only from the 1560s that English sailors began to take an interest in global exploration.

Explorers were Attracted by Economic Opportunities

1) Spanish trade with its colonies was very profitable. This attracted English privateers (men with their own ships) — they hoped to profit by trading with Spain's colonies and raiding Spanish settlements and ships.

2) John Hawkins was the first English privateer to join the Atlantic slave trade. In the 1560s, he made three slave-trading voyages. He bought slaves in west Africa and sold them to Spanish colonies. The Spanish didn't want the English to trade with these colonies, so his actions fuelled tensions between England and Spain (see p.87).

> Elizabeth encouraged English merchants to take part in long-distance trade and privateering, and to try and establish English colonies in the Americas (see p.79). She wanted England to compete with Spain globally.

3) Hawkins' first two voyages were very profitable, but on his last expedition he was confronted by Spanish ships in the battle of San Juan de Ulúa and most of his fleet was destroyed.

4) From the 1570s, English merchants also looked for routes to Asia, like the North West passage around the top of North America. In 1591, James Lancaster sailed to India around the Cape of Good Hope (the southern tip of Africa). After this, the East India Company was set up in 1600 to trade with Asia.

New Technology made Longer Journeys possible

1) As the Portuguese and Spanish began to explore the seas, they developed better navigational techniques. They learnt how to navigate by the position of the stars or the Sun using an instrument called a sea astrolabe.

2) In 1561, a key Spanish book, 'The Art of Navigation' by Martin Cortés, was translated into English. This gave English sailors detailed information about how to navigate across the Atlantic using a sea astrolabe.

3) From the 1570s, the English built larger, longer ships. These were better-suited to long ocean voyages, as they were faster, more stable and easier to navigate. They could also carry larger cargoes, making their voyages more profitable.

> Other innovations improved navigation. The log and line helped sailors to estimate their speed with more accuracy from the 1570s. English navigator John Davis invented the backstaff in the 1590s, which was easier to use and more accurate than the sea astrolabe. There were also improvements in map-making, which made maps and naval charts more detailed and reliable.

Francis Drake was the Second man ever to sail Around the World

1) Francis Drake was John Hawkins' cousin, and had travelled with Hawkins on two of his slave-trading expeditions. Between 1577 and 1580, Drake circumnavigated the world (sailed all the way around it).

2) Drake probably wasn't trying to sail around the world. It seems that he was sent by Elizabeth to explore the coast of South America, looking for opportunities for English colonisation and trade.

3) Drake explored the South American coastline, raiding many Spanish settlements as he went. In the Pacific, he captured two very valuable Spanish treasure ships. In order to get this treasure safely home, Drake had to return by a different route — the Spanish were blocking the way that he had come.

4) Instead, Drake sailed west, across the Pacific to Indonesia. He then made his way across the Indian Ocean, went round the Cape of Good Hope and back to England.

> Drake was involved in many other important naval expeditions. E.g. in 1587 he led a raid on the Spanish port of Cadiz (p.87), and in 1588 he played a key role in the defeat of the Spanish Armada. He died of disease in 1596 while trying to conquer Spanish colonies in the Americas.

5) Drake was knighted by Elizabeth on his ship, the Golden Hind. This royal recognition and the wealth that Drake brought back encouraged more English sailors to go on long-distance journeys.

Circumnavigation — taking the roundabout route...

'Francis Drake's circumnavigation of the globe made him the most successful English sailor of Elizabeth's reign'. Explain how far you agree with this statement. [16]

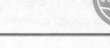

The Elizabethans, 1558-1603

Elizabethan Sailors

After Drake's circumnavigation, England tried to challenge Spain's dominance as an imperial power by establishing a colony in North America. But creating a permanent settlement turned out to be pretty tricky...

Drake's Circumnavigation was a Huge Achievement

Drake's expedition was only the second successful global circumnavigation, and the first by an English sailor. He and his crew had to overcome some major challenges in order to complete the expedition.

1) Navigating across vast oceans was extremely difficult. Elizabethan sailors knew how to use the Sun and stars to work out how far north or south of the equator they were (their latitude), but they couldn't measure how far east or west they had travelled (their longitude).

2) Many of the places Drake visited had never been explored by European sailors before, so there were no detailed maps or charts to help him navigate.

> The challenges of navigation, bad weather and disease had to be faced by all Elizabethan sailors who set out on long-distance voyages.

3) Many sailors died of disease during long journeys — one of Drake's ships had to be abandoned after crossing the Atlantic because so many of the crew had died.

4) Bad weather could blow ships off course, or even sink them. Storms destroyed one of Drake's ships as it attempted to sail around the bottom of South America, and forced another to turn back to England.

Raleigh's attempts to Colonise Virginia were Unsuccessful

> Walter Raleigh was a member of a gentry family from Devon. His family were involved with international exploration, and Raleigh first visited America in 1578. From the early 1580s, Raleigh had a powerful position at court as one of Elizabeth's 'favourites'.

1) In 1584, Elizabeth gave Raleigh permission to explore and colonise unclaimed territories. She wanted him to establish a colony on the Atlantic coast of North America.

2) In 1585, Raleigh sent 108 settlers to establish a permanent colony on Roanoke Island, Virginia (Raleigh named his colony after Elizabeth, who was known as the 'Virgin Queen'). However, the settlers (or planters) soon ran low on supplies, and when Francis Drake visited Roanoke in 1586, most of them abandoned the colony and returned to England.

Comment and Analysis

An English colony would have challenged Spain's dominance in the Americas and could be used as a base for attacking Spanish treasure ships. The colony might also provide opportunities for trade.

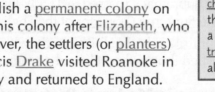

Roanoke Island, Virginia

3) A second group of planters reached Roanoke in 1587. They were expecting supplies from England in 1588, but the fleet was delayed by the Spanish Armada (see p.88).

4) When the supply ships reached Roanoke in 1590, all the planters had disappeared. They were never found, and Roanoke became known as the 'Lost Colony'.

5) Raleigh was partly responsible for the colony's failure — his funds were too limited and the whole project was poorly planned. However, other factors like bad luck and a lack of supplies also played a part.

Raleigh's Career had Ups and Downs

1) Despite the failure of the Roanoke colony, Raleigh remained one of Elizabeth's 'favourites'.

2) However, in 1592 he was disgraced when Elizabeth found out that he had secretly married one of her ladies-in-waiting. As a punishment, Raleigh was banished from court and briefly imprisoned.

3) This wasn't the end of his career though — after his release he continued to play an important role in politics. He became a Member of Parliament and was still heavily involved with the Royal Navy.

As Raleigh learned, if you fail to plan, you plan to fail...

Make a timeline of Walter Raleigh's career. Include all the key events of his attempts to colonise Virginia and details of what happened to him after the failure of the Roanoke colony.

The Religious Settlement

By 1558, England had experienced decades of dizzying religious changes. Elizabeth's religious 'settlement', passed in 1559, aimed to put a stop to these changes and bring religious stability to England.

There had been constant Religious Changes since the 1530s

When Elizabeth became queen in 1558, England had suffered 30 years of religious turmoil, with the national religion switching repeatedly between Catholicism and Protestantism.

Henry VIII
Until the 1530s, England was a Catholic country, and most people were Catholics. However, in the early 1530s Henry VIII broke away from the Roman Catholic Church. He rejected the Pope's authority and made himself head of the Church of England.

Edward VI
Edward VI was a strong supporter of Protestantism. When he became king, he tried to reform the English Church to make it more Protestant.

Mary I
Mary I was a devout Catholic. As queen, she made England Catholic again — she restored the Pope as head of the English Church and removed Edward's protestant reforms. Protestants were harshly persecuted under Mary — more than 280 were executed, and many more fled to Protestant countries in Europe.

Elizabeth had been raised as a Protestant. She was deeply religious and committed to Protestantism. But she was also determined to end the constant religious changes of the last 30 years by creating a stable and lasting religious settlement.

Protestants questioned the authority of the Pope and rejected some Catholic beliefs — e.g. they believed that Christians were saved by faith, not by good deeds. They encouraged ordinary people to read the Bible by translating it from Latin, and thought churches should be plain and simple, unlike highly decorated Catholic churches.

The Religious Settlement was designed for Religious Stability

The Act of Supremacy gave Elizabeth Control over the Church

1) Henry VIII and Edward VI had used the title Supreme Head of the Church of England. In her Act of Supremacy (passed in 1559), Elizabeth altered this title to make herself the Supreme Governor of the English Church.

2) This gave Elizabeth control of the English Church, without actually calling her its 'Head'. This compromise satisfied those who believed a woman couldn't lead the Church.

The Act of Uniformity made Moderate Protestant Reforms

The Act of Uniformity and the Royal Injunctions, both passed in 1559, imposed moderate Protestant reforms on the English Church, but they also made some concessions to English Catholics:

Reforms
- Going to church was compulsory — there were fines for missing a church service.
- A new Book of Common Prayer was issued, which had to be used in all churches.
- All parishes had to have a copy of the Bible in English.

Concessions
- The wording of the communion service (an important Christian ceremony) was kept deliberately vague, so that it could be accepted by both Protestants and Catholics.
- Churches were allowed to keep some decorations, and priests had to wear certain Catholic vestments (robes).

Comment and Analysis
The religious settlement made England a Protestant country, but allowed some elements of Catholic belief and practice to continue. This 'middle way' was designed to satisfy the majority, who held moderate religious beliefs and were willing to make some compromises for the sake of peace and stability. But it couldn't win over the more extreme Catholics or the Puritans (see p.81).

Sometimes the 'middle way' is the only way...

Divide a piece of paper into two. Jot down the key features of the Act of Supremacy on one side and the Act of Uniformity and the Royal Injunctions on the other.

REVISION TASK

Early Challenges to the Religious Settlement

Elizabeth's religious settlement faced many <u>challenges</u> in the <u>1560s</u>. Some were more serious than others.

The Puritans were Committed Protestants

1) For the Puritans, Elizabeth's religious settlement was only a <u>first step</u>, and they wanted her to make <u>further reforms</u> to remove all traces of Catholicism from the English Church.

2) Many <u>Puritans</u> had fled England when Mary I was in power (see p.80). While in exile in Protestant parts of Europe, some had come into contact with the teachings of leading reformers like <u>Martin Luther</u> and <u>John Calvin</u>.

3) The <u>Vestment Controversy</u> of the 1560s was a serious Puritan challenge to the religious settlement. Puritan priests <u>refused</u> to wear the <u>surplice</u>, a white vestment used by Catholics, which the Royal Injunctions had made compulsory (see p.80).

4) Elizabeth tolerated this at first, but in <u>1565</u> she ordered the Archbishop of Canterbury to ensure that all priests wore the surplice. Those Puritans who still refused <u>lost their jobs</u> or were <u>imprisoned</u>.

> Many of the <u>Protestant bishops</u> appointed from 1559 <u>supported</u> the Puritans and were in favour of <u>further reforms</u>. However, the Archbishop of Canterbury, <u>Matthew Parker</u>, was a <u>moderate</u> who helped Elizabeth to uphold the '<u>middle way</u>' of the religious settlement.

> The Puritans challenged the religious settlement <u>again</u> later in Elizabeth's reign — see p.86.

Many members of the Nobility continued to practise Catholicism

1) A large proportion of the <u>nobility</u> were still <u>Catholic</u>. The compromises in the religious settlement won some of them around, but others <u>refused</u> to attend <u>church services</u> — they were known as <u>recusants</u>.

2) The <u>Catholic nobility</u> was <u>influential</u> in areas outside the south-east, especially <u>Lancashire</u>. They used their strong local power bases to <u>protect Catholics</u> and maintain their <u>traditional religious practices</u>.

3) These Catholic nobles posed a potential <u>threat</u> to the religious settlement — there was a risk that they might try to <u>overthrow</u> Elizabeth and <u>restore Catholicism</u>.

4) To minimise this threat, Elizabeth <u>did not</u> force the Catholic nobility to attend church services. As long as they didn't make a public show of their beliefs, they were allowed to <u>continue practising Catholicism</u>.

> The <u>threat</u> posed by the Catholic nobility became <u>more serious</u> when <u>Mary, Queen of Scots</u>, (a Catholic claimant to the English throne) arrived in England in <u>1568</u> (p.82).

France and Spain were Distracted by Domestic Difficulties

1) There was a risk that the <u>Catholic</u> rulers of <u>France</u> or <u>Spain</u> might try to <u>reverse</u> the <u>religious settlement</u> and <u>replace</u> Elizabeth with a <u>Catholic monarch</u>. However, neither country was really in a position to challenge the religious settlement during the 1560s.

2) The threat of a <u>French invasion</u> was serious in the first years of Elizabeth's reign, but <u>faded</u> with the start of the <u>French Wars of Religion</u> in <u>1562</u>.

3) In the <u>1560s</u>, <u>Spain</u> was facing a growing <u>revolt</u> in the <u>Netherlands</u>. To prevent an alliance forming between England and the Protestant Netherlands, Spain tried to stay on <u>good terms</u> with Elizabeth and <u>avoided</u> challenging her religious settlement.

> **Comment and Analysis**
>
> The <u>Catholic aspects</u> of the settlement encouraged Catholic countries and the Pope to think that <u>Elizabeth</u> might eventually <u>return to Catholicism</u>. This helped to <u>reduce</u> the threat of a <u>foreign challenge</u> during the early years of the settlement.

The Papacy Lacked Military Support

1) The Pope had the power to <u>excommunicate</u> Elizabeth (<u>expel</u> her from the Catholic Church). This might encourage <u>Catholic</u> countries to <u>invade</u> England. It could also encourage <u>rebellion at home</u> by releasing Elizabeth's Catholic subjects from their duty of loyalty to her.

2) However, neither France nor Spain had the <u>military resources</u> to invade England, and there was <u>no clear support</u> for a revolt against Elizabeth at home, so the Pope <u>didn't take any action</u> against her in the 1560s.

Despite the settlement, things took a while to settle down...

Do you agree that foreign opposition was the most serious threat to the Elizabethan religious settlement in the 1560s? Explain your answer. [16]

The Elizabethans, 1558-1603

Mary, Queen of Scots

Even though Elizabeth and Mary, Queen of Scots, were <u>cousins</u>, Elizabeth wasn't too pleased when Mary arrived in England for an <u>unexpected visit</u> in <u>1568</u>. In fact, she was so unimpressed, she put Mary in prison...

Mary, Queen of Scots, had a Strong Claim to the English Throne

1) Mary was the only child of <u>James V of Scotland</u>. She was related to the <u>Tudors</u> through her grandmother, <u>Margaret Tudor</u>. Margaret was Henry VIII's sister, the wife of James IV and mother of James V.

2) As a granddaughter of Margaret Tudor, Mary had a <u>strong claim</u> to the <u>English throne</u>. Because Mary was a Catholic, her claim was <u>supported</u> by many <u>English Catholics</u>.

3) Mary became <u>queen of Scotland</u> in 1542 when she was just six days old. Her mother acted as regent (she ruled on Mary's behalf), while Mary was raised in <u>France</u>.

4) In 1558, when Mary was 15 years old, she married the heir to the French throne. However, her husband died suddenly in <u>1560</u>, and Mary <u>returned to Scotland</u>.

Comment and Analysis

Mary wanted to be named as <u>heir</u> to the <u>English throne</u>, but Elizabeth was <u>unwilling</u> to do this. She feared that making Mary her heir would <u>encourage Catholic plots</u>, both at home and abroad, to overthrow her and make Mary queen.

Mary Fled to England in 1568

1) In <u>1565</u> Mary married the Scottish nobleman <u>Lord Darnley</u>. The marriage was not a happy one. Darnley hated Mary's personal secretary, <u>David Rizzio</u>, and became convinced that the two were having an <u>affair</u>. In 1566 a group of Scottish nobles, accompanied by Darnley, <u>stabbed Rizzio to death</u>.

2) In <u>1567</u>, Darnley was <u>murdered</u>. Many people believed that <u>Mary</u> and her close friend, the <u>Earl of Bothwell</u>, were behind the murder. Their suspicions seemed to be confirmed when <u>Mary married Bothwell</u> a few months later.

3) This marriage was <u>unpopular</u> with the Scottish nobles, who <u>rebelled</u> against Mary. They <u>imprisoned</u> her and forced her to <u>abdicate</u> (<u>give up the throne</u>) in favour of her one-year-old son, James. In <u>1568</u>, Mary <u>escaped</u> from prison and raised an army. Her forces were <u>defeated</u> in battle and she <u>fled</u> south to <u>England</u>.

> Some people (including <u>Elizabeth</u>) thought that the Scottish nobles had <u>no right</u> to <u>overthrow</u> Mary. As a result, they <u>didn't accept</u> her <u>abdication</u>, and still viewed her as the <u>legitimate</u> queen of Scotland.

Mary was Imprisoned, but still posed a Threat

1) Mary hoped that Elizabeth would help her <u>regain control</u> of <u>Scotland</u>. Elizabeth was <u>not</u> willing to do this — Mary's <u>claim</u> to the <u>English throne</u> meant that there would be a constant <u>threat of invasion</u> from the north if Mary regained power in Scotland.

2) Instead, Elizabeth had Mary <u>imprisoned</u> and set up an <u>inquiry</u> to investigate whether she had been involved in <u>Darnley's murder</u>.

3) Elizabeth <u>didn't</u> want the inquiry to find Mary <u>guilty</u>. A guilty verdict would lend <u>support</u> to the actions of the <u>Scottish nobles</u>, who had <u>overthrown</u> Mary, their <u>legitimate queen</u>.

> The so-called '<u>Casket Letters</u>' were presented to the inquiry. They included several letters apparently written by Mary to Bothwell, which <u>implicated</u> the pair in Darnley's murder. Mary's supporters insisted that the letters were <u>forgeries</u>, but most members of the inquiry believed they were <u>genuine</u>.

4) However, Elizabeth <u>didn't</u> want a <u>not-guilty</u> verdict either, because this would force her to <u>release</u> Mary. Once free, Mary might use her claim to the English throne to try and <u>overthrow Elizabeth</u>.

5) In the end, the inquiry <u>didn't</u> reach a <u>verdict</u> — this enabled Elizabeth to keep Mary in <u>captivity</u>. Elizabeth hoped that <u>imprisoning</u> Mary would <u>prevent</u> her becoming the centre of <u>Catholic plots</u>, but Mary's presence caused <u>problems</u> for Elizabeth throughout the next <u>20 years</u> (see p.83-85).

Elizabeth really wasn't a fan of uninvited guests...

Why was Mary, Queen of Scots, a threat to Queen Elizabeth I? Explain your answer. [12]

The Northern Rebellion

Mary, Queen of Scots, had barely been in England five minutes when she began causing trouble for Elizabeth.

The Northern Nobles were unhappy for Several Reasons

1) Many northern nobles were still committed Catholics. They wanted to see the restoration of Catholicism in England under a Catholic monarch. The arrival of Mary, Queen of Scots, in 1568 (see p.82) gave them hope that Elizabeth could be replaced with Mary.

2) Elizabeth had confiscated large areas of land from the Earl of Northumberland and shared them between Northumberland's main rival in the north and a southern Protestant. Northumberland was also angry that Elizabeth had claimed all the profits from copper mines discovered on his estates.

3) Elizabeth had reduced the power of the northern nobles and increased her control in the north. In part, she did this through the Council of the North, which helped to govern the region. Under Elizabeth, the Council was controlled by southern Protestants. The northern nobles deeply resented this.

4) The northern nobles blamed Elizabeth's advisors for these policies. They believed that some Privy Councillors, especially William Cecil (see p.70), had become too powerful. They wanted to remove these 'evil counsellors' and replace them with men who would be more sympathetic to their interests.

The Northern Rebellion broke out in November 1569

1) In 1569, the Duke of Norfolk (the wealthiest landowner in England) hatched a plan to marry Mary, Queen of Scots, and have her recognised as Elizabeth's heir. This plan was supported by Catholic nobles, including the Earls of Northumberland and Westmorland, because it meant that Elizabeth would be succeeded by a Catholic queen.

2) When the plan was uncovered, the Earls feared they would be executed for their involvement. In a desperate attempt to escape punishment, they rebelled and tried to overthrow Elizabeth.

3) In November 1569, the Earls captured Durham, where they celebrated Catholic Mass in the cathedral. They then marched south, probably making for Tutbury in Derbyshire, where Mary was imprisoned.

4) Before the rebels reached Tutbury, a large royal army forced them to retreat. Many of their troops deserted, and the two Earls fled to Scotland. Elizabeth showed the rebels little mercy. Westmorland fled abroad, but Northumberland was executed, as were at least 400 rebel troops.

The revolt was a Serious Threat to Elizabeth's rule

1) The Northern Rebellion was the most serious rebellion of Elizabeth's reign. It posed a major threat to Elizabeth's rule and showed the danger that Mary, Queen of Scots, represented as a rallying point for English Catholics.

2) News of the rebellion created widespread fear among English Protestants about the threat posed by Catholics, and contributed to growing anti-Catholic feelings. These views were fuelled by memories of the harsh persecution of Protestants during the reign of Queen Mary I.

3) There was little support for the revolt among the rest of the Catholic nobility and ordinary people — when given a choice between Elizabeth and their religion, most Catholics chose to support the Queen. 1569-70 was the last time that English Catholics tried to remove Elizabeth by force.

> ### Comment and Analysis
>
> The Northern Rebellion sought to protect the long-standing independence of the northern nobles, but in the end it increased government control in the north of England. After the revolt, many rebels had their lands confiscated. The Council of the North was also strengthened under the leadership of the Puritan, Henry Hastings, Earl of Huntingdon.

Those northern earls were revolting...

As well as knowing what happened in Elizabethan England, you also need to know why things happened — so be sure to learn what caused events like the Northern Rebellion.

84

The Catholic Threat

The Catholic threat got even <u>worse</u> throughout the <u>1570s</u> and early <u>1580s</u>.
As a result, Elizabeth and her government became less and <u>less tolerant</u> of Catholicism.

The Pope Expelled Elizabeth from the Catholic Church

1) In <u>1570</u>, Elizabeth was <u>excommunicated</u> (<u>expelled</u> from the Catholic Church) by the Pope. This meant Catholics no longer had to <u>obey</u> the Queen and were encouraged to <u>overthrow</u> her.

> The excommunication was meant to <u>strengthen</u> the <u>Northern Rebellion</u>, but news of it didn't arrive until <u>after</u> the revolt had <u>collapsed</u>.

2) Together with the Northern Rebellion (see p.83), the excommunication <u>changed</u> Elizabeth's <u>attitude</u> towards Catholics. They were now seen as potential <u>traitors</u>, so Elizabeth and her government became <u>less tolerant</u> of <u>recusancy</u> (refusal to go to church) by Catholics.

3) In response to the excommunication, <u>Parliament</u> passed the <u>Treasons Act</u> in <u>1571</u>. Under this Act, anyone who claimed that Elizabeth <u>wasn't</u> England's <u>legitimate ruler</u> could face the <u>death penalty</u>.

Missionary Priests strengthened English Catholicism

1) In <u>1568</u>, William Allen founded a <u>missionary college</u> at <u>Douai</u> (now in France) to train English Catholic priests. Once trained, these missionary priests would return to England and <u>secretly</u> minister to English Catholics. The first missionary priests reached England in <u>1574</u>.

2) In <u>1580</u>, the missionaries <u>Robert Parsons</u> and <u>Edmund Campion</u> (who had both trained at a missionary college in <u>Rome</u>) entered the country. Campion was <u>executed</u> for <u>treason</u> in December <u>1581</u>.

3) In the <u>1560s</u>, Elizabeth had <u>tolerated recusancy</u> because she believed that English Catholicism would gradually <u>die out</u> as the religious settlement became more firmly established.

4) However, the arrival of the <u>missionary priests</u> from the 1570s <u>changed</u> things — with the support of these highly-committed missionaries, it was now <u>unlikely</u> that Catholicism in England would just <u>fade away</u> on its own. This <u>strengthening</u> of Catholicism was a <u>major threat</u> to the religious settlement.

> In response to the threat from missionary priests, Parliament passed two anti-Catholic Acts in <u>1581</u>. These Acts:
> • Massively <u>increased</u> the <u>fines</u> for <u>recusancy</u>, making them too expensive for most ordinary Catholics.
> • Introduced <u>fines</u> and <u>prison sentences</u> for people who said or attended <u>Catholic Mass</u>.
> • Made it treason (which was punishable by death) to <u>convert</u> to Catholicism or persuade others to convert.
> • Introduced <u>prison sentences</u> and the <u>death penalty</u> for anyone who encouraged <u>rebellion</u>.

Catholic Plots aimed to put Mary on the English Throne

1) Between 1571 and 1585, there were several <u>Catholic plots</u> to <u>assassinate</u> Elizabeth and replace her with Mary, Queen of Scots. They included the <u>Ridolfi Plot</u> (<u>1571</u>), the <u>Throckmorton Plot</u> (<u>1583</u>) and the <u>Babington Plot</u> (<u>1586</u>, see p.85).

> Letters sent by <u>Mary</u> <u>implicated</u> her in the <u>Ridolfi Plot</u>. In 1572 <u>Parliament</u> urged Elizabeth to <u>execute</u> Mary for her part in the plot. Elizabeth <u>refused</u> — she was <u>reluctant</u> to execute someone she saw as a <u>legitimate monarch</u> (p.82).

2) The plots involved Catholic conspirators in <u>England</u> and <u>Europe</u>. They were supported by the <u>Pope</u> and Catholic rulers, especially King <u>Philip II</u> of Spain.

3) The plots were a <u>real threat</u> to Elizabeth's rule and her religious settlement (p.80). Mary's <u>strong claim</u> to the throne (p.82) made them seem <u>credible</u>, and <u>Philip II's</u> involvement meant there was a risk they would lead to a Spanish <u>invasion</u>.

Comment and Analysis

<u>Missionary priests</u> supported the Catholic <u>plots</u> to assassinate Elizabeth. They wanted <u>England</u> to return to <u>Catholicism</u> and believed this could <u>only</u> be achieved if <u>Elizabeth</u> was <u>removed</u>.

4) However, <u>none</u> of the plots succeeded. This was partly because there was <u>little public support</u> for a Catholic revolution (as the Northern Rebellion had shown). Also, by the 1580s Elizabeth's Principal Secretary, <u>Francis Walsingham</u>, had established a highly efficient <u>spy network</u>, which ensured that the plots were <u>uncovered</u> before they were carried out.

Don't lose the plot, just learn this page...

Write a couple of sentences to explain why each of the following factors was a threat to Elizabeth and her religious settlement: excommunication, missionary priests, Catholic plots.

The Catholic Threat

In 1586, Walsingham used his spy network to prove that Mary had supported the Babington Plot. His evidence persuaded Elizabeth to put Mary on trial and execute her for treason.

Persecution of Catholics Increased in the 1580s

1) In 1584, the Dutch Protestant leader, William the Silent, was assassinated by a Catholic (see p.87). Combined with the arrival of missionary priests and the Catholic plots against Elizabeth, this assassination made the government even more concerned about the Catholic threat in England.

2) As a result, persecution of Catholics increased. Anti-Catholic laws were enforced more strictly than they had been earlier in Elizabeth's reign, and in 1585 Parliament passed two new laws:

   - Mary, Queen of Scots, wouldn't be allowed to become queen if Elizabeth was assassinated. It was hoped that this would put a stop to the plots involving Mary.

   - Missionary priests had 40 days to leave the country. Any priests who didn't leave could be executed, as could anyone who tried to help them.

   > The anti-Catholic laws of 1581 (see p.84) and 1585 led to the execution of more than 120 Catholic priests and the deaths of many more in prison.

The Babington Plot led to the Execution of Mary, Queen of Scots

1) In 1586, Francis Walsingham used his spy network to gather evidence of Mary, Queen of Scots' involvement in the Babington Plot. He intercepted and decoded Mary's letters, including one which approved plans to assassinate the Queen and free Mary from prison.

2) Mary had been implicated in Catholic plots before, but Elizabeth had always refused to take action against her. The evidence gathered by Walsingham finally persuaded her to put Mary on trial.

3) In October 1586, Mary was found guilty of treason and sentenced to death. Despite the guilty verdict, Elizabeth was very reluctant to execute Mary. Parliament and the Privy Council believed that the execution was vital to weaken the Catholic threat and protect the religious settlement, so they put pressure on Elizabeth to sign Mary's death warrant.

4) After hesitating for several months, Elizabeth eventually agreed to the execution. Mary was executed on 8th February 1587.

Comment and Analysis

Elizabeth was reluctant to execute Mary because she was queen of Scotland. Elizabeth believed that monarchs ruled by Divine Right (see p.71), so she felt she had no right to execute a legitimate monarch. She also feared that executing Mary would undermine her own claim to rule by Divine Right and might fuel more plots against her.

Mary's execution Reduced the Threat from Catholics at Home...

The execution of Mary, Queen of Scots, removed the Catholic threat to Elizabeth at home. English Catholics now had no-one to rally around, and they lost hope of ever overthrowing Elizabeth and reversing the religious settlement. There were no more major Catholic plots during Elizabeth's reign.

...but it Increased the Threat from Abroad

1) In 1587, relations with Spain were at a low point — the two countries were now at war over the Netherlands, and King Philip II had been preparing for an attack on England since 1585 (see p.87). Mary's execution made the situation worse. Philip was now even more determined to invade.

2) There was also a danger that Mary's son, James VI of Scotland might seek revenge for his mother's death. There were fears that he would form an alliance with other Catholic powers in order to invade England.

The Babington Plot wasn't very well executed...

Give an account of the ways missionary priests affected England in the 1570s and 1580s. [8]

The Puritan Threat

As if the Catholic threat wasn't bad enough, the religious settlement also faced a threat from the other end of the religious spectrum. The Puritans were committed Protestants who wanted to purify the English Church.

The Puritans wanted to make the English Church More Protestant

1) As committed Protestants, the Puritans were strongly anti-Catholic. They thought that the English Church should be free from all traces of Catholicism.

2) They believed that preaching (explaining the word of God) was very important. They thought that all priests should be well educated so that they'd be able to preach. At the time, this was unusual — many priests lacked education and didn't preach at all.

3) The Puritans also encouraged the education of ordinary people, so that they would be able to read and understand the Bible for themselves. They were very strict about godly living (obeying all of God's commandments).

Comment and Analysis

For Elizabeth, the religious settlement of 1559 was final and couldn't be changed. She wanted everyone to accept the settlement, so she saw Puritan demands for further reforms as a serious threat.

Some Puritans were more radical. They wanted to get rid of the Church hierarchy of archbishops, bishops, etc. This view was a threat to Elizabeth because it called into question her authority as Supreme Governor of the Church — the head of the hierarchy.

Puritans believed that Christians should live a restrained lifestyle. They opposed anything encouraging playfulness or idleness. This included sports and popular pastimes, like cock-fighting and drinking. They also disliked public celebrations, even for religious events like Christmas.

The 'Prophesyings' taught Priests how to Preach

1) By the 1570s, the Puritans were concerned about the lack of educated priests who were able to preach. So they introduced the 'prophesyings' — a kind of training to teach priests how to preach.

2) Elizabeth thought that the 'prophesyings' would encourage more Puritan opposition to the religious settlement. In 1576, she ordered the Archbishop of Canterbury, Edmund Grindal, to put a stop to them.

3) Grindal (a moderate Puritan) thought the 'prophesyings' were good for the Church, so he refused to obey Elizabeth's order. This made Elizabeth furious. She suspended Grindal and put him under house arrest.

Archbishop Whitgift tried to Suppress Puritanism

1) In 1583, Grindal died and Elizabeth made John Whitgift Archbishop of Canterbury. With Elizabeth's support, Whitgift launched an attack on Puritan clergy — all priests had to accept the regulations of the Church of England or face suspension. Between 200 and 300 Puritan priests were suspended.

Comment and Analysis

Whitgift's campaign faced some opposition from the Privy Council and Parliament. Elizabeth overcame this by threatening to dismiss any council members who opposed it, and refusing to let Parliament discuss the matter.

2) Whitgift's campaign made some Puritans feel that there was no hope of reforming the Church of England. Instead, they decided to break away and form a separate church.

3) These Puritan separatists were seen as a major threat to the religious settlement. The government introduced censorship laws to prevent them spreading their ideas, and in 1590 several of their leaders were arrested.

4) The threat from Puritan separatists probably wasn't as serious as Elizabeth and her government thought. There weren't many separatists and they didn't have the support of any powerful members of the elite. Most Puritans were moderates who worked within the Church of England.

The Puritans wanted the Church to be pure and simple...

The different religious groups in Elizabethan England can be pretty confusing. Think about what the Puritans believed, and how they were different from Catholics and moderate Protestants.

War with Spain

England and Spain tried to stay on good terms, but the growing tensions between them eventually led to war.

There were Political, Religious and Economic tensions with Spain

King Philip II of Spain had been married to Queen Mary I of England, and the two countries had been allies. Elizabeth and Philip tried to maintain good relations, but tensions between them gradually began to grow.

Political

Spain was a great imperial power. Philip ruled Spain, the Netherlands, parts of Italy and (from 1581) Portugal. He also had a large empire in the Americas. By the 1570s, England was starting to have ambitions for an empire of its own (p.78). This led to growing rivalry and tension between the two countries.

Religious

Philip was a devout Catholic and disliked Elizabeth's religious settlement. He became involved in several Catholic plots against Elizabeth in the 1570s and 1580s (p.84), which damaged Elizabeth's trust in him.

Economic

Elizabeth encouraged privateers to trade illegally with Spanish colonies, raid Spanish ships and attack the treasure fleets carrying gold and silver from the New World to Spain.

In the 1560s an English fleet, commanded by John Hawkins, traded with Spanish colonies, even though Spain had banned them from doing so. This led to the Battle of San Juan de Ulúa in 1568. Francis Drake also raided many Spanish colonies in South America during his round-the-world voyage of 1577-80 (p.78-79).

England and Spain eventually went to War over the Netherlands

1) In 1581, Protestant rebels in the Netherlands declared independence from Spain. In 1584 the rebel leader, William the Silent, was assassinated, and the revolt was in danger of being defeated.

2) Elizabeth decided to help the rebels — in 1585 she signed the Treaty of Nonsuch, which promised military assistance. Religious, economic and military factors influenced her decision:

- Elizabeth wanted to protect Dutch Protestantism and prevent Philip forcing Catholicism on the Netherlands.
- English exports to Europe were vital to the English economy, and many English goods reached the European market via Dutch ports, especially Antwerp. Elizabeth needed to ensure that English merchants would have access to the Dutch ports.
- If the rebels were defeated, Philip might use the Netherlands as a base for an invasion of England.

3) Philip saw the Treaty of Nonsuch as a declaration of war on Spain. In response, he began building a huge fleet (an Armada) that he planned to use to invade England.

Drake was sent to Disrupt Spanish Preparations for the Armada

1) Elizabeth sent Francis Drake to spy on Spanish preparations and attack their ships and supplies. In April 1587, Drake attacked the Spanish port of Cadiz. He destroyed around 30 ships and seized many tonnes of supplies.

2) This delayed the Armada by more than a year. Obtaining fresh supplies and weapons was very expensive and seriously strained Spain's finances.

3) During his raid, Drake captured planks made from seasoned wood, which were needed to make the barrels used to carry food and water.

4) As a result, the Spanish had to make their barrels from unseasoned wood, which couldn't preserve food and water very well. This caused supply problems for the Armada and affected the morale of Spanish troops and sailors. Fresh water supplies were lost and many tons of food rotted as the fleet sailed to England in 1588.

Comment and Analysis

Drake described his raid on Cadiz as 'singeing the King of Spain's beard'. He meant that he had inflicted temporary damage on King Philip's Armada, but hadn't destroyed it entirely — it would 'grow back' in time.

The Americas — a whole New World of commercial rivalry...

England's relationship with Spain was a major headache for Elizabeth throughout her reign. Make sure you understand how and why the relationship changed over time.

EXAM TIP

The Spanish Armada

The Spanish Armada was launched in 1588, but right from the start, things didn't go according to plan....

The Armada Planned to meet the Duke of Parma at Dunkirk

1) By the spring of 1588, the Spanish Armada was complete. The Armada was a huge fleet of around 130 ships, manned by approximately 8000 sailors and carrying an estimated 18,000 soldiers.

2) Philip appointed the Duke of Medina Sidonia to lead the Armada. Philip respected the Duke's high social status and trusted him to obey instructions. However, the Duke had little military or naval experience.

3) The Spanish had thousands more soldiers stationed in the Netherlands under the leadership of the Duke of Parma. Philip's plan was for the Armada to meet Parma's army at Dunkirk. The combined forces would then sail across the Channel to England under the protection of the Armada's warships.

The English managed to Scatter Spain's ships

1) The Armada set out in May 1588. In July, it was sighted off Cornwall. English ships set sail from Plymouth to attack the Armada, but they caused little damage. Only two Spanish ships were lost, and they were destroyed by accident.

2) Having sailed up the Channel, Medina Sidonia anchored at Calais to wait for Parma's troops. However, Parma and his men were being blockaded by Dutch ships and weren't able to reach the coast in time.

> **Things went from bad to worse for Spain...**
> * That night, England sent eight fireships (ships loaded with flammable materials and set alight) among the anchored Spanish ships. The Spanish sailors panicked and headed for the open sea. The weather made it impossible for them to return to their defensive position at Calais.
> * The English advanced, and the following battle lasted for many hours. Five Spanish ships were sunk, and the rest of the fleet was forced to sail away from the French coast into the North Sea.

The Armada's Journey back to Spain was a Disaster

1) Medina Sidonia decided to call off the attack on England and return to Spain by sailing round Scotland and Ireland. The Spanish sailors were unfamiliar with this very dangerous route, and they encountered several powerful Atlantic storms.

2) Many ships sank or were wrecked on the Scottish and Irish coasts. Those ships that completed the journey ran short of supplies, and many men died of starvation and disease. Less than half the fleet and fewer than 10,000 men made it back to Spain.

The war with Spain Continued until 1604

1) Despite the defeat of the Armada, continued tension between England and Spain helped to sustain the war. Spain was determined to end the Protestant rebellion in the Netherlands and bring the country back under Spanish control. Elizabeth continued supporting the rebels, which angered Philip.

2) England was still attacking Spanish ships off the coast of Spain and in the Caribbean (see p.78), while Spain launched two more unsuccessful Armadas in 1596 and 1597.

3) However, by the end of the 16th century, the conflict was beginning to drain English and Spanish resources. In 1604, they signed a peace treaty, which brought an official end to the war.

> The victory of 1588 encouraged England's development as a strong naval power to rival Spain. It also boosted Elizabeth's popularity and strengthened the Protestant cause — it was seen as a sign that God favoured Protestantism.

The defeat of the Armada — a great English victory...

The Armada was an important event in the war with Spain — you need to learn the story well.

Revision Summary

That's the Elizabethans all done and dusted — time to test your knowledge with a quick revision summary.
- Try these questions and <u>tick off each one</u> when you <u>get it right</u>.
- When you've done <u>all the questions</u> for a topic and are <u>completely happy</u> with it, tick off the topic.

Elizabeth's Court and Parliament (p.66-72) ☑

1) Describe Queen Elizabeth I's character.
2) Explain what the term 'patronage' means.
3) Why was Elizabeth under pressure to find a husband?
4) Explain why France was a threat to Elizabeth at the start of her reign.
5) Name three important members of Court who became Elizabeth's 'favourites'.
6) What was the role of the Privy Council?
7) What were Parliament's main functions?
8) Give three ways in which Elizabeth and her Privy Council managed Parliament.
9) Who was Robert Devereux? Briefly describe his rebellion against Elizabeth.
10) How did Elizabeth's Privy Council change towards the end of her reign?

Life in Elizabethan Times (p.73-79) ☑

11) Why was the problem of poverty growing in Elizabethan England?
12) Describe how the Poor Laws of 1597 and 1601 treated the deserving and undeserving poor.
13) Give four ways in which members of the Elizabethan elite spent their growing wealth.
14) Give two reasons that family was considered important to Elizabethan society.
15) What was a petty school?
16) Why were some people opposed to the theatre?
17) Who was John Hawkins?
18) What did Francis Drake do between 1577 and 1580? Why was this a major achievement?
19) Who organised the attempted colonisation of Virginia in the 1580s?
20) Why is Roanoke known as the 'Lost Colony'?

Troubles at Home and Abroad (p.80-88) ☑

21) Name the two Acts of the Elizabethan religious settlement.
22) Why did the Puritans oppose the religious settlement?
23) Why did Mary, Queen of Scots, have a strong claim to the English throne?
24) Give three reasons for the 1569 Northern Rebellion.
25) How did Elizabeth's government respond to the threat posed by missionary priests?
26) Name three Catholic plots against Elizabeth.
27) Why was Elizabeth reluctant to execute Mary, Queen of Scots?
28) Explain how radical Puritans wanted to change the Church.
29) Who was John Whitgift? What was his role in dealing with the Puritan threat?
30) Why were there growing tensions between England and Spain in the 1570s and 1580s?
31) Why did England and Spain go to war in 1585?
32) Explain what the phrase 'the singeing of the King of Spain's beard' means.
33) Give two consequences of the defeat of the Spanish Armada for England.

The Monarchy Under Threat

The <u>German Empire</u> was created in 1871 and lasted until 1918. It was ruled by <u>Kaiser Wilhelm II</u> from 1888.

The Constitution made the Kaiser very Powerful

When the <u>German Empire</u> was created in 1871, its constitution made the <u>Kaiser</u> the most <u>powerful</u> figure in government. A German parliament called the <u>Reichstag</u> was also created, but in reality it held <u>little</u> power.

- **Kaiser** — <u>Inherits</u> his position and rules like a <u>king</u>. Controls the <u>army</u> and <u>foreign policy</u>. Appoints and dismisses a <u>Chancellor</u> who runs the <u>government</u>. Can <u>dissolve</u> the Reichstag and overrule the <u>Bundesrat</u>.

- **Bundesrat** — Its consent is needed for <u>all</u> <u>legislation</u>. It includes representatives from each <u>state</u> in the German Empire.
- **Reichstag** — Can <u>pass</u> or <u>reject</u> legislation handed down by the <u>Bundesrat</u>. Its members are elected by the public.

1) Kaiser Wilhelm II <u>didn't</u> believe in democracy and <u>disliked</u> working with the <u>Reichstag</u>. He preferred to place his trust in the <u>army</u>, and often relied on military advisors to help him make <u>important decisions</u>.

2) The Prussian army played an important role in Germany's unification in 1871. Wilhelm II was strongly influenced by its <u>prestige</u> and <u>power</u>, and adopted a system of <u>militarism</u> — this meant <u>strengthening</u> Germany's military (e.g. its army and navy) and using it to <u>increase</u> Germany's influence.

> Before 1871, Germany was made up of lots of independent states — one of these was called <u>Prussia</u>.

Social problems Increased and Germans wanted Reforms

Germany's economy <u>grew</u> rapidly from <u>1890</u> to <u>1914</u> and became more <u>industrialised</u>. New <u>jobs</u> were created, the population in Germany's <u>cities</u> grew and the working classes gained more economic power.

1) The working classes <u>expanded</u> and began to demand better <u>working conditions</u> and <u>representation</u>. This led to a rise in <u>socialism</u> — a political ideology promoting <u>equality</u> and <u>public ownership</u> of industry.

2) The government didn't want to pass <u>reforms</u> to improve <u>working</u> and <u>living conditions</u>, as it was <u>afraid</u> of causing a <u>socialist revolution</u> that could bring down the <u>government</u> and the <u>German class system</u>. As a result, groups who promised <u>change</u> became <u>more popular</u>.

In 1887, the Social Democratic Party (SPD) had <u>11</u> seats in the Reichstag, but by 1903 it had <u>81</u>. Trade unions (groups set up by employees to defend their rights) became more popular too — by 1914, membership stood at about <u>3.3 million</u>.

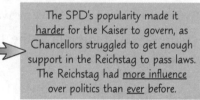

The SPD's popularity made it <u>harder</u> for the Kaiser to govern, as Chancellors struggled to get enough support in the Reichstag to pass laws. The Reichstag had <u>more influence</u> over politics than <u>ever</u> before.

Comment and Analysis

The SPD had <u>different</u> political views to the Kaiser. It wanted to improve conditions for the <u>working classes</u> and disagreed with the <u>privileges</u> held by the <u>military</u> and the <u>monarchy</u>.

Wilhelm tried to Divert Attention away from Socialism

1) The Kaiser tried to reduce <u>discontent</u> among the working classes by introducing limited <u>social reforms</u>.

2) In 1897, he adopted a foreign policy called '<u>Weltpolitik</u>' — this aimed to expand Germany's <u>territory</u>, <u>army</u> and <u>navy</u>. The Kaiser hoped to <u>distract</u> attention from socialism and <u>increase</u> support for the <u>monarchy</u>.

The Navy Laws made people feel patriotic...
- In <u>1898</u>, the first Navy Law was passed. Its eventual aim was to build up Germany's navy to <u>rival</u> Great Britain's.
- In <u>1900</u>, the Reichstag passed another Navy Law, which put a <u>17 year</u> navy expansion programme into place.

The government used propaganda (see p.103) to promote the Navy Laws and inspire <u>patriotism</u> among the German people. The laws were <u>popular</u>, and socialist opposition to them was seen as <u>unpatriotic</u>. In the elections of 1907, the SPD <u>lost</u> 36 seats in the Reichstag.

3) Despite the Kaiser's efforts, by <u>1912</u> the SPD was the <u>largest party</u> in the Reichstag. The Kaiser had managed to <u>keep</u> his power, but the SPD's <u>growth</u> showed that there was an increasing desire for <u>democracy</u> amongst the German people.

Social and economic change shifted the balance of power...

The Reichstag's increasing power meant the Kaiser had to consider the will of the working classes.

(EXAM TIP)

The War Ends

World War I lasted from 1914-1918. During the war, political parties agreed to support the government. However, by 1918 Germany was experiencing widespread unrest, which eventually resulted in a revolution.

World War I had a Devastating Impact on Germany

1) Towards the end of the war, people in Germany were undergoing severe hardship. The Allies had set up naval blockades which prevented imports of food and essential goods — by 1918, many people faced starvation.

2) Public opinion had turned against Kaiser Wilhelm II and there were calls for a democracy. Germany's people were war-weary — they were tired of fighting and wanted an end to the war. There was widespread unrest.

- In November 1918, some members of the German navy rebelled and refused to board their ships.
- In Hanover, German troops refused to control rioters.
- A Jewish communist called Kurt Eisner encouraged a general uprising, which sparked mass strikes in Munich.

A British cartoon from 1917. German civilians queue for food as an over-fed official walks past them. The cartoonist is highlighting the difference between the lifestyle of Germany's rich officers and that of the rest of its struggling population.

Social Unrest turned into Revolution

1) By November 1918, the situation in Germany was almost a civil war. A huge public protest was held in Berlin, and members of the SPD (Social Democratic Party) called for the Kaiser's resignation.

2) Kaiser Wilhelm abdicated (resigned) on 9th November 1918. On the same day, two different socialist parties — the Social Democratic Party and the Independent Social Democratic Party (USPD) — declared a republic.

A republic is a country ruled without a monarch (king or queen) — power is held by the people via elected representatives.

3) On November 10th, all the state leaders that had been appointed by the monarchy left their posts. New revolutionary state governments took over instead. The monarchy had been abolished and Germany had the chance to become a democracy.

Germany was made up of 18 states, and each had its own government. The national government decided national affairs, and state governments dealt with more local affairs.

The signing of the armistice

- On 11th November 1918, a ceasefire to end the First World War was agreed. The Allies (Britain, France and the USA) signed an armistice (truce) with Germany.
- The new republic was under pressure to sign. The government didn't think Germany could continue fighting — its people were starving and military morale was low.
- The armistice wasn't supported by some right-wing Germans, who saw the truce as a betrayal. They believed Germany could still win the war.

The Socialists set up a Temporary Government

1) After the abdication of the Kaiser, Germany was disorganised. Different political parties claimed control over different towns.

2) A temporary national government was established, consisting of the SPD and the USPD. It was called the Council of People's Representatives.

3) It controlled Germany until January 1919, when elections were held for a new Reichstag (parliament) — see p.92.

Revolutions pop up in history over and over and over again...

Give two reasons for the German revolution in 1918. [4]

Germany, 1890-1945

The Weimar Republic

The <u>Weimar Republic</u> was the first time Germany had ever been governed as a <u>democracy</u>. It was designed to give the German people a <u>voice</u>. However, there were <u>major flaws</u> in its constitution that made it <u>weak</u>.

The Weimar Republic was formed

1) The Council of People's Representatives organised elections in <u>January 1919</u> to create a new parliament. Germany was now a <u>democracy</u> — the <u>people</u> would say how the country was run.

2) <u>Friedrich Ebert</u> became the first President, with <u>Philip Scheidemann</u> as Chancellor. Ebert was leader of the <u>SPD</u>, a moderate party of socialists.

3) In February 1919, the members of the new <u>Reichstag</u> met at <u>Weimar</u> to create a new <u>constitution</u> for Germany. This was the beginning of a new period of Germany's history that historians call the <u>Weimar Republic</u>.

> The constitution decided how the government would be <u>organised</u>, and established its main <u>principles</u>.

The Weimar Constitution made Germany More Democratic...

The new constitution <u>reorganised</u> the German system of government.

> <u>Proportional representation</u> is where the proportion of <u>seats</u> a party wins in parliament is roughly the same as the <u>proportion</u> of the total <u>votes</u> they win.

President
- Elected <u>every 7 years</u>.
- Chooses the <u>Chancellor</u> and is <u>head of the army</u>.
- Can <u>dissolve</u> the Reichstag, call new elections and <u>suspend</u> the constitution.

> The President was <u>elected</u> by the German people, and so were the <u>parties</u> in the Reichstag. The President had the <u>most</u> power, but the Chancellor was in charge of the day-to-day running of <u>government</u>.

Reichstag
- The new German <u>Parliament</u>.
- Members are elected <u>every 4 years</u> using <u>proportional representation</u>.

Reichsrat
- Second (less powerful) house of parliament.
- Consists of members from each <u>local region</u>.
- Can <u>delay measures</u> passed by the Reichstag.

1) The new constitution was designed to be as <u>fair</u> as possible. Even <u>very small</u> political parties were <u>given seats</u> in the Reichstag if they got 0.4% of the vote or above.

2) The constitution <u>allowed women</u> to vote for the first time, and <u>lowered</u> the voting age to 20 — <u>more Germans</u> could vote and the German public had <u>greater power</u>.

...but the Consitution had Weaknesses

Even though the new constitution was <u>more democratic</u>, it wasn't very <u>efficient</u>.

1) <u>Proportional representation</u> meant that even parties with a very small number of votes were guaranteed to get into the Reichstag. This meant it was <u>difficult</u> to make decisions because there were so <u>many parties</u>, and they all had <u>different points of view</u>.

2) When a decision couldn't be reached, the <u>President</u> could <u>suspend</u> the constitution and pass laws without the Reichstag's consent.

> The President's ability to force through his <u>own decision</u> was known as '<u>Article 48</u>'.

3) This power was only supposed to be used in an <u>emergency</u>, but became a useful way of getting around disagreements that took place in the Reichstag. This meant it <u>undermined</u> the new democracy.

The Weimar Republic was vulnerable from the beginning...

When you're writing an answer in the exam, make sure you develop the points you make. For example, don't just say that Weimar Republic was weak — explain why it was weak.

Early Unpopularity

The <u>Treaty of Versailles</u> was signed in <u>June 1919</u>. The treaty was very <u>unpopular</u> in Germany and many Germans <u>resented</u> the new government for <u>accepting</u> its terms — not exactly a great start for the Republic.

President Ebert signed the Treaty of Versailles

1) After the armistice, a peace treaty called the <u>Treaty of Versailles</u> was imposed on Germany.

2) The <u>terms</u> of the treaty were mostly decided by the <u>Allied leaders</u> — David Lloyd George (Britain), Georges Clemenceau (France) and Woodrow Wilson (USA).

> **Comment and Analysis**
>
> Since the President had signed the Treaty of Versailles, the Weimar Republic became <u>associated</u> with the <u>pain</u> and <u>humiliation</u> it caused.

> The new German government <u>wasn't invited</u> to the peace conference in 1919 and had <u>no say</u> in the <u>Versailles Treaty</u>. At first, Ebert <u>refused</u> to sign the treaty, but in the end he had little choice — Germany was too <u>weak</u> to risk restarting the conflict. In June 1919, he accepted its terms and signed.

The Terms of the Versailles Treaty were Severe

1) Article 231 of the treaty said Germany had to take the <u>blame</u> for the war — the <u>War-Guilt Clause</u>.

> Many Germans <u>didn't agree</u> with this, and were <u>humiliated</u> by having to accept total blame.

2) Germany's armed forces were <u>reduced</u> to 100,000 men. They weren't allowed any armoured vehicles, aircraft or submarines, and could only have six warships.

> This made Germans feel <u>vulnerable</u>.

3) Germany was <u>forced to pay</u> £6600 million in reparations — payments for the damage caused by German forces in the war. The amount was decided in 1921 but was <u>changed</u> later.

> The heavy reparations seemed <u>unfair</u> to Germans and would cause <u>lasting damage</u> to Germany's economy.

4) Germany <u>lost</u> its empire — areas around the world that used to belong to Germany were now called <u>mandates</u>. They were put under the control of countries on the winning side of the war by the <u>League of Nations</u> — an organisation which aimed to settle international disputes <u>peacefully</u>.

> People <u>opposed</u> the losses in territory, especially when people in German colonies were <u>forced</u> to become part of a <u>new nation</u>.

5) The German military was banned from the <u>Rhineland</u> — an area of Germany on its western border with France. This left Germany <u>open to attack</u> from the west.

Germany Felt Betrayed by the Weimar Republic

The Treaty of Versailles caused <u>resentment</u> towards the Weimar Republic.

1) Germans called the treaty a '<u>Diktat</u>' (a treaty forced upon Germany), and many <u>blamed Ebert</u> for accepting its terms.

> The <u>Weimar politicians</u> involved in signing the armistice became known as the '<u>November Criminals</u>'.

2) Some Germans believed the armistice was a <u>mistake</u> and that Germany could have <u>won</u> the war. They felt '<u>stabbed in the back</u>' by the Weimar politicians, who brought the Treaty of Versailles upon Germany <u>unnecessarily</u>.

> **Comment and Analysis**
>
> The Treaty of Versailles played an important part in the <u>failure</u> of the Weimar Republic. It <u>harmed</u> the Republic's <u>popularity</u>, and created <u>economic</u> and <u>political unrest</u> that hindered the government for years.

This German cartoon demonstrates Germany's feelings towards the Treaty of Versailles. The Allies are shown as demons, out for revenge.

Germans felt 'stabbed in the back' by the government...

Explain why the Weimar Republic struggled to gain popular support. You could write about unemployment and/or the Treaty of Versailles. You also need to include your own knowledge. [12]

Years of Unrest

The first four years of the Weimar Republic (1919-1923) were dominated by political, social and economic unrest. This unrest created hardship for the German people, and fuelled criticism of Ebert's government.

There was Widespread Discontent in Germany

1) By 1919, thousands of Germans were poor and starving, and an influenza epidemic had killed thousands.
2) Many Germans denied they had lost the war and blamed the 'November Criminals' who had agreed to the armistice and the Treaty of Versailles.
3) Others who were blamed for losing the war included communists and Jews.
4) The government was seen as weak and ineffective — the Treaty of Versailles made living conditions worse.

Soon there were Riots and Rebellions

The government faced threats from left-wing and right-wing political groups.

The extreme left wanted a revolution...
- In January 1919, communists led by Karl Liebknecht and Rosa Luxemburg tried to take over Berlin. They took control of important buildings like newspaper headquarters, and 50,000 workers went on strike in support of the left-wing revolution. This became known as the Spartacist Revolt.
- Ebert asked for help from the right-wing Freikorps (ex-German soldiers) to stop the rebellion. Over 100 workers were killed. The Freikorps' use of violence caused a split on the Left between the Social Democratic Party and the communists.

The right also rebelled against the Weimar government...
- In March 1920, some of the Freikorps themselves took part in the Kapp Putsch ('Putsch' means revolt) — led by Wolfgang Kapp. They wanted to create a new right-wing government.
- The Freikorps marched into Berlin to overthrow the Weimar regime. But German workers opposed the putsch and staged a general strike. Berlin was paralysed and Kapp was forced to give up.
- Even after the putsch failed, threats to the government remained. In 1922, some former Freikorps members assassinated Walter Rathenau — he'd been Foreign Minister and was Jewish.

> As Germany's economic problems got worse after the war, anti-Semitic (anti-Jewish) feelings increased.

In 1923 Germany Couldn't Pay its Reparations

1) By 1923, Germany could no longer meet the reparations payments set out by the Treaty of Versailles.
2) France and Belgium decided to take Germany's resources instead, so they occupied the Ruhr — the richest industrial part of Germany. This gave them access to Germany's iron and coal reserves. The occupation led to fury in Germany, and caused a huge strike in the Ruhr.
3) German industry was devastated again. Germany tried to solve her debt problem by printing more money, but this plunged the economy into hyperinflation.
4) In 1918, an egg cost ¼ of a Mark. By November 1923, it cost 80 million Marks.

> Hyperinflation happens when production can't keep up with the amount of money in circulation, so the money keeps losing its value.

The consequences of hyperinflation
- Germany's currency became worthless. Nobody wanted to trade with Germany, so shortages of food and goods got worse.
- Bank savings also became worthless. The hardest hit were the middle classes.

> By 1923, even basic necessities were hard to get hold of. The German people were undergoing immense hardship, which they'd now come to associate with the rise of the Weimar Republic.

Hyperinflation — sounds good for blowing up balloons...
Write a list of the problems facing the Weimar Republic in the period 1918-1923.

Early Stages of the Nazi Party

Hitler entered German politics around the time the Weimar Republic was formed. By the time the Nazi Party was founded in 1920, he was growing in influence. In 1923, he tried to overthrow the Weimar government.

Adolf Hitler became the Voice of the German Workers' Party

1) Hitler began his political career in the German Workers' Party — a nationalist party led by Anton Drexler. He joined the party in January 1919, when he was in the German army. He gained a reputation as a passionate and skilled speaker, and crowds gathered to hear him talk.

2) In 1920, the party was re-branded as the National Socialist German Workers' Party (the Nazi Party). In July 1921, Hitler became its leader.

> In 1919, the party had about 60 members. By the end of 1920, it had about 2000.

The Nazi Party Developed its Identity

As the Nazi Party grew in popularity, it established an identity that appealed to as many people as possible.

1) In February 1920, the Nazi Party promoted its policies in the 'Twenty-Five Point Programme'. The Programme stressed German superiority and promoted anti-Semitism (prejudice against Jews).

2) The party wanted to raise pensions and improve health and education — but only for Germans. It also rejected the Treaty of Versailles. Promoting German greatness gave the party a nationwide appeal.

3) In 1921, Hitler founded his own party militia called the SA ('storm troopers'). The SA were political thugs — they carried out violent anti-Semitic attacks and intimidated rival political groups. Many were scared of them, but some Germans admired them. The milita also gave many ex-soldiers a job and a purpose.

Hitler tried to Overthrow the Government in the Munich Putsch

In 1923, the Weimar Republic was in crisis:

Hitler thought the time was right to attempt a putsch (revolt)...
- In 1923, things were going badly for the Weimar Republic — it seemed weak.
- Hyperinflation was at its peak and there were food riots.
- Many Germans were angry at the French and Belgian invasion of the Ruhr (see p.94). When the government stopped resisting by ending the strike there in 1923 (see p.96), discontent increased.

GERMANY

Munich.

In November 1923, the Nazis marched on Munich...
- Hitler's soldiers occupied a beer hall in the Bavarian city of Munich where local government leaders were meeting. He announced that the revolution had begun.
- The next day, Hitler marched into Munich supported by his storm troopers. But news of the revolt had been leaked to the police, who were waiting for Hitler. The police fired on the rebels and the revolt quickly collapsed.

1) Hitler was imprisoned for his role in the Munich Putsch and the Nazi Party was banned. However, his trial gave him publicity. He wrote a book in prison called 'Mein Kampf' ('My Struggle') describing his beliefs and ambitions.

2) Mein Kampf spread Nazi ideology — millions of Germans read it. It introduced Hitler's belief that the Aryan race (including Germans) was superior to all other races, and that all Germans had a right to 'Lebensraum' (more space to live).

3) In 1926, Hitler held a conference with the Nazi leadership at Bamberg. He was worried that the party had become divided — some members wanted the party to go in a more socialist direction. He made it clear that the party would only follow his agenda.

> The ban on the Nazi Party was lifted in February 1925. However, it suffered a dip in support from 1924 to 1928 due to the improving economic situation in the mid 1920s (see p.96). Economic unrest was a key reason why people supported Nazi ideology.

Hitler was charismatic and stood for German greatness...

Some historians interpret the Munich Putsch as a failure for the Nazi Party, but others think it ended up helping Hitler. Jot down a couple of reasons in support of each view.

REVISION TASK

Recovery

In 1923, Gustav Stresemann became <u>Chancellor</u> of the Weimar Republic. His <u>domestic</u> and <u>international</u> policies helped the German economy to recover, resulting in the '<u>Golden Years</u>' of the Weimar Republic.

Stresemann introduced a New Currency

1) Gustav Stresemann was <u>Chancellor</u> of the Weimar Republic between <u>August</u> and <u>November 1923</u>. He made important changes to help Germany to recover from its economic crisis.

2) In September 1923, he <u>ended the strike</u> in the Ruhr. This <u>reduced tension</u> between Germany, France and Belgium, and meant the government could stop <u>compensation payments</u> to strikers.

3) In November 1923, Stresemann replaced the German Mark with the <u>Rentenmark</u> to stabilise Germany's currency.

4) Stresemann created the '<u>great coalition</u>' — a group of moderate, pro-democracy socialist parties in the Reichstag who agreed to <u>work together</u>. This allowed Parliament to make decisions <u>more quickly</u>.

Stresemann wanted International Cooperation

In November 1923, Stresemann became <u>Foreign Minister</u>. He tried to cooperate more with other countries and build better <u>international relationships</u>. Germany's economy prospered as a result.

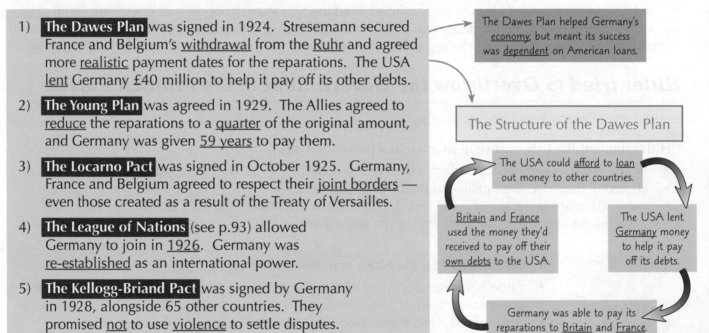

1) **The Dawes Plan** was signed in 1924. Stresemann secured France and Belgium's <u>withdrawal</u> from the <u>Ruhr</u> and agreed more <u>realistic</u> payment dates for the reparations. The USA <u>lent</u> Germany £40 million to help it pay off its other debts.

2) **The Young Plan** was agreed in 1929. The Allies agreed to <u>reduce</u> the reparations to a <u>quarter</u> of the original amount, and Germany was given <u>59 years</u> to pay them.

3) **The Locarno Pact** was signed in October 1925. Germany, France and Belgium agreed to respect their <u>joint borders</u> — even those created as a result of the Treaty of Versailles.

4) **The League of Nations** (see p.93) allowed Germany to join in <u>1926</u>. Germany was <u>re-established</u> as an international power.

5) **The Kellogg-Briand Pact** was signed by Germany in 1928, alongside 65 other countries. They promised <u>not</u> to use <u>violence</u> to settle disputes.

The Dawes Plan helped Germany's <u>economy</u>, but meant its success was <u>dependent</u> on American loans.

The Structure of the Dawes Plan

The USA could <u>afford</u> to <u>loan</u> out money to other countries.

The USA lent <u>Germany</u> money to help it pay off its debts.

Germany was able to pay its reparations to <u>Britain</u> and <u>France</u>.

<u>Britain</u> and <u>France</u> used the money they'd received to pay off their <u>own debts</u> to the USA.

Germany had begun to Recover — but Depended on US Money

1) Life was beginning to <u>look better</u> for Germany thanks to the work of Stresemann.

2) But he <u>died</u> in October <u>1929</u>, just before the disaster of the <u>Wall Street Crash</u> — a massive stock market crash in the USA which started a global economic depression.

3) The plans he had agreed would only work if the <u>USA</u> had <u>enough money</u> to keep lending to Germany — but after the crash, it didn't. Things were suddenly going to <u>get worse again</u> (see p.98).

Comment and Analysis

Germany's economic recovery helped <u>restore faith</u> in the Weimar Republic — there was strong support for pro-Weimar political parties in the <u>1928 elections</u>.

No need to Strese, mann — it's all under control...

Stresemann had a positive impact on the Weimar Republic and on the lives of many Germans, but he didn't solve all of Germany's problems — the economy was still very unstable.

EXAM TIP

Changes Under the Weimar Republic

Despite political, social and economic unrest, life did improve for some under the Weimar Republic.

Living standards Improved for the Working Classes

During the 'Golden Years', living standards improved in the Weimar Republic. This was a result of Germany's economic prosperity, but also of the reforms which took place throughout the 1920s.

What Improved	How It Improved
Unemployment	The unemployed were more protected. In 1927, the government introduced unemployment insurance. Workers could pay into the scheme and would receive cash benefits if they became unemployed.
Wages	The working classes became more prosperous. Wages for industrial workers rose quickly in the late 1920s.
Housing	The government launched mass housing projects. More than 2 million new homes were built between 1924 and 1931. This also provided extra employment.

Comment and Analysis

Not everyone benefited from higher standards of living. The middle classes felt ignored by the Weimar government and their resentment made it easier for the government's political opponents to gain support.

Despite these changes, some problems remained:

1) Higher living standards could only be maintained with a strong economy, and Germany's was fragile.

2) The changes mainly helped the working classes — the middle classes couldn't access the welfare benefits.

Women gained more Freedoms

Women were given more freedom and greater access to public life under the Weimar Republic.

1) Politically, women were given more representation. They were awarded the vote and could enter politics more easily —between 1919 and 1932, 112 women were elected to the Reichstag.

2) Women showed that they were capable workers during the war, and the number of young women working increased.

3) The traditional role of women began to change. New female sports clubs and societies sprang up, and women had more opportunities.

4) Divorce became easier, and the number of divorces rose.

Comment and Analysis

These changes fuelled right-wing criticism — some German nationalists thought giving women more power and freedom threatened traditional family life and values in Germany.

The Weimar Republic had many Cultural Achievements

1) The Weimar Republic was a period of creativity and innovation in Germany. Freedom of expression generated new ideas. Artists began to question traditional forms and styles, especially ones that focused on authority and militarism.

2) There were advances in the arts — some developments were bold and new, like the drama of Bertholt Brecht. The Bauhaus School of design was highly influential, especially in fine arts and architecture.

3) There were also important changes in music, literature and cinema. German films were successful — e.g. 'Metropolis' directed by Fritz Lang.

4) The Weimar Republic encouraged new ways of critical thinking at places like Frankfurt University, and a cabaret culture developed in Berlin.

Not all Germans liked the rejection of traditional forms and values in Weimar culture. Some were afraid it symbolised a loss of German tradition.

It wasn't all doom and gloom...

'There were no great changes to German society under the Weimar Republic.'
To what extent do you agree with this view? [20]

Germany, 1890-1945

The Great Depression

In 1929, the Great Depression hit Germany. The desperation it caused in the 1920s and 1930s meant that the German people were willing to consider any political party that promised something different.

The Wall Street Crash Ended economic Recovery

In October 1929, the Wall Street stock market in America crashed. It sparked an international economic crisis (the Great Depression) and meant the USA couldn't afford to prop up the German economy any longer.

1) Germany's economic recovery between 1924 and 1929 was built on unstable foundations. The biggest problem was that it was dependent on loans from the USA, which had been agreed in the Dawes Plan (see p.96).

2) After the Wall Street Crash, the USA couldn't afford to lend Germany money anymore. It also wanted some old loans to be repaid.

- Germany's economy collapsed without American aid. Industrial production went into decline — factories closed and banks went out of business.
- There was mass unemployment. In October 1929 1.6 million people were out of work, and by February 1932 there were over 6 million.
- The government also cut unemployment benefits — it couldn't afford to support the large numbers of Germans out of work.

> This made many Germans angry with the government.

3) By 1932, many parts of society were discontent with the Weimar government. Its failure to deal with unemployment meant it lost some backing from the working classes who'd been a key part of its support.

Extremist parties became More Popular

Popular discontent with the Weimar government and economic instability created an opportunity for extremist parties to grow. The KPD (the Communist Party of Germany) increased in influence.

1) The KPD was founded in December 1918 and wanted a workers' revolution. The communists promised to represent workers' needs and make German society more fair.

2) This helped the KPD to gain a lot of support from unemployed Germans during times of economic crisis.

3) When the Great Depression hit Germany in 1929, the KPD competed with the Nazi Party for the support of Germans who had been hit hard by the economic crisis.

4) Between 1928 and 1932, membership of the KPD grew from 130,000 to almost 300,000. However, Nazi Party membership grew even more rapidly — soon the KPD got left behind.

Comment and Analysis

Some historians think the Nazi Party's rise to power wasn't guaranteed — in the 1930s, both left and right-wing political parties increased in popularity in Germany.

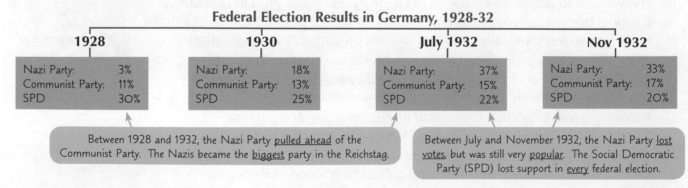

Federal Election Results in Germany, 1928-32

1928	1930	July 1932	Nov 1932
Nazi Party: 3%	Nazi Party: 18%	Nazi Party: 37%	Nazi Party: 33%
Communist Party: 11%	Communist Party: 13%	Communist Party: 15%	Communist Party: 17%
SPD 30%	SPD 25%	SPD 22%	SPD 20%

> Between 1928 and 1932, the Nazi Party pulled ahead of the Communist Party. The Nazis became the biggest party in the Reichstag.

> Between July and November 1932, the Nazi Party lost votes, but was still very popular. The Social Democratic Party (SPD) lost support in every federal election.

Revision couldn't get any cheerier...

Describe the changes in federal election results between 1928 and 1932. What do they show about the changing popularity of the three different political parties?

The Nazi Rise

The Nazi Party was able to take advantage of the discontent and anger created by the Great Depression.

The Nazi Party Appealed to many Different Groups in Society

The Nazis promised a more prosperous and less humiliating future, which was very popular among the German people — by 1930, membership had grown to over 300,000.

1) After the onset of the Depression, the Nazi Party's popularity soared. Hitler's promise to make Germany great again appealed to the growing ranks of unemployed and young people who wanted a brighter future.

2) Some people also supported the Nazis' anti-communist and anti-Jewish views. They saw communists and Jews as scapegoats, blaming them for Germany's economic problems.

3) Some wealthy businessmen who had lost out in the Great Depression turned to the Nazi Party. They approved of the Nazis' anti-communist stance and wanted the economic prosperity Hitler had promised.

Comment and Analysis

After the Depression hit Germany, more Germans began to vote. Participation in elections increased by around 10% between 1928 and 1932. Many of these new voters were attracted by the changes the Nazi Party promised.

The Nazi Party was well organised...

- Hitler's private army, the SA (see p.95), gave the party a military feel, which made it seem organised and disciplined. His authority over the SA and his undisputed role as head of the Nazi Party made the Nazis seemed strong in comparison to the Weimar government.
- Propaganda was very efficient. It often focused on regional issues and targeted specific groups. This made individuals feel valued by the Nazi Party and stole votes from smaller parties.

Hitler's Personality attracted Support

Interviews with Germans who lived through this period suggest that Hitler's personality was an important factor in the Nazis' popularity.

1) Hitler was patriotic and energetic, and was able to effectively get across his enthusiasm to his supporters. His speeches brought hope to those who listened.

2) In the 1932 election campaigns, Hitler was depicted as Germany's saviour. He stood up to the Weimar government and opposed communism.

3) He came across as a strong leader, which created a sharp contrast with the politicians of the Weimar governments. Hitler's authority over the SA and his undisputed role as head of the Nazi Party attracted support — many Germans had now lost faith in democracy.

A Nazi election poster from April 1932. The text reads 'Our last hope: Hitler'.

Here are two different interpretations of Hitler's rise to power. There's evidence to support both opinions.

Interpretation 1: After the onset of the Great Depression, Germans were willing to support any strong extremist party as an alternative to the democratic Weimar government.

After the Great Depression, both the Nazi Party and the Communist Party became more popular, and support for moderate parties like Social Democratic Party dropped off.

Interpretation 2: There was only one credible party to turn to after the Great Depression hit — the Nazi Party. It was the only party with a charismatic leader who had mass appeal.

The Nazi Party grew more rapidly than any other party after 1928. Hitler's passion and energy made the Nazis stand out, and support for the KPD simply couldn't keep up.

Hitler's personality was magnetic — it attracted support...

EXAM TIP

If you're asked to discuss interpretations or statements, then it's a good idea to read through them carefully and think clearly about what each suggests. For more, see p.134-136.

Establishing a Dictatorship

As the Depression got worse, political instability grew. Several parties were competing for power in the elections of 1932 (see p.98). In 1933, the Nazis would emerge on top. Hitler's rise continued.

Hitler Gained Power in Elections... with the aid of a Political Deal

1) By April 1932, conditions had worsened. The country was desperate for a strong government.

2) President Hindenburg had to stand for re-election because his term of office had run out. He was a national hero, but Hitler decided to run against him. Despite claiming he'd win easily, Hindenburg didn't win a majority in the first election. In the second ballot he won 53%, beating Hitler's 36.8%.

3) In July 1932, the Nazis won 230 seats in the elections for the Reichstag — more than any other party. Hitler demanded to be made Chancellor, but Hindenburg didn't trust Hitler and refused to appoint him.

4) Then in the election of November 1932, the Nazis seemed to be losing popularity — they lost 34 seats.

5) But Hitler struck a deal with another politician, Franz von Papen — if Papen would persuade Hindenburg to make Hitler Chancellor, Hitler would make Papen Vice-Chancellor.

6) Hindenburg agreed to Papen's suggestion, thinking that he could control Hitler. But Hitler used his new powers to call another election in March 1933, hoping to make the Nazis even stronger in the Reichstag.

Comment and Analysis

Hindenburg hoped that Hitler would be less extreme once he was actually in power. He also hoped that Hitler wouldn't be able to repair the economy — meaning he (Hindenburg) might be able to regain popularity and power.

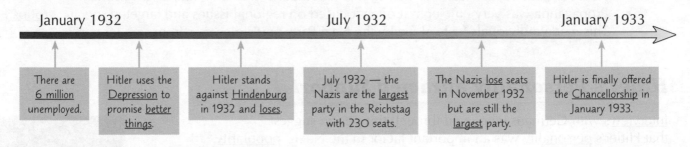

January 1932   July 1932   January 1933

There are 6 million unemployed.	Hitler uses the Depression to promise better things.	Hitler stands against Hindenburg in 1932 and loses.	July 1932 — the Nazis are the largest party in the Reichstag with 230 seats.	The Nazis lose seats in November 1932 but are still the largest party.	Hitler is finally offered the Chancellorship in January 1933.

The Nazis used Dirty Tricks to Win in 1933

1) In the elections of 1933, the Nazis took no chances:

- They controlled the news media, and opposition meetings were banned.
- They used the SA to terrorise opponents.
- When a fire broke out in the Reichstag building, Hitler blamed the communists. He used the fire to claim that communists were a threat to the country and to whip up anti-communist feelings. Hitler was even given emergency powers to deal with the supposed communist threat — he used these powers to intimidate communist voters.

2) The Nazis won 288 seats but didn't have an overall majority. So Hitler simply made the Communist Party (who had 81 seats) illegal.

3) This gave him enough support in Parliament to bring in the Enabling Act, passed with threats and bargaining in March 1933. This let him govern for four years without Parliament.

4) Trade unions were banned in May 1933. Then in July 1933, all political parties, apart from the Nazi party, were banned. Germany had become a one-party state.

Comment and Analysis

The emergency powers granted to Hitler were a turning point — they mark the first step towards making Germany a dictatorship. Hitler justified them by saying that they were necessary to protect the German people. This meant he faced little opposition from the German public.

The Nazis — gaining power...

In the exam, remember to consider people's circumstances and the limited knowledge they had at the time. Most Germans had no idea what the Nazi Party would grow into after it gained power.

Achieving Total Power

Hitler was more powerful, but he still had <u>enemies</u>. He wanted to <u>remove</u> them to secure his <u>dictatorship</u>.

The SA was a Threat to Hitler

1) The <u>SA</u> had <u>helped</u> Hitler come to power, (see p.100) but Hitler now saw it as a <u>threat</u>.

2) Its members were very loyal to <u>Ernst Röhm</u>, the SA's leader. Hitler was worried that Röhm was becoming <u>too powerful</u> — by 1934 the SA had more members than the German army.

3) The SA was also <u>unpopular</u> with the leaders of the <u>German army</u> and with some <u>ordinary Germans</u>.

The 'Night of the Long Knives' — Hitler removes his enemies

1) <u>Ernst Röhm</u> was the biggest threat to Hitler, but Hitler was also worried about <u>other members</u> of the Nazi Party who <u>disagreed</u> with his views.

2) On the 29th-30th June 1934, Hitler sent men to <u>arrest</u> or <u>kill</u> Röhm and other leaders of the SA. Hitler also used this opportunity to remove some of his <u>political opponents</u>. Altogether, several hundred people were <u>killed</u> or <u>imprisoned</u>.

3) Hitler claimed that those who had been killed had been <u>plotting</u> to <u>overthrow</u> the government, so he declared their murders legal.

4) This became known as the '<u>Night of the Long Knives</u>', and was a triumph for Hitler.

5) It stamped out all potential <u>opposition</u> within the Nazi Party and sent a powerful message to the party about Hitler's <u>ruthlessness</u> and <u>brutality</u>. It also showed that Hitler was now free to act <u>above the law</u>.

Comment and Analysis

Most Germans <u>wouldn't</u> have known exactly what had happened on the 'Night of the Long Knives' until a few days later, when Hitler declared the events legal. Even then, there was <u>little outcry</u>. It's likely that some people <u>believed</u> Hitler's claims that the violence was necessary to <u>protect</u> the country. Others were <u>too scared</u> to speak out.

Hitler took full control of National and Local government

1) In August 1934, <u>Hindenburg died</u>. Hitler used the opportunity to <u>combine</u> the posts of Chancellor and President, and also made himself Commander-in-Chief of the army.

2) He called himself <u>Der Führer</u> (the leader) — this was the beginning of the <u>dictatorship</u>.

3) At this point, Germany was <u>reorganised</u> into a number of provinces. Each province was called a <u>Gau</u> (plural: Gaue), with a Gauleiter (a loyal Nazi) in charge of each.

4) Above them were the <u>Reichsleiters</u>, who <u>advised</u> Hitler, e.g. <u>Goebbels</u> who was in charge of propaganda, and <u>Himmler</u> who was chief of the German police.

5) At the top and in absolute <u>control</u> was the <u>Führer</u> — Hitler.

6) Every aspect of life was carefully <u>controlled</u>, and only <u>loyal</u> Nazis could be <u>successful</u>.

The Führer
↓
Reichsleiters
↓
Gauleiters
↓
Other Officials

Gauleiters were appointed by <u>Hitler</u>, which ensured he had control over the <u>lower levels</u> of the party.

These included <u>local</u> and <u>district</u> party leaders.

Comment and Analysis

When the Nazis took over, some Germans were glad that someone was at last <u>taking control</u> after the chaos and political weaknesses of the Weimar years.

The <u>army</u> had to swear an <u>oath of allegiance</u> to Hitler, instead of pledging to protect Germany. Some <u>German workers</u> were also forced to take an <u>oath of obedience</u>, promising loyalty to Hitler. Those who refused could lose their jobs.

The Nazis — eliminating opposition...

You need to know how Hitler secured his power to become Führer. Write a summary of the steps he took to consolidate his position between January 1933 and August 1934.

The Machinery of Terror

The Nazis aimed to make Germany a <u>totalitarian state</u> (where the government controls <u>all aspects</u> of life).

Germany became a Police State

1) The Nazis wanted <u>complete control</u> over the <u>machinery of government</u> and <u>people's lives</u>.

2) Hitler's Enabling Act of 1933 (see p.100) allowed the government to <u>read</u> people's mail, <u>listen in</u> on their phone calls, and <u>search</u> their homes without notice.

3) The <u>Law for the Reconstruction of the Reich</u> (1934) gave the Nazis total power over local governments.

4) There were <u>laws</u> to sack civil servants who didn't support the Nazis and accept their rules.

5) The Nazis also made changes to the <u>justice system</u>. <u>Judges</u> didn't have to be 'fair' and unbiased. Instead, they were expected to make rulings that were in line with <u>Nazi Party policy</u>.

6) The <u>Sicherheitsdienst</u> (SD) was the Nazi intelligence service. It was initially run by <u>Reinhard Heydrich</u> — he aimed to bring every German under continual supervision.

The legal system was far from fair...
- In 1933, the Nazis set up <u>special courts</u> where the basic rights of those accused were <u>suspended</u> — they couldn't <u>appeal</u> or <u>question</u> evidence given against them.
- In 1934, Hitler established the <u>People's Court</u> in Berlin, which held trials for important <u>political</u> crimes. Defendants were nearly always found <u>guilty</u>.

People could be Terrorised into Conforming

The government was also prepared to use <u>terror</u> and even <u>violence</u> against the German people.

1) The <u>SS</u> (<u>Schutzstaffel</u>) began as a bodyguard for Hitler. It expanded massively under the leadership of Himmler during the 1930s. Its members were totally loyal to Hitler, and feared for their <u>cruelty</u>.

2) Himmler was also in charge of the <u>secret police</u> — the <u>Gestapo</u>. The Gestapo's job was to protect the German public, but their methods included harsh <u>interrogations</u> and <u>imprisonment</u> without trial.

3) Local <u>wardens</u> were employed to make sure Germans were loyal to the Nazis. Members of the public were encouraged to <u>report disloyalty</u>. Many were arrested by the Gestapo as a result.

4) After 1933, <u>concentration camps</u> were created across Germany and its territories to hold political prisoners and anybody else considered dangerous to the Nazis. Some of these were later turned into <u>death camps</u>.

Security Police search a car in Berlin on the orders of the Gestapo.

Not everyone lived in Constant Terror

1) Most Germans were prepared to <u>go along with</u> the new regime. Some people accepted the new rules out of <u>fear</u>.

2) Others went along with them because they <u>believed in their aims</u>, even if they didn't approve of the Nazis' <u>brutal methods</u>.

Comment and Analysis

For those that <u>didn't fit in</u> with the Nazi ideals (e.g. Jews), life under the SS and the Gestapo could be terrifying. But Hitler was <u>supported</u>, <u>not feared</u>, by many Germans.

The Nazis exercised control using any means necessary...

Turn this page over, then try to scribble down as much as you can remember about the Nazi police state. If you get stuck, think how you might've been treated if you were a political enemy.

Nazi Propaganda

The Nazis also used lots of very sophisticated <u>propaganda</u> to help them control German people's lives.

Propaganda aims to Control how people Think

Propaganda means spreading information that <u>influences</u> how people <u>think</u> and <u>behave</u>. It gives only certain <u>points of view</u> and often <u>leaves out key facts</u>. The <u>Nazis</u> used <u>propaganda</u> to get support in Germany. <u>Dr Joseph Goebbels</u> was in charge of the Nazis' 'propaganda machine'. He founded the <u>Ministry of Public Enlightenment and Propaganda</u> in 1933. It <u>controlled</u> music, theatre, film, literature and radio.

Nazi propaganda took Simple Ideas and Repeated them

1) Nazi propaganda was used to <u>unite</u> the German people and convince them that the Nazis would make Germany <u>strong</u>. The Nazis encouraged a return to <u>traditional</u> German <u>values</u> and German <u>culture</u>.

2) The Nazis' propaganda also said that <u>Jews</u> and <u>communists</u> were the biggest cause of <u>Germany's problems</u>. One Nazi paper claimed that Jews <u>murdered children</u> for the Passover Feast.

3) Germans were encouraged to <u>hate</u> the countries that signed the <u>Treaty of Versailles</u> (see p.93). Many Germans felt angry and humiliated by the <u>Treaty of Versailles</u>, so Hitler's promises to reverse the treaty and make Germany great again were very <u>popular</u>.

> Some historians say Nazi propaganda was better at <u>reinforcing</u> people's <u>existing attitudes</u> than making them believe <u>something different</u>. For example, after the <u>political weakness</u> of the Weimar Republic, people found the image of Hitler as a <u>strong</u> leader appealing.

4) Goebbels created the '<u>Hitler Myth</u>', which made Hitler seem like a god and the saviour of Germany. This was the '<u>cult of the Führer</u>'.

The Nazis used the Media as a tool of Propaganda

The Nazis used <u>censorship</u> to prevent Germans from seeing or hearing anything that gave a <u>different message</u> to their propaganda.

The Nazis sold <u>cheap radios</u> and <u>controlled broadcasts</u>. By 1939 about 70% of households had a radio, which gave the Nazis a <u>voice</u> in most people's homes. According to Goebbels, radio was a way to <u>control</u> the German people.

By 1944, <u>82%</u> of German daily newspapers were controlled by the Nazis This meant the Nazis could decide what was published in the papers.

The Nazis also produced hundreds of <u>films</u>. Many films showed the <u>strengths</u> of the Nazis and Hitler, and the <u>weaknesses</u> of their <u>opponents</u>.

Propaganda told people what was <u>expected</u> of them. This poster from <u>1935</u> states that 'the German student' fights for the Führer and for the German people. Posters showing the <u>evil of Germany's enemies</u> and the <u>power of Hitler</u> were also common.

Comment and Analysis

The Nazis used <u>culture</u> to promote their values. <u>Modern art</u> was banned, in favour of realistic paintings that fit with Nazi ideology. Modern art was labelled '<u>degenerate</u>' and exhibitions were created to show people how 'bad' it was. The Nazis celebrated the works of '<u>German</u>' composers, such as Wagner, but much <u>modern classical music</u>, works by <u>Jewish composers</u>, and <u>jazz</u> were all attacked.

Nazi propaganda could involve Spectacular Displays

1) The Nazis used <u>public rallies</u> to spread their propaganda. The annual <u>Nuremberg Rallies</u> focused on speeches by leading Nazis, like Hitler and Goebbels.

2) Events like the <u>1936 Berlin Olympics</u> were used to show off German wealth and power. But the success of non-Aryan athletes like African-American gold medal winner <u>Jesse Owens</u> undermined Hitler's message.

3) Nazi power was shown through <u>architecture</u> — grand new buildings appeared in Nuremberg and Berlin.

Radio Nazi — broadcasting to you wherever you are...

In the exam, you might need to think about why propaganda had such a big impact on many Germans. Think about why it was attractive, who it targeted and how powerful it was.

Nazis and the Church

The Nazi Party publicly <u>supported</u> religious freedom, but in reality saw Christianity as a <u>threat</u>.

Hitler wanted to Reduce the Church's Power

1) In the 1930s, most Germans were <u>Christians</u> and the Church was very <u>influential</u>. During the Weimar Republic, the state and the Church had worked <u>closely</u> together and the Church was involved in national matters like <u>education</u>.

2) Some prominent Nazis were <u>anti-Christian</u> and Nazi ideology disagreed with the <u>role</u> the Church had traditionally had in society.

3) Hitler thought religion should comply with the <u>state</u> and wanted churches to promote <u>Nazi ideals</u>. He was also worried that some members of the Church might publicly <u>oppose</u> Nazi policies.

4) The Nazi Party was careful to maintain <u>support</u> from the <u>Catholic</u> and <u>Protestant</u> Churches during its rise to power because they were so <u>popular</u>. However, as Hitler consolidated his totalitarian state, his <u>control</u> over churches <u>increased</u>.

The Catholic Church was Persecuted

1) In July 1933, an agreement called the <u>Concordat</u> was signed between the <u>Pope</u> and the <u>Nazi government</u>. Hitler promised <u>not</u> to interfere with the Catholic Church if the Church agreed to <u>stay out</u> of German politics.

Comment and Analysis

The Concordat reassured Christians that Hitler was <u>consolidating</u> ties with the Catholic Church, but he was actually <u>restricting</u> its power.

2) The Catholic Church was now <u>banned</u> from speaking out against the Nazi Party, but Hitler soon <u>broke</u> his side of the deal.

- The Nazi Party started to <u>restrict</u> the Catholic Church's role in <u>education</u>.
- In 1936 all crucifixes were removed from <u>schools</u> and by 1939 <u>Catholic education</u> had been destroyed.

- The Nazis began arresting <u>priests</u> in 1935 and put them on trial.
- Catholic newspapers were <u>suppressed</u> and the Catholic Youth group was <u>disbanded</u>.

3) In 1937, the Pope <u>spoke out against</u> Hitler in a letter to Catholic Churches in Germany. The view of the Church had <u>changed</u>, but many German Catholics were <u>too scared</u> to speak out against the Nazi Party.

Catholics tried to protect their religion by <u>avoiding confrontation</u> with the Nazi Party.

The Nazi Party Controlled the Protestant Church

The Protestant Church was <u>reorganised</u> and fell under <u>Nazi control</u>.

1) When Hitler became Chancellor in 1933, there were 28 independent Protestant Churches. These Churches were politically <u>divided</u> — some formed a group known as the '<u>German Christians</u>'. They supported Hitler and favoured an <u>anti-Semitic</u> version of Christianity.

2) The Nazi Party <u>backed</u> this version of Christianity and believed all Christians should follow its <u>principles</u>. In 1936, all Protestant Churches were <u>merged</u> to form the <u>Reich Church</u>.

The Reich Church 'Nazified' Christianity...

The Reich Church replaced the symbol of a <u>cross</u> with the Nazi <u>Swastika</u>, and the Bible was replaced by '<u>Mein Kampf</u>' (see p.95). Only <u>Nazis</u> could give sermons and the Church <u>suspended</u> non-Aryan ministers.

Comment and Analysis

Not everyone supported the Reich Church — it was opposed by a Protestant group called the '<u>Confessing Church</u>' (see p.105).

3) The Reich Church was an attempt to increase <u>state control</u> over the Protestant Church and make a <u>National Socialist</u> version of Christianity.

The Nazis wanted the state to come first...

You might get sources in the exam that give different viewpoints on Nazi religious policies. Don't forget that Catholic and Protestant Christians were treated differently by the Nazis.

Opposition to the Nazis

The Nazis had a tight grip on Germany, but some opposition remained.

The Political Left opposed Hitler, but was Divided and Weak

1) Once in power, the Nazis had banned other political parties, including those on the political left, such as the Communist Party (KPD) and the Social Democratic Party (SPD).

2) But members of these parties formed underground groups to try and organise industrial unrest (e.g. strikes). These networks were often infiltrated by the Gestapo, and party members could be executed.

3) Their impact was also limited because the different parties of the left were divided and didn't cooperate.

Some members of the Church Opposed the Nazis

There was little opposition to the Nazis in Germany from Christian groups. But a number of Church members did oppose the Nazis, even though they risked being sent to concentration camps (see p.102):

1) Martin Niemöller was a Protestant pastor, a former U-boat (submarine) captain, and a one-time Nazi supporter. He objected to Nazi interference in the Church, and was one of the founders of the Confessing Church. He used a sermon in 1937 to protest against the persecution of Church members, and as a result spent several years in concentration camps.

> The Confessing Church protested against Hitler's attempt to unite the different Protestant Churches into one Reich Church (see p.104).

2) Another key member of the Confessing Church was Dietrich Bonhoeffer, a Protestant philosopher and pastor who opposed the Nazis from the beginning. He joined the resistance, helped Jews escape from Germany and planned to assassinate Hitler. He was caught and imprisoned, then executed just weeks before the fall of the Nazis.

3) Clemens August von Galen was the Catholic Bishop of Münster, who used his sermons to protest against Nazi racial policies and the murder of the disabled. His protests didn't stop the killing, but they did force the Nazis to keep them secret. Only the need to maintain the support of German Catholics stopped the Nazis from executing him.

The Edelweiss Pirates and Swing Kids were Youth Movements

1) The Edelweiss Pirates was the name given to groups of rebellious youths who rejected Nazi values.
   - They helped army deserters, forced labourers and escaped concentration camp prisoners.
   - At first the Nazis mostly ignored them, but cracked down after they started distributing anti-Nazi leaflets. Many members were arrested, and several were publicly hanged.

2) The Swing Kids (or Swing Youth) were groups of young people who rebelled against the tight control the Nazis had over culture, acting in ways considered 'degenerate' by the Nazi regime (e.g. listening to American music and drinking alcohol). They were mostly considered a nuisance rather than a threat, but some members were arrested and even sent to concentration camps.

Comment and Analysis

German opposition to the Nazis didn't really threaten their dominance, but it did mean the Gestapo was kept busy tracking down people who had distributed anti-Nazi leaflets, held secret meetings, committed acts of sabotage, etc.

Comment and Analysis

Other Germans expressed their dissatisfaction with the Nazi regime in 'low level' ways — e.g. by grumbling about the government or spreading rumours. Not everyone considers this genuine opposition, but even this was probably risky.

If you weren't with the Nazis, you were against them...

Write the headings 'political opposition', 'religious opposition' and 'opposition from youths' on a piece of paper. Cover this page, then jot down as much as you can remember about each one.

Work and Home

The Nazis encouraged <u>women</u> to be <u>homemakers</u> and tried to provide <u>jobs</u> for <u>men</u>.

Women were expected to raise Large Families

1) The Nazis didn't want <u>women</u> to have too much freedom. They believed the role of women was to provide <u>children</u> and support their families <u>at home</u>.

2) Women were <u>banned</u> from being <u>lawyers</u> in 1936, and the Nazis did their best to stop them following other professions.

> This didn't quite go to plan for the Nazis — after 1939, the war caused a <u>shortage of workers</u>, which meant lots of women had to <u>go back to work</u> (see p.109).

3) The <u>League of German Maidens</u> spread the Nazi idea that it was an honour to produce <u>large families</u> for Germany. Nazis gave <u>awards</u> to women for doing this and encouraged more women to marry by offering <u>financial aid</u> to married couples.

4) Women were expected to dress <u>plainly</u> and were <u>discouraged</u> from wearing make-up and smoking. At school, girls studied subjects like <u>cookery</u>. It was stressed that they should choose '<u>Aryan</u>' husbands.

Public Works and Rearmament meant Unemployment Fell

1) Hitler started a huge <u>programme</u> of <u>public works</u>, which helped to reduce unemployment — e.g. from 1933 jobs were created as a result of the construction of <u>autobahns</u> (motorways).

2) <u>All</u> men between 18 and 25 could be <u>recruited</u> into the <u>National Labour Service</u> and given jobs. Industrial output increased and <u>unemployment</u> fell.

3) Hitler also brought in <u>military conscription</u> and encouraged German <u>industry</u> to manufacture more <u>ships</u>, <u>aircraft</u>, <u>tanks</u> and <u>weapons</u> for the military. This <u>rearmament</u> meant further falls in <u>unemployment</u>.

4) Trade unions were banned (see p.100), and workers had to join the Nazis' <u>Labour Front</u> instead. The Labour Front acted like one big trade union, but it was controlled by the Nazis. Workers <u>couldn't</u> go on <u>strike</u> or campaign for better conditions, and <u>wages</u> were relatively <u>low</u>.

Comment and Analysis

Although <u>unemployment fell</u> after the Depression, the Nazis <u>fiddled</u> with the <u>statistics</u> to make it look lower than it really was — e.g. they didn't count <u>women</u> or <u>Jewish</u> people without jobs in the official unemployment statistics.

Many groups in society Felt Better Off

1) The Nazis made efforts to maintain the support of German <u>workers</u>. They wanted workers to feel <u>important</u> and believe that they were an essential part of the <u>Volksgemeinschaft</u>.

> 'Volksgemeinschaft' means a <u>community</u> of people working hard towards the same <u>aims</u>.

- The Nazis introduced the <u>Volkswagen</u> (the 'people's car') as a luxury people could aspire to own.
- They also introduced '<u>Strength through Joy</u>' — a scheme which provided workers with <u>cheap holidays</u> and leisure activities.
- The '<u>Beauty of Labour</u>' scheme encouraged factory owners to <u>improve conditions</u> for workers.

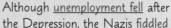

2) Many in the <u>middle classes</u> also felt <u>better off</u>, e.g. small-business owners were able to advance more in society than previously.

3) But even though many people felt better off, workers and small-business owners had <u>lost out</u> in some ways.
- The cost of living rose by about <u>25%</u> — but wages didn't go up.
- Workers didn't have the <u>right</u> to <u>strike</u> or <u>resign</u>.
- <u>Small businesses</u> had to pay <u>high taxes</u>.

Comment and Analysis

During the <u>Depression</u>, one third of all workers had been <u>unemployed</u>. Many Germans had been <u>desperate</u>, so life under the Nazis did feel genuinely <u>better</u> for them.

Hitler reduced unemployment — and gained popularity...

It's important to remember that for some Germans life really did get better under the Nazi Party.

EXAM TIP

Young People

An important key to Nazi success was controlling the minds of Germany youth.

Youth Movements helped produce Committed Nazis

1) Hitler knew that loyalty from young people was essential if the Nazis were to remain strong.

2) Youth movements were a way of teaching children Nazi ideas —
so they would be loyal to the Nazi Party when they grew up.

The Hitler Youth seemed exciting...

- The Hitler Youth was founded in 1926. Boys aged fourteen and over were recruited to the movement. It became all but compulsory in 1936 and lasted until 1945.
- Boys wore military-style uniforms and took part in physical exercise preparing for war. High-achieving boys might be sent to Hitler Schools to be trained as loyal Nazi leaders.
- They also went on camping trips and held sports competitions. Some of those who took part said the organisation was fun, made them feel valued and encouraged a sense of responsibility.

The League of German Maidens was for girls...

- The League of German Maidens was the female branch of the Hitler Youth, aimed at girls aged between fourteen and eighteen.
- Girls were trained in domestic skills like sewing and cooking.
- Sometimes they took part in physical activities like camping and hiking. This gave girls new opportunities that were normally reserved for boys.

Comment and Analysis

After 1936, all other youth organisations were banned and it was almost impossible for children to avoid joining the Hitler Youth. However, towards the end of the 1930s, attendance actually decreased as activities adopted an increasingly military focus.

Education across Germany was 'Nazified'

1) Education in schools meant learning Nazi propaganda. Most teachers joined the Nazi Teachers' Association and were trained in Nazi methods. Children had to report teachers who did not use them.

2) Subjects were rewritten to fit in with Nazi ideas. Children were taught to be anti-Semitic (prejudiced against Jews) — for example, Biology courses stated that Jews were biologically inferior to 'Aryans'. History courses explained that the First World War was lost because of Jews and communists.

3) Physical education became more important for boys to prepare them for joining the army. They sometimes even played games with live ammunition.

4) In universities, students burned anti-Nazi and Jewish books, and Jewish lecturers were sacked. Jewish teachers were also dismissed from public schools.

German children were always being bombarded with Nazi propaganda. Erika Mann, a German who opposed the Nazis, described Nazi education in Germany. 'Every child says 'Heil Hitler!' from 50 to 150 times a day...[it] is required by law; if you meet a friend on the way to school, you say it; study periods are opened and closed with [it]... [The Nazis'] supremacy over the German child...is complete.'

German Youth eventually became involved in Fighting the War

1) During the Second World War, members of the Hitler Youth contributed to the war effort — for example, helping with air defence work, farm work and collecting donations for Nazi charities.

2) Towards the end of the war, many Hitler Youth members ended up fighting alongside adults. They were known for being fierce and fanatical fighters.

The Nazis' attempts to impose their ideology on children weren't always effective. See p.105 and p.111 for more about how unofficial youth movements resisted Hitler and the Nazis.

The Hitler Youth — not everyone's favourite youth group...

Imagine you're a teacher in Nazi Germany. Write an account of how your job might have changed after the Nazis gained power in 1933.

Nazi Racial Policy

The Nazi belief in the idea of a 'master race' caused a huge amount of harm.

Hitler wanted to 'Cleanse' Germany of 'Inferior' groups

1) Most Nazis believed that Germans were members of a superior ancient race called the 'Aryans'. Hitler thought people who were not pure Aryans (e.g. Jews) did not belong in Germany, and had no part to play in the new German Empire.

2) He wanted to 'cleanse' the German people by removing any groups he thought 'inferior'. Jews were especially targeted, but action was also taken against other groups.

> Hitler always claimed the Jews were responsible for many of Germany's problems.

- Many Romani (gypsies) and Slavs (an ethnic group from central and eastern Europe) were sent to concentration camps. The Nazis believed that they were racially inferior.
- The Nazis murdered or sterilised many people who had mental or physical disabilities.
- Many people of mixed race were also sterilised against their will.
- Homosexual people were sent to concentration camps in their thousands. In 1936 Himmler, Head of the SS, began the Central Office for the Combating of Homosexuality and Abortion.

The Nazis Changed the Law to Discriminate against Jews

1) In 1933, the SA organised a national boycott of Jewish businesses, which resulted in Nazi-led violence against Jews. The violence wasn't popular with the German people, so the Nazis decided to use the legal system to persecute Jews instead.

2) Over time, the number of jobs that Jews were banned from gradually increased.

3) The Nuremberg Laws of 1935 were based on the idea that Jews and Germans were biologically different. They removed many legal rights from Jews and encouraged 'Aryan' Germans to see them as inferior.

- The Nuremberg Laws stopped Jews being German citizens.
- They banned marriage between Jews and non-Jews in Germany.
- They also banned sexual relationships between Jews and non-Jews.

> Some Jews were given passports enabling them to leave Germany but preventing them from returning.

4) Jews were later forced to close or sell their businesses, and they were banned from all employment.

5) By 1938, all Jewish children had been banned from attending German schools and Jews were no longer allowed in many public places, including theatres and exhibitions.

> The Nazis' racial policies aimed to isolate Jews from the rest of society. 'Aryan' Germans were even encouraged to break off friendships with Jews and avoid any contact with Jewish people.

Kristallnacht — the 'Night of the Broken Glass'

1) In November 1938, a German diplomat was murdered in Paris by a Jew.

2) There was anti-Jewish rioting throughout Germany — thousands of Jewish shops were smashed and almost every synagogue in Germany was burnt down. In the days that followed, thousands of Jews were arrested and sent to concentration camps.

3) The Nazis claimed that the events of Kristallnacht were a spontaneous reaction by the German people to the Paris murder. In fact, they had been planned and organised by the Nazi government. Few ordinary Germans had participated.

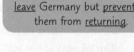

Comment and Analysis

Kristallnacht was a turning point in the Nazi persecution of Jews — it was the first widespread act of anti-Jewish violence in Nazi Germany. After Kristallnacht, conditions for German Jews got even worse.

Nazi Germany — a climate of cruelty and fear...

Fold a piece of paper in half. On one side, jot down all the different types of people who were persecuted as a result of the Nazis' racial policies, and on the other list how they were treated.

Germany's War Economy

Hitler had always planned a war to provide Lebensraum (more space to live) for the German people. But Germany wasn't at full strength when the Second World War broke out in 1939.

The Nazi Economy had to Prepare for War

1) Hitler transformed the German economy to prepare the country for war.

2) A Four-Year Plan was started in 1936, concentrating on war preparations. The Nazis needed to quickly build up industries making weapons and chemicals, and increase Germany's agricultural output.

3) Hermann Göring was put in charge of the economy. He aimed to make Germany self-sufficient — this meant producing enough goods to not need imports from other countries. ←

> Supplies to Germany had been blocked during the First World War, causing severe shortages. By becoming self-sufficient, Hitler hoped to avoid this problem in future wars.

4) Many workers were retrained to do jobs that would help the war effort, such as producing weapons and working in chemical plants.

5) But Hitler knew that ultimately Germany would need to conquer new territories and capture their resources to become genuinely self-sufficient.

The Outbreak of War forced Changes in the Economy

1) When war broke out in 1939, the German economy wasn't ready. More changes were needed.

2) A quarter of the workforce was already working in war industries, especially weapons production. Two years later this had become three-quarters.

3) A lot of German workers were conscripted into the army, so the Nazis had to use foreign workers to keep the economy going. This included civilians from occupied territories, prisoners of war and slave labourers — see p.112.

4) Eventually, in 1942, after several years of fighting, Hitler put Albert Speer in charge of the war economy.

> - Speer focused the economy completely on the war effort.
> - He improved efficiency and greatly increased weapons production.
> - Germany also used raw materials from occupied lands to support its production.

Daily Life in Germany was Affected by the War

Germans had to make sacrifices to help the war effort:

1) Wages were less than they had been before the Nazis took control and working hours increased.

2) Rationing affected people's quality of life. Food and clothes rationing began in 1939, but while Germany was winning the war, most goods could still be bought easily.

- Rationing meant that some people ate better than they had before the war, though it soon became impossible to eat meat every day. ←

> Toilet paper and soap became difficult to get hold of too. And to save fuel, the use of warm water was restricted to two times per week. Germans also made use of 'ersatz' (or 'substitute') goods. For example, ersatzkaffee ('substitute coffee') was made from acorns or other types of seed.

- Later in the war, things became harder for ordinary Germans. By 1942, German civilians were living on rations of bread, vegetables and potatoes — these rations decreased as the war progressed (and were much less than British rations).

3) More women and children had to work, especially after 1941 when German forces suffered some heavy defeats in Russia.

> By 1944, 50% of the German workforce were women (up from 37% in 1939).

Life under the Nazis got worse — even for Germans...

Explain how the German economy was affected by the outbreak of World War Two. [8]

EXAM QUESTION

The Impact of Total War

Food rationing was one thing. But the impact of <u>total war</u> on German civilians went way beyond that.

'Total War' involves Soldiers and Civilians

1) A lot of wars are fought between two <u>armies</u>. The term '<u>total war</u>', on the other hand, is often used to describe conflicts where <u>all</u> of a country's resources are considered part of the war effort.

2) So a total war is also a battle between countries' <u>economies</u>, their <u>scientists</u>, their <u>industries</u>, and their <u>civilians</u>. World War II is usually considered to have been a total war.

Germans were More Heavily Affected later in the war

1) After some <u>heavy defeats</u> in 1942, Germany prepared itself for <u>total war</u>. In a speech at the <u>Berlin Sportpalast</u> (sports arena) in February 1943, <u>Goebbels</u> stated:

> **Comment and Analysis**
>
> Hitler had hoped that the wars he was starting would be <u>short</u> (<u>quick victories</u>). This would have meant <u>less disruption</u> to normal life.

'Total war is the demand of the hour... The danger facing us is enormous. The efforts we take to meet it must be just as enormous... We can no longer make only partial and careless use of the war potential at home and in the parts of Europe that we control. We must use our full resources.'

2) This meant that <u>all</u> of Germany's resources had to be directed to help with the <u>war effort</u>.

- <u>Non-essential</u> production (production that wasn't vital to the war effort) stopped, and small non-essential businesses closed. Workers were used in <u>war-related</u> industries instead.
- <u>Civilian clothes</u> and <u>consumer goods</u> were no longer manufactured.
- <u>Rationing</u> was a fact of life in Germany from the very start of the war (see p.109). Food supplies for ordinary families became much more <u>restricted</u> later on.

> German women never fought on the <u>front line</u> — they took mainly <u>clerical</u> and <u>administrative</u> roles. However, many women did help to operate Germany's <u>anti-aircraft</u> defences and served in <u>signals units</u> on the front line.

- More <u>women</u> were expected to <u>work</u> or join the <u>army</u>.
- Eventually, males between the ages of 13 and 60 who weren't already serving in the military had to join the <u>Volkssturm</u> — a part-time defence force (a sort of German 'Dad's Army').

Bombings Killed Thousands and left many more Homeless

1) From <u>1940</u>, Germany <u>rapidly prepared</u> for <u>bombing</u>. Hundreds of community <u>air raid shelters</u> were built.

2) <u>Auxiliary hospitals</u> and emergency <u>first-aid stations</u> were also established to care for civilian injuries.

3) From <u>1942</u>, the British and American air forces began bombing German cities more <u>heavily</u>. Around <u>half a million</u> German civilians were killed, and many more were made <u>homeless</u>.

4) Germany was later flooded with <u>refugees</u> from other <u>German territories</u> and from cities like Dresden, Berlin and Hamburg, which were all <u>heavily bombed</u>.

5) Germany struggled to deal with the growing number of <u>refugees</u>. There was <u>little help</u> for people displaced by the war — most struggled to find <u>food</u> and <u>shelter</u>.

> German cities were attacked using <u>incendiary bombs</u> — these were designed to cause huge <u>fires</u>. Hamburg and Dresden were both fire-bombed.

Dresden, after an Allied air raid in February 1945.

Germany had to throw everything behind the war effort...

Remember, total war wasn't what the Nazis had wanted. They had hoped for short wars and prepared accordingly. But things hadn't gone at all as the Nazis had planned.

Growing Opposition

As the <u>war</u> went on, and especially as things started to go <u>worse</u> for Germany, <u>opposition</u> to Hitler grew.

There were some anti-Nazi Protest Movements

1) The <u>Kreisau Circle</u> was an anti-Nazi movement led by <u>Helmuth von Moltke</u> and <u>Yorck von Wartenburg</u>.

   - The group was <u>against</u> violence, so they didn't <u>actively resist</u> the Nazis. Instead they discussed how to make Germany a <u>better country</u> after the Nazis had fallen. Some members of the Circle tried to <u>inform</u> Allied governments about the <u>dangers</u> and <u>weaknesses</u> of Nazi control.
   - In <u>1944</u>, members of the Kreisau Circle, including <u>Moltke</u>, were <u>arrested</u> and <u>executed</u>.

2) The <u>Rosenstrasse protest</u> took place in Berlin after the authorities had rounded up some of the last Jewish men left in the city — many of them married to 'Aryan' German women.

   - When the men's wives discovered what had happened, they went to the building in <u>Rosenstrasse</u> ('Rose Street') where their husbands were being held.
   - For several days, the women gathered outside the building and <u>protested</u>. Eventually Goebbels ordered the Jewish men to be <u>released</u>.

   Comment and Analysis

   This was one of the few <u>successful</u> anti-Nazi public protests. It's thought that the men were released because Goebbels saw it as the <u>simplest way</u> to quickly end the protest without attracting too much attention. He also thought the Jews would soon be <u>killed</u> anyway.

3) Underground networks of <u>communists</u> operated in Germany after 1941. They mostly <u>gathered information</u> about Nazi brutality and <u>distributed leaflets</u>.

Some young people joined the White Rose group

1) The <u>White Rose</u> group (active between 1942 and 1943) was an opposition movement of students and lecturers from <u>Munich University</u>. Among the leaders were brother and sister <u>Hans</u> and <u>Sophie Scholl</u>.

2) Some male members of the group had served in the army and had been horrified by the <u>atrocities</u> carried out by the German army, including the <u>mass killing</u> of Jews.

3) The group used <u>non-violent</u> methods to protest against Nazi <u>discrimination</u> against <u>minorities</u> — they wrote anti-Nazi <u>graffiti</u> and distributed anti-Nazi <u>leaflets</u> to encourage opposition. In <u>1943</u>, the group organised the first <u>public</u> anti-Nazi <u>demonstration</u>.

4) Many of the group were later <u>arrested</u> by the Gestapo. Several were tortured and <u>executed</u>, including <u>Hans</u> and <u>Sophie Scholl</u>.

Comment and Analysis

At her trial, Sophie Scholl stated that everything she had written in the leaflets was also known by <u>many others</u>, but they <u>didn't dare</u> to say anything about it.

Resistance in the Army grew during the war

1) There had been <u>plots against Hitler</u> by army officers before the war. These became <u>more serious</u> when some became convinced Hitler was going to lead Germany to <u>defeat</u>.

2) One of the most famous army plots was the <u>July plot</u> of <u>1944</u>. <u>Claus von Stauffenberg</u> (along with other German officers) <u>planned</u> to <u>kill Hitler</u> and install a <u>moderate</u> government, which would include members of the Kreisau Circle.

3) During a meeting, Stauffenberg left a <u>bomb</u> in a <u>briefcase</u> by Hitler's chair. However, someone <u>moved</u> the briefcase. The bomb exploded, but Hitler was <u>unhurt</u>.

4) Most of the plotters were quickly <u>captured</u> and <u>executed</u>.

It wasn't easy to stand against the Nazis...

Describe two examples of opposition faced by the Nazi Party during World War II. [4]

Nazi Rule in Eastern and Western Europe

The Nazis conquered territory to the <u>west</u> and <u>east</u> of Germany, but <u>didn't</u> treat all areas <u>equally</u>.

Nazi rule in the West was Relatively Humane

1) Hitler had hoped to <u>quickly</u> knock <u>western</u> European countries like France and Britain out of the war, <u>before</u> invading countries in the east to provide Germany with '<u>Lebensraum</u>' (see p.95). But the western countries <u>didn't</u> all surrender — e.g. Britain fought on. So a <u>long occupation</u> of western countries followed.

> However, the Nazis would certainly <u>respond brutally</u> to any resistance, and arrests, detentions and imprisonment in concentration camps were <u>common</u>.

2) Life in any Nazi-occupied country was far from pleasant, and <u>Jews</u> were especially <u>persecuted</u> in all territories under Nazi rule. But the Nazis <u>didn't</u> attempt to <u>exterminate</u> occupied countries' entire populations in the <u>west</u>.

3) It was the <u>resources</u> of these occupied countries in the west that Germany most wanted — <u>raw materials</u>, <u>agricultural produce</u>, and <u>industrial goods</u>. This led to <u>extreme shortages</u> for inhabitants of those countries.

4) Germany also needed <u>manpower</u>. Citizens of occupied countries were <u>forced</u> to <u>work</u> for the Nazis in Germany. The work was hard, but conditions were generally <u>reasonable</u> for workers from <u>western Europe</u>.

5) There were also other <u>rules</u> that people in <u>occupied countries</u> had to live by:

> Being <u>hostile</u> to <u>Germans</u>, listening to <u>foreign propaganda</u> and <u>communicating</u> with Germany's enemies were forbidden. Owning a <u>weapon</u> or a <u>radio</u>, <u>taking photographs outdoors</u>, <u>gathering</u> with others without permission and displaying <u>flags</u> were all banned too.

Nazi rule in the East was Brutal and Cruel

1) In occupied countries in <u>eastern Europe</u>, life could be <u>much harder</u>.

> In 1940, <u>Himmler</u> said, 'All Poles will disappear from this world. It is imperative that the great German nation considers the <u>elimination</u> of all Polish people as its chief task.'

- The Nazis thought of the east as <u>Lebensraum</u> for the 'Aryan master race' — it was intended eventually to become part of the <u>Greater Germanic Reich</u>.

- This meant it had to be '<u>cleansed</u>' of non-Aryan populations. <u>Jews</u> and <u>Slavic</u> populations (e.g. Poles and Russians) were especially <u>targeted</u>.

- The Nazis thought some members of these populations might be suitable for '<u>Germanisation</u>' (absorption into the German population), but those considered <u>unsuitable</u> would be <u>killed</u>.

> In 1939, <u>Hitler</u> told his commanders to kill 'without pity or mercy, all men, women, and children of Polish descent or language'.

2) When Germany invaded the Soviet Union in 1941, <u>Einsatzgruppen</u> (see p.113) followed the German army with orders to <u>kill</u> every <u>Jew</u> they found.

3) <u>Forced labourers</u> from the east were essentially <u>slaves</u>, and endured <u>terrible conditions</u>. About <u>2 million</u> non-Jewish <u>Poles</u> were forced into slave labour.

> **Comment and Analysis**
>
> The <u>different treatment</u> stemmed from the Nazis' belief that people in the <u>west</u> were of <u>Germanic</u> origin (they were '<u>Aryans</u>', just like the Germans). People in the <u>east</u>, on the other hand, were thought to be '<u>biologically inferior</u>'.

People Resisted or Collaborated in different ways

The <u>types</u> of action that people took in the face of Nazi rule can be grouped into different categories:

> **Acts of genuine resistance** are actions that tried to <u>hinder</u> the <u>Nazi war effort</u>, or <u>help Jews</u> or the <u>Nazis' enemies</u> — using either <u>violent</u> or <u>non-violent</u> methods. For example, French and Polish <u>resistance movements</u> supplied <u>information</u> to the countries fighting Germany, and <u>disrupted</u> German communications.

> **Acts of collaboration** are actions that <u>helped</u> the Nazis. Whole <u>governments</u> could collaborate (e.g. the <u>Vichy government</u> in <u>southern France</u>, which <u>voluntarily</u> persecuted Jews, deporting tens of thousands of them to Nazi death camps), or it could be <u>individuals</u>. Acts of collaboration ranged from doing German soldiers' <u>laundry</u> and <u>denouncing</u> fellow citizens, through to taking part in <u>mass killings</u>.

> **Acts of accommodation** are actions that <u>didn't</u> <u>help</u> the Nazis, but <u>didn't hinder</u> them or <u>help their victims</u> either. It's often called being a <u>bystander</u>.

The Nazis didn't treat everyone the same...

'Life in Nazi occupied areas was universally brutal and harsh.' To what extent do you agree? *[18]*

The Holocaust

The Holocaust is the name given to the mass murder of Jews by the Nazis.
The Nazis called their plan to kill Europe's Jews the 'final solution'.

The Final Solution was the Genocide of Europe's Jews

1) Large numbers of German Jews had been sent to concentration camps since the Nazis came to power. After the conquest of countries in western Europe, many more Jews had been deported to camps. When Germany invaded Poland and the Soviet Union, even more Jews fell under Nazi control.

2) The Nazis planned to deport them to a Jewish reservation in German-occupied Poland — but the idea was dropped because the area couldn't possibly hold all of Europe's Jews. Instead Jews were to be killed. This was described as the 'final solution to the Jewish question.'

3) As a temporary measure, the Nazis created ghettos — small areas of towns and cities where Jews were to be gathered together, away from the rest of the population.

4) Conditions in the ghettos were terrible. Many people died of disease or starved. Some were used for slave labour, e.g. in weapons factories.

5) After the Nazis invaded the Soviet Union, Einsatzgruppen followed the German army. These were units of SS soldiers whose job was to murder 'enemies' of the Nazi state in occupied eastern Europe. They were a key part of the final solution and killed in huge numbers, especially in Poland and the Soviet Union.

The largest ghetto was in Warsaw. In this picture, Jewish police are separating different members of the population.

Death Camps were built to Kill People on an Industrial Scale

1) To slaughter on the scale the Nazis required, death camps were built in Eastern Europe. Heinrich Himmler, head of the SS, was in overall charge of this operation.

2) The camps included gas chambers to carry out the mass murder, and crematoria to burn the bodies.

3) The plan was to kill around 11 million people — all of the Jews living in Nazi-controlled territory.

4) People were transported to the camps from all over Nazi-occupied Europe. They could take luggage and even paid for their own train tickets — the Nazis wanted to hide their intentions to prevent panic.

5) Mainly Jewish people were killed, but other groups were targeted as well, for example Slavs (e.g. Russians and Poles), Romani, black people, homosexuals, disabled people and communists.

It's Hard to understand How this Mass Murder happened

1) By the end of the war, the Nazis had killed approximately 6 million Jews and countless other people.

2) Before the war ended, orders went out to destroy the camps — but there wasn't time.

3) After the war, people around the world found it hard to believe that this inhuman, cold-blooded extermination had taken place, and that so many soldiers were involved. It has been argued that they might have gone along with the Nazi leadership for various reasons:

- The Nazi guards felt they had to 'do their duty' and obey orders. They might have feared their leaders, or just felt that obeying orders was the right thing to do.

- Jews may not have been regarded as fully human — so killing them didn't matter to guards.

> ### Comment and Analysis
> The world only discovered the horror of the death camps as the Allies advanced in 1945. Some historians claim there's evidence leaders like Churchill were told about the camps — but didn't believe the facts.

The 'final solution' — the ultimate madness...

What was the most vital factor in the decision to kill Europe's Jews rather than segregate them?
a) Nazi racial policy b) the size of Europe's Jewish population [12]

Revision Summary

Well, that's Germany all wrapped up — now have a crack at a revision summary to see how much stuck.
- Try these questions and <u>tick off each one</u> when you <u>get it right</u>.
- When you've done <u>all the questions</u> for a topic and are <u>completely happy</u> with it, tick off the topic.

Germany and the Growth of Democracy, 1890-1929 (p.90-97) ☑

1) Describe how the government of the German Empire was structured under Kaiser Wilhelm. ☑
2) Why did the Kaiser face difficulties ruling Germany between 1890 and 1914? ☑
3) Describe the events of the German Revolution in 1918. ☑
4) Name the three separate bodies of the Weimar government and describe what each one did. ☑
5) Give five terms from the Treaty of Versailles and explain why they were unpopular in Germany. ☑
6) Give two examples of unrest that occurred under the Weimar Republic between 1919 and 1922. ☑
7) What was the Munich Putsch? Why did it fail? ☑
8) How did Gustav Stresemann try to build better international relationships? ☑
9) How did life improve for the working classes and women under the Weimar Republic? ☑

Hitler's Rise to Power, 1929-1934 (p.98-101) ☑

10) What was the Great Depression? ☑
11) Describe the trends in federal election results in Germany between 1928 and 1932. ☑
12) Give three examples of social groups that were particularly drawn to the Nazis and explain why. ☑
13) Describe how Hitler rose to the position of Chancellor. ☑
14) What was the Enabling Act? When was it introduced? ☑
15) What happened on the 'Night of the Long Knives'? ☑

The Experiences of Germans under the Nazis, 1933-1939 (p.102-108) ☑

16) Describe three powers the Nazis had that suggested Germany had become a police state by 1934. ☑
17) What were the aims of Nazi propaganda? ☑
18) What was the Reich Church? ☑
19) Name two members of the Church who opposed the Nazis. ☑
20) What expectations did the Nazi Party have of women? ☑
21) How was education in Germany affected while the Nazis were in power? ☑
22) What were the Nuremberg Laws? Why were they important? ☑
23) Describe the events of Kristallnacht. ☑

The Second World War, 1939-1945 (p.109-113) ☑

24) What changes were made to the Nazi economy after the outbreak of World War Two? ☑
25) Describe one way in which daily life was affected by Nazi rule before the outbreak of war. ☑
26) What is 'total war'? How did it affect German civilians? ☑
27) Who was Claus von Stauffenberg? What did he do to oppose Nazi rule? ☑
28) How was Nazi occupation different in eastern and western Europe? ☑
29) What is a ghetto? Describe the role of ghettos in the Holocaust. ☑
30) What was the role of Einsatzgruppen? ☑
31) Name four groups of people who were targeted for execution in the Nazi death camps. ☑

The Grand Alliance

The Grand Alliance was made up of the 'big three' allies from World War Two — Britain, the USA and the USSR. They were united by their desire to defeat Nazi Germany, but as the war ended, tensions emerged.

The 'Big Three' discussed Europe's Future at Tehran and Yalta

1) In 1943, the Grand Alliance held a conference in Tehran. The talks focused mainly on plans to defeat the Nazis. But the allies also started to discuss what would happen to Europe and Germany after the war.

2) Britain and the USA were politically very different from the USSR and there were tensions between the three allies. These were put aside during the war as they fought a common enemy (Germany).

3) The British Prime Minister Winston Churchill and US President Franklin D. Roosevelt agreed the USSR could claim a 'sphere of influence' in Eastern Europe after the war was over. Eastern European countries would be subject to Soviet policies and ideas.

> The USSR (Union of Soviet Socialist Republics) was also known as the Soviet Union.

4) The Grand Alliance made more decisions about the future of Europe at the Yalta Conference in February 1945:

   - Free elections would be held in previously occupied countries in Eastern Europe.
   - The United Nations (UN) would replace the failed League of Nations.

Comment and Analysis

The allies had different interpretations of a 'free' election. To the USA and Britain, it meant lots of political parties competing for votes. But Stalin (the leader of the USSR) believed only communist parties should run in elections as they were the only parties that truly represented the people.

Potsdam revealed the First Cracks in the Grand Alliance

After Germany surrendered in May 1945, the allied leaders met again at Potsdam over July and August. They wanted to work on the finer details of their plans for Germany and Europe.

Some important agreements were made at Potsdam...
- The new boundaries of Poland were agreed.
- The 'big three' plus France would divide Germany and Berlin between them.
- Nazi leaders would be tried for war crimes at Nuremberg.

1) Some things remained undecided. For example, Germany would be divided into four zones (one each for Britain, France, the USA and the USSR) — but the allies didn't decide if, or when, the zones could rejoin and form a country again.

2) Tensions were high. Roosevelt had died and Harry Truman had succeeded him as US President — Truman was more suspicious of the USSR and less willing to compromise.

> Britain also had a new leader — Clement Attlee replaced Churchill mid-conference.

3) Britain and the US were also alarmed by Stalin's actions in Poland — he had installed a government consisting of only pro-communist members. Britain and the US felt this went against the Yalta agreement.

The USA and the USSR had very Different Ideologies

The tension between the USA and the USSR was partly caused by their very different beliefs — the USSR was communist, while the USA was capitalist. Both countries also feared the other's intentions.

1) Communism meant state control of industry and agriculture. The USA, by contrast, valued private enterprise — the 'American Dream' was that anyone could work their way to the top.

2) The USSR only allowed one political party — the Communist Party. The USA valued political freedom.

3) Communism aimed at world revolution, and so it was seen by Americans as a danger to their democracy. However, the communists also feared worldwide American influence.

'East' and 'West' had different perspectives...

Summarise the tension in the Grand Alliance between 1943 and July 1945.
Include how the allies' relationships altered and why their attitudes changed.

The Two Superpowers

The USSR and the USA emerged from the Second World War as the <u>two</u> biggest <u>powers</u> in the world. But they were very <u>suspicious</u> of one another, and began to interpret each other's actions as <u>threats</u>.

The USA kept their Atom Bomb a Secret

The atom bomb caused devastation in Hiroshima.

1) <u>Japan</u> was on Germany's side in the war, and <u>continued to fight</u> after Germany <u>surrendered</u> in May 1945. In August 1945, the USA dropped two <u>atom bombs</u> on Japan — <u>destroying</u> the cities of <u>Hiroshima</u> and <u>Nagasaki</u>.

2) The atom bombs meant that military help from the USSR <u>wasn't needed</u> to defeat Japan. President Truman also <u>refused</u> to allow the USSR to take part in the US <u>occupation</u> of Japan.

3) The USA had kept the exact nature of the atom bomb a <u>secret</u> from the USSR at <u>Potsdam</u> in July 1945 (although Stalin's spies had passed on many details).

4) These nuclear weapons boosted the <u>status</u> of the USA. For four years it was the world's <u>only</u> nuclear power. Stalin saw the development of the atom bomb as an attempt to <u>intimidate</u> the USSR, and was angry that the USA had managed to <u>surpass</u> Soviet technology.

5) The atom bombs <u>increased the rivalry</u> between the USA and the USSR. The USSR sped up the development of its own atomic bomb, starting an <u>arms race</u> between the two countries (see p.119).

The USSR became Influential in Eastern Europe

1) At the end of the Second World War, the <u>Red Army</u> (the USSR's army) occupied <u>Eastern Europe</u>. These countries would pass into the USSR's <u>sphere of influence</u> after the war.

2) Between 1945 and 1948, Stalin installed pro-Soviet 'puppet' governments in Poland, Hungary, Romania, Bulgaria and Czechoslovakia.

- For a while it seemed that <u>Czechoslovakia</u> might remain democratic. But when the Communist Party seemed likely to lose ground in the next election, it <u>seized power</u> in February 1948.

- The <u>exception</u> to Soviet domination was <u>Yugoslavia</u>, which had freed itself from the Germans <u>without</u> the Red Army. Yugoslavia was communist but more <u>open</u> to the <u>West</u>. Its leader, <u>Tito</u>, argued with Stalin over political interference. Stalin cut off aid but <u>didn't invade</u>.

There was an 'Iron Curtain' between East and West

Countries under the <u>influence</u> of the USSR became known as its '<u>satellite states</u>' (in pink).

1) Increasing tensions between the USA and the USSR became known as the '<u>Cold War</u>'. There was no direct fighting — both sides were <u>afraid</u> of another war, espccially after 1949, when the USSR had its own nuclear weapons.

2) Countries in <u>Western Europe</u> tended to support the <u>USA</u>. Most countries in <u>Eastern Europe</u> were dominated by the <u>USSR</u>. In a famous speech in 1946, Winston Churchill warned there was an '<u>Iron Curtain</u>' dividing Europe.

Comment and Analysis

Churchill's '<u>Iron Curtain</u>' speech demonstrates the <u>breakdown</u> of the Grand Alliance — Britain and the USA now viewed the USSR as a <u>threat</u>, not an <u>ally</u>.

My two favourite superpowers — flying and being invisible...

In the exam, try to explain people's actions by considering the way they would have looked at a situation. Here, each country is acting for reasons that made sense to the people in charge.

EXAM TIP

Mutual Suspicion

The Cold War was a period of international tension — with each side suspicious of the other.

The 'Long' and 'Novikov' telegrams were detailed Reports

By 1946, tensions between the superpowers were high. Each country issued secret telegrams about the other.

1)   The telegrams were detailed reports describing the motivations and intentions of the other country.

The Long Telegram (February 1946)

- Issued to President Truman about the USSR.
- It said that Stalin had given a speech in favour of the destruction of capitalism.
- It warned of the USSR trying to weaken and divide Western powers, while building the strength of its own military.

The Novikov Telegram (September 1946)

- Issued to Stalin about the USA.
- The report claimed that the USA was pursuing world supremacy.
- It warned that the USA was trying to limit the influence of the USSR in Europe.

2)   Neither country seemed to know for certain what the other was thinking.
The reports panicked the Russian and American governments and
accelerated the Cold War — the findings seemed to confirm their worst fears.

Truman Acted to Contain the Communist Threat

President Truman was extremely worried about the spread of communism to Western Europe.
Many countries were undergoing economic hardships, which he thought might make communism look
more appealing. The USA decided to intervene in Europe to try and contain the spread of communism.

The Truman Doctrine (announced March 1947)

The USA pledged to support any nation threatened by a communist takeover.
This support could be diplomatic, military or financial. For example, the USA
gave $400 million of aid to Turkey and Greece to stop communism spreading.

The Marshall Plan (announced June 1947)

This promised $17 billion of aid to European countries to help rebuild their economies
— the areas of Germany under Western occupation benefited massively. Stalin,
however, ordered all of his satellite states to reject the plan. He believed the USA was
using economic incentives to lure Eastern European states away from the USSR.

The USSR Reacted by creating the Cominform

Stalin felt threatened by the Truman Doctrine, and reacted by strengthening and uniting his allies.

1)   The Cominform (Communist Information Bureau) was set up in
1947. The organisation brought together all European communist
parties and placed them under the control of the USSR.

2)   The Comecon (the Council for Mutual Economic Assistance) was
established in 1949. It countered the Marshall Plan by nationalising
industries, collectivising agriculture and offering economic aid.

Stalin hoped this would encourage economic development in Eastern
Europe and discourage trade with the West. It also appeased the
countries that had been ordered to refuse Marshall aid.

Comment and Analysis

Marshall Plan aid ensured that
a lot of Western Europe became
allied with the USA. Stalin's
retaliation — his creation of the
Cominform and, later, the
Comecon — strengthened his
alliances in Eastern Europe.

The Cold War was tense — but preferable to a hot one...

*In your own words, summarise what the USA and the USSR believed about each other after
the Long and Novikov Telegrams were sent, and how this might have affected their actions.*

The Berlin Crisis

Tension over the division of Germany had been building since the Potsdam Conference, and finally spilled over in the Berlin crisis in 1948. It resulted in an even larger rift between the two great powers.

In 1948 the USSR and the West Clashed over Berlin

Berlin was in East Germany. The French, British and US sectors formed West Berlin, while the Soviet sector was called East Berlin.

1) Immediately after the war, there were four zones of occupied Germany, and four zones in Berlin. In 1947, the USA and Britain agreed to combine their zones to form 'Bizonia'. The next year, the French agreed to add their zone.

2) The new western zone had a single government, and in June 1948 introduced a new currency to help economic recovery.

3) This alarmed the USSR. Stalin did not want a unified western zone on his doorstep. West Berlin's strong capitalist economy embarrassed the USSR, and made communism look weak.

4) As a result, Stalin decided to blockade Berlin to try to force the West to withdraw from West Berlin.

5) In June 1948, he ordered that all road, rail and canal links between West Berlin and the outside world should be cut off.

Comment and Analysis

Stalin wanted to force the West to withdraw from Berlin altogether. The Western powers believed that if this happened, the Soviet Union would be tempted to invade West Germany.

The Western powers wouldn't give up West Berlin...

• The West decided to bypass the blockade and fly in supplies. This became known as the Berlin Airlift, and lasted for 318 days.

• By 1949, 8000 tons of supplies were being flown in each day.

• Tegel airport was built in West Berlin to accommodate the large volume of flights. It meant supplies could be delivered in even greater numbers.

After the crisis, Germany was Divided in Two

1) When it became clear that the West was determined not to withdraw from Berlin, Stalin had to lift the blockade. It was also clear that Germany would remain divided.

2) In 1949, two separate states were formed — West Germany (Federal Republic of Germany) and communist East Germany (German Democratic Republic).

Comment and Analysis

The end of the Berlin blockade increased tensions as Stalin hadn't lifted the blockade willingly. The allies appeared strong, and had discredited and humiliated Stalin.

The Two Powers formed Military Alliances

1) Stalin's blockade during the Berlin crisis showed how unprepared the West would be if there was a conflict with the USSR.

2) As a consequence, the Western Powers decided to form a military alliance. In 1949, NATO (the North Atlantic Treaty Organisation) was created.

3) All members of NATO agreed to respond together if any member of the alliance was attacked.

> The USSR saw the formation of NATO as a real threat.

• In 1955, the USSR established the Warsaw Pact to rival NATO. All the USSR's satellite states (except Yugoslavia) became members.

• Its main aims were to improve the defensive capability of Eastern Europe and strengthen relations.

• There were now two power blocs in Europe — NATO and the Warsaw Pact.

> Members of the Warsaw Pact formed the so-called 'Eastern Bloc'.

The West had made Stalin look weak...

Explain how important the Berlin Crisis was for relations between the US and the USSR. [8]

The Arms Race

In the Cold War, the USA and the USSR tried to gain an advantage by forming <u>military alliances</u> and developing ever more <u>powerful weapons</u>. The aim was to 'look strong' to <u>deter</u> the other from attacking.

The USA and the USSR began an Arms Race

1) During the Cold War, the USA and the USSR worked to develop the most powerful weapons they could — there was an <u>arms race</u>.

2) Neither side really wanted to <u>use</u> these weapons, but <u>both</u> felt the other <u>couldn't</u> be allowed to gain an <u>advantage</u>. The fear was that if either gained a <u>significant</u> military advantage, that country might be tempted to trigger a war to take advantage of it.

3) Instead, a <u>stand-off</u> developed where both countries <u>didn't dare</u> act against the other, but didn't dare get '<u>left behind</u>', either.

4) This <u>competition</u> sometimes spilled over into other areas. For example, when the USSR launched the first satellite into space, the USA quickly developed one of its own. This '<u>space race</u>' led to the USSR sending the <u>first</u> man into space in 1961, and to the USA sending astronauts to the <u>Moon</u> in 1969.

Both countries developed Nuclear Stockpiles

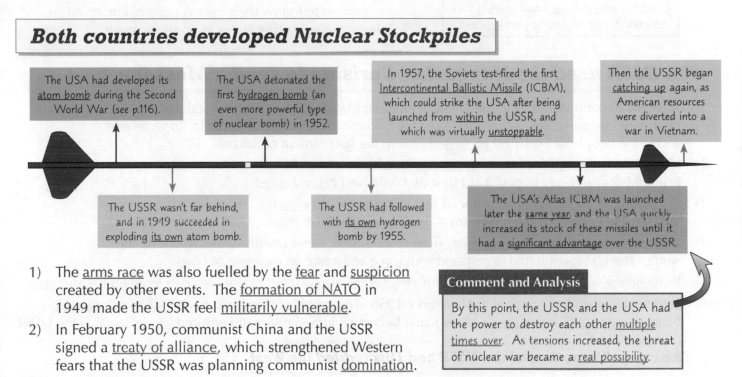

The USA had developed its <u>atom bomb</u> during the Second World War (see p.116).

The USA detonated the first <u>hydrogen bomb</u> (an even more powerful type of nuclear bomb) in 1952.

In 1957, the Soviets test-fired the first <u>Intercontinental Ballistic Missile</u> (ICBM), which could strike the USA after being launched from <u>within</u> the USSR, and which was virtually <u>unstoppable</u>.

Then the USSR began <u>catching up</u> again, as American resources were diverted into a war in Vietnam.

The USSR wasn't far behind, and in 1949 succeeded in exploding <u>its own</u> atom bomb.

The USSR had followed with <u>its own</u> hydrogen bomb by 1955.

The USA's Atlas ICBM was launched later the <u>same year</u>, and the USA quickly increased its stock of these missiles until it had a <u>significant advantage</u> over the USSR.

1) The <u>arms race</u> was also fuelled by the <u>fear</u> and <u>suspicion</u> created by other events. The <u>formation of NATO</u> in 1949 made the USSR feel <u>militarily vulnerable</u>.

2) In February 1950, communist China and the USSR signed a <u>treaty of alliance</u>, which strengthened Western fears that the USSR was planning communist <u>domination</u>.

Comment and Analysis

By this point, the USSR and the USA had the power to destroy each other <u>multiple times over</u>. As tensions increased, the threat of nuclear war became a <u>real possibility</u>.

Khrushchev raised hopes of 'Peaceful Co-existence'

In 1953, Stalin <u>died</u> and another member of the Communist Party, <u>Nikita Khrushchev</u>, took power.

Comment and Analysis

Because Khrushchev continued to develop weapons, the West still felt <u>threatened</u> and the arms race <u>didn't</u> slow down.

1) Khrushchev said he wanted '<u>peaceful co-existence</u>' with the West. His words brought hope that there would be a '<u>thaw</u>' in the Cold War.

2) But Khrushchev remained <u>very competitive</u> with the USA.

3) He wanted communism to spread, but thought the best way to achieve this was to clearly demonstrate its <u>superiority</u> — not defeat the West in a war.

The rivalry between the USA and the USSR kept on going...

Remember to give evidence to back up your points. For this page, you could use the sequence of 'tit for tat' weapons developments to show how neither side dared fall behind in the arms race.

Divisions in Eastern Europe

Not all of the USSR's satellite states had <u>willingly</u> accepted communism, and the USSR soon faced unrest.

Unrest began to Stir in the Eastern Bloc

1) When Khrushchev came to power, he made a speech <u>criticising</u> Stalin's policies and brought in measures to '<u>de-Stalinise</u>' the USSR. These included the <u>abolition</u> of the <u>death penalty</u> and the <u>freeing</u> of <u>political prisoners</u> jailed under Stalin's regime.

2) Some satellite states hoped that their countries would also become 'de-Stalinised'. Khrushchev abolished the <u>Cominform</u> (see p.117), meaning that states in Eastern Europe would have more <u>political</u> and <u>economic freedom</u> from the USSR.

> Communism created a lot of <u>economic hardship</u> — poor living conditions increased <u>anti-Soviet</u> sentiment.

> **Comment and Analysis**
>
> Khrushchev wanted the Eastern Bloc to remain <u>communist</u> — he just <u>didn't agree</u> with Stalin's approach to communism. He thought that giving satellite states more <u>economic independence</u> would <u>stabilise</u> their communist regimes, but his plan <u>backfired</u>.

3) These moves allowed <u>tensions</u> in the <u>satellite states</u> to rise to the surface. Not all states had <u>chosen</u> communism, and saw the changes as a chance to <u>loosen</u> ties with the USSR.

4) In 1956, there was an <u>uprising</u> in Poland. The USSR threatened to intervene, but eventually allowed the new government to follow their <u>own version</u> of communism. This <u>encouraged</u> other states to consider revolt.

The USSR used the Hungarian Uprising to send a Message

1) After the Second World War, the USSR helped put <u>Mátyás Rákosi</u>, a brutal Stalinist, in charge of Hungary. His <u>authoritarian</u> regime became increasingly unpopular. In October 1956, the people of Budapest <u>protested</u> against the government of Rákosi.

2) Khrushchev <u>allowed</u> the liberal <u>Imre Nagy</u> to take over from Rákosi as Hungarian Prime Minister. Nagy hoped that Hungary could be a <u>neutral state</u>.

3) In November 1956, Nagy announced that Hungary would <u>withdraw</u> from the Warsaw Pact and hold free elections — <u>ending communism</u> there.

4) If Hungary was allowed to <u>turn away</u> from communism, other satellite states might do the same. The USSR felt it had to respond with <u>force</u> and make an <u>example</u> of Nagy.

5) Khrushchev, who had only held power for <u>two years</u>, also wanted to use the crisis to <u>assert</u> his <u>authority</u>.

6) Soviet tanks <u>invaded</u> Hungary in November 1956. Thousands of Hungarians were <u>killed</u> or <u>wounded</u>. Nagy was <u>arrested</u> and <u>hanged</u>. János Kádár became Prime Minister and ensured <u>loyalty</u> towards the USSR.

The crisis Strengthened the USSR and Discredited the West

1) Khrushchev's brutal response to Hungary demonstrated to satellite states that disloyalty <u>wouldn't</u> be tolerated. It also showed the Western powers that the USSR was <u>still in control</u>.

2) It was a <u>turning point</u> for Khrushchev — his actions <u>reasserted his authority</u> over the satellite states and destroyed any <u>illusions</u> in the West that his leadership signified a '<u>thaw</u>' in the Cold War.

Western Reactions
- There was a <u>lack of intervention</u> from Western countries. They <u>condemned</u> the USSR's actions, but thought that helping Hungary would risk a <u>nuclear war</u>.
- The UN asked the USSR to <u>withdraw</u> from Hungary, but Kádár refused to take part in discussions. The situation remained <u>unresolved</u>.

> **Comment and Analysis**
>
> The Western powers' reputation as upholders of democracy was <u>discredited</u>. Their <u>inaction</u> sent a clear message to Eastern Europe that they <u>wouldn't</u> receive Western help to move away from the USSR. The UN was shown to be <u>weak</u>.

The USSR kept a tight hold on its satellite states...

Explain the significance of the Hungarian Uprising as a factor in keeping the Eastern European satellite states loyal to the USSR. [8]

EXAM QUESTION

The Berlin Question

The 1950s saw more communication between the two superpowers, but underlying tensions remained.

There were some Steps to Improve East-West Relations...

President Eisenhower succeeded President Truman in January 1953, while Khrushchev came to power in September. This provided an opportunity to create a fresh start — there were several encouraging steps towards defusing tensions between the two powers:

- The USA and the USSR met in Geneva in 1955 and agreed to communicate more openly.
- In 1955, the USSR officially recognised the Federal Republic of Germany (West Germany) as a state.
- Khrushchev also freed some prisoners and reduced censorship in the USSR.

...but Berlin remained a Source of Tension

1) After the Berlin crisis in 1948 (see p.118), West Berlin was a unified zone and continued to develop economically, benefiting from a new currency and American (Marshall Plan) aid.

2) The situation in East Berlin was very different — the USSR had drained it of resources and its economy was slow to develop. Many people wanted to leave and go to the more prosperous West Berlin instead.

By 1961, at least 3 million East Germans had emigrated from East Berlin to West Berlin.

3) The situation was hugely embarrassing for Khrushchev, as it suggested that people preferred life under capitalism to communism.

4) It also threatened East Germany's economy, as many of those who left were skilled workers in search of a better life.

5) The refugee crisis in Berlin led Khrushchev to issue his 'Berlin Ultimatum' in 1958. He demanded that US, British and French troops leave West Berlin within six months. West Berlin would become a free city.

6) Eisenhower refused the ultimatum. Khrushchev took no further action, but the Berlin issue wasn't solved.

The Soviet attitude towards Berlin...
- The USSR felt threatened by the economic success in West Berlin.
- East Berlin had become dependent on trade links with West Berlin.
- The USSR worried the West was trying to use its strong economy to interfere in Eastern Europe.

The Western attitude towards Berlin...
- After the Berlin Airlift, West Berlin became a symbol of democracy — it had to be supported or the West would lose credibility.
- People fleeing from East Berlin suited the West — it was good propaganda because it made communism look weak.

Khrushchev and Eisenhower held a Summit in 1959

1) In 1959, Khrushchev became the first communist leader to visit the USA. The meeting symbolised a new spirit of co-operation and communication between the two powers.

2) At the meeting they discussed Berlin. Eisenhower still didn't agree to withdraw from West Berlin, but did agree to discuss the matter more deeply.

3) The leaders decided to meet in Paris the following year. Although no firm decisions had been made, the arrangement of another summit promised to continue the optimistic dialogue they had started.

Both powers refused to compromise on Berlin...

You need to show you understand how events are connected. Here you could show how the superpowers' attitudes towards Berlin were shaped by the Airlift or West Berlin's economic success.

The Berlin Wall

In 1961, around <u>2000</u> Germans crossed over from East to West Berlin every day. When it became clear that the situation wasn't going to be solved <u>diplomatically</u>, Khrushchev constructed the <u>Berlin Wall</u>.

Talks about Berlin Broke Down...

1) President Eisenhower and Khrushchev had agreed to discuss the <u>Berlin question</u> at the <u>Paris Summit</u> in 1960. Days before the summit was due to take place, the USSR shot down a U2 <u>American spy plane</u> over <u>Soviet territory</u>.

2) Eisenhower <u>denied</u> that it was a spy plane, but the USSR then produced the pilot (alive) and the plane's wreckage as evidence. When the USA <u>refused</u> to apologise, Khrushchev <u>walked out</u> of the Paris Summit.

3) The U2 incident <u>hindered</u> further negotiations about Berlin. Both countries met again at <u>Vienna</u> in June 1961 — by this time, John F. Kennedy had replaced Eisenhower as US President.

4) Kennedy vowed to take a <u>tougher</u> approach towards communism. He <u>refused</u> to <u>compromise</u> over Berlin, and <u>no</u> resolution was reached.

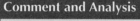

Comment and Analysis

After the <u>Vienna Summit</u>, the USSR believed that problems in Berlin wouldn't be resolved by <u>negotiation</u>. This sparked the creation of the <u>Berlin Wall</u>.

...so the Berlin Wall was Put Up

1) Khrushchev felt he had to <u>act</u> to stem the flow of refugees out of East Berlin. On 13th August 1961, a 27-mile <u>barrier</u> was built across the city of Berlin overnight, <u>separating</u> East from West.

2) It was fortified with <u>barbed wire</u> and <u>machine gun</u> posts, and was later strengthened and made into a more <u>permanent</u> barrier. Military <u>checkpoints</u> policed any movements into or out of East Berlin.

3) Before the wall, East Berliners had entered West Berlin freely. After the wall, they could no longer go to <u>work</u> in West Berlin and were instantly <u>separated</u> from friends and relatives.

A photo of the newly-built Berlin Wall.

4) Citizens from East and West Berlin were <u>rarely</u> allowed through the military checkpoints and anyone who tried to <u>escape</u> East Berlin was <u>shot</u>.

The Berlin Wall helped Stabilise the situation in Europe

After the Berlin Wall was put up, Cold War tensions over Berlin <u>stabilised</u>.

'It's <u>not</u> a very nice solution, but a wall is a hell of a lot <u>better</u> than a war.' — President Kennedy, 1961.

The West condemned Khrushchev, but was actually relieved...

• Immediately after the Berlin Wall appeared, Soviet and Western troops were positioned <u>either side</u> of the wall, but then both powers agreed to <u>back down</u>.
• The USA <u>condemned</u> the building of the wall, but took no further military action.
• Kennedy was actually <u>relieved</u> — he'd been preparing for a <u>confrontation</u> of some sort.

1) The wall succeeded in <u>stopping</u> mass emigration to West Berlin. It also gave East Germany the opportunity to <u>rebuild</u> its economy, and <u>strengthen</u> itself as a communist state.

2) In the West, the Berlin Wall became a symbol of <u>oppression</u> and the <u>failure</u> of <u>communism</u>. In the USSR, it was seen as a sign of <u>strength</u>.

3) President Kennedy visited West Berlin in 1963 and gave a famous <u>speech</u> stating his solidarity with West Berlin and its people. He declared 'Ich bin ein Berliner' (I am a Berliner).

The wall cemented the divide between East and West Berlin...

Write a summary of the events that led to the construction of the Berlin Wall in 1961.

The Cuban Missile Crisis

As tension was increasing over Berlin, the USA also began to have problems closer to home. <u>Cuba</u> had long been the USA's economic <u>ally</u>, but revolution brought the <u>communist threat</u> to the USA's doorstep.

The Cuban Revolution in 1959 Worried the USA

1) Since 1952, Cuba had been <u>ruled</u> by Batista, a ruthless military <u>dictator</u>, who allowed American businessmen and the Mafia to make <u>huge profits</u> in a country where <u>most people</u> lived in <u>poverty</u>.

2) In 1956, a rebel called <u>Fidel Castro</u> began a <u>guerrilla war</u>. By 1959, he had enough support to take Cuba's capital, Havana, and <u>successfully</u> overthrew the government.

> In a '<u>guerrilla war</u>', small military units use tactics like <u>raids</u> to fight a larger opponent.

3) This revolution <u>worried</u> the USA. The USA had a long <u>economic history</u> with Cuba. It owned <u>half</u> of Cuba's land and held most of the <u>shares</u> in all <u>Cuban industries</u>.

4) The USA felt it had a <u>right</u> to be <u>involved</u> in Cuba's affairs. But Cubans had grown to <u>resent</u> American influence in their country — they didn't feel like an <u>independent</u> state.

> The USA had <u>occupied</u> Cuba from 1898 to 1902. When Cuba became <u>independent</u>, the two countries maintained <u>close economic ties</u>.

The USA Accidentally pushed Castro Closer to the USSR

1) When Castro seized power in 1959, he <u>nationalised US companies</u> and <u>increased taxes</u> on goods <u>imported</u> from <u>America</u>. This angered the USA.

> 'Nationalisation' means taking a <u>privately owned industry</u> and placing it under <u>public ownership</u>.

2) Eisenhower was concerned that Castro's drive towards <u>public ownership</u> showed that he was <u>moving towards communism</u>.

3) He threatened to <u>stop importing</u> Cuban sugar. Sugar was Cuba's <u>main</u> source of wealth, and the USA was sure that Castro would <u>back down</u>.

4) Instead, Castro signed a <u>trade agreement</u> with the <u>USSR</u> — the USSR promised to buy all sugar exports. All remaining American <u>property</u> in Cuba was <u>confiscated</u>.

5) In January 1961, the USA <u>severed</u> all <u>diplomatic relations</u> with Cuba — the new US President John Kennedy no longer <u>recognised</u> Castro's government.

> **Comment and Analysis**
>
> Khrushchev wanted to <u>help</u> Castro, who was <u>sympathetic</u> towards communism. He also saw an opportunity to <u>gain influence</u> near US soil.

By 1961, Cuba had consolidated its ties with the USSR. As Cuba was only 100 miles from the USA, the communist threat had come dangerously close.

Rebels backed by the USA Invaded Cuba at the Bay of Pigs

Kennedy couldn't let a <u>communist state</u> emerge <u>next to</u> America — he <u>intervened</u>.

1) In 1961, Kennedy authorised an <u>invasion</u> of Cuba by anti-Castro rebels.

2) In April 1961, the rebels landed in the <u>Bay of Pigs</u>, but they were easily <u>defeated</u> and the USA didn't help — it was a bit of a <u>fiasco</u>.

3) The USA was <u>humiliated</u>, and had pushed Cuba <u>even closer</u> to the USSR.

> **Tensions continued to grow...**
>
> • The invasion led Castro to decide that Cuba needed Soviet <u>military assistance</u> to defend itself. This sparked one of the biggest <u>crises</u> of the Cold War — the <u>Cuban Missile Crisis</u> (see p.124).
>
> • In December 1961, <u>Castro</u> publicly announced that he was a <u>communist</u>, confirming US fears.

The Bay of Pigs invasion wasn't Kennedy's finest moment...

In the exam you get marks for how well you organise your ideas. Make sure you've got a clear argument in your head before you start to write your answer — it's best to jot down a plan first.

The Cuban Missile Crisis

Khrushchev agreed to <u>help</u> Castro and began to build nuclear missile sites in <u>Cuba</u>.

Khrushchev planned to put Nuclear Missiles in Cuba

1) In September 1961, Cuba <u>asked the USSR</u> for weapons to defend itself against <u>further American intervention</u>. By July 1962, Khrushchev had decided to put <u>nuclear missiles</u> in Cuba.

2) Although Khrushchev already had missiles that <u>could reach</u> the USA, missiles in Cuba would allow him to launch a <u>nuclear attack</u> on all of central and eastern USA with <u>very little warning</u>.

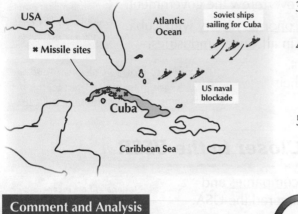

3) In October 1962, American U2 <u>spy planes</u> spotted that nuclear <u>missile bases</u> were being built in <u>Cuba</u>.

4) President Kennedy <u>demanded</u> that Khrushchev <u>dismantle</u> the missile bases and ordered a <u>naval blockade</u> of Cuba. All Soviet ships were to be <u>stopped</u> and <u>searched</u> to prevent missiles being transported to the island.

5) As tensions grew, US bombers were put in the air carrying <u>nuclear bombs</u> and the USA prepared to <u>invade</u> Cuba. The world was on the brink of <u>nuclear war</u>.

Comment and Analysis

The USA had placed missiles in Turkey <u>right next</u> to the USSR in April 1962. In Khrushchev's eyes, putting missiles in Cuba was a <u>reasonable</u> response.

On 27th October 1962, Khrushchev made a deal to <u>dismantle</u> the missile bases in Cuba and ordered his <u>ships</u> to <u>turn around</u>. In exchange the USA <u>lifted</u> the <u>blockade</u>, promised to <u>not invade</u> Cuba — and <u>secretly</u> agreed to <u>remove</u> their <u>missiles</u> from <u>Turkey</u>.

The crisis Significantly Altered the Course of the Cold War

The Cuban Missile Crisis was <u>important</u> because it forced everybody to face up to how quickly a tense situation could become an absolute catastrophe. In the short term, efforts were made to <u>defuse tensions</u> and <u>improve communication</u> between the powers.

- In 1963, a telephone '<u>hotline</u>' was established between <u>Washington</u> and <u>Moscow</u>. This enabled the two superpowers to <u>talk directly</u> and more <u>quickly</u> in the event of a crisis.
- All nuclear missiles were <u>removed</u> from <u>Cuba</u>, and then from <u>Turkey</u> by April 1963.
- <u>Kennedy</u> emerged from the crisis as a <u>hero</u> who had <u>stood up</u> against the threat of communism.
- <u>Khrushchev</u>, however, was <u>discredited</u> — he'd forced the USA to <u>remove their missiles</u> from Turkey, but had agreed to keep the deal a <u>secret</u>. In the eyes of the public he'd <u>failed</u> and he <u>resigned</u> in 1964.

In the long term, the crisis prompted <u>new measures</u> to bring the build up of nuclear weapons <u>under control</u>.

1) **The Limited Test Ban Treaty** was signed by <u>both powers</u> in 1963. It stated that all future <u>tests</u> of nuclear weapons had to be carried out <u>underground</u> to avoid polluting the air with <u>nuclear radiation</u>.

> The Cuban Missile Crisis was one of the most <u>dangerous events</u> in the Cold War, but it also marked the beginning of a period of '<u>détente</u>' (see p.127).

2) **The Outer Space Treaty** was drawn up in 1967. It <u>forbade</u> countries (including the USSR and the USA) from placing <u>weapons of mass destruction</u> in <u>space</u>.

3) **The Nuclear Non-Proliferation Treaty** came into force in 1970. Both superpowers agreed <u>not to supply</u> nuclear weapons or related technology to countries that <u>didn't</u> already have nuclear arms. The treaty also encouraged nuclear <u>disarmament</u>, but it allowed countries to use nuclear technology for <u>peaceful</u> purposes (e.g. energy).

Signing that Non-Profiterole Treaty must've taken guts...

What was the significance of the Cuban Missile Crisis for the development of the Cold War? [8]

The Prague Spring

In 1968, discontent within the Soviet Eastern Bloc stirred again. Czechoslovakia wanted more freedom from Moscow, and decided to move away from Soviet influence in a rebellion known as 'the Prague Spring'.

There was Opposition to Soviet Control in Czechoslovakia

1) Tension had been building in Czechoslovakia. It had become a communist state in 1948 and its policies were heavily influenced by the USSR.

2) It was a member of the Warsaw Pact, which discouraged trade with countries outside the Eastern Bloc and promoted Soviet-style communism.

> Soviet policies such as collectivisation and centralisation slowed economic progress in Czechoslovakia.

3) There was growing discontent about the extent of external control over Czechoslovakian affairs. In 1956, students and writers protested at the lack of free speech and free movement in the country.

Dubcek wanted to Move Away from Soviet policies

1) In January 1968, Alexander Dubcek became the leader of the Communist Party in Czechoslovakia. Dubcek wanted Czechoslovakia to follow its own version of communism.

2) In April 1968, he introduced a series of reforms that went against Soviet-style communism.

Dubcek's Reforms

- Travel to the West was made available for all.
- The border with West Germany was re-opened.
- All industry became decentralised.
- Trade unions and workers were given more power.
- Freedom of speech and opposition parties were allowed.

> Decentralisation meant that companies were no longer controlled by Communist party officials — workers and local authorities were given more power.

3) Many of the reforms were aimed at improving the performance of Czechoslovakia's economy — partly by developing closer relations with the West.

4) This worried the USSR — it didn't want any Western involvement in its Eastern Bloc.

5) Even though some reforms moved away from Soviet policy, Dubcek was still a communist. He promised that Czechoslovakia would stay in the Warsaw Pact and remain a loyal ally to Moscow.

6) For four months, Dubcek's new policies were tolerated by the USSR, and Czechoslovakia enjoyed relative freedom. This period is known as the 'Prague Spring'.

The USSR was Under Pressure to Intervene

1) The USSR grew increasingly concerned about Dubcek's reforms. Dubcek promised he was still loyal to Moscow, but his new policies meant that the USSR had less control over Czechoslovakia.

2) The leader of the USSR, Leonid Brezhnev, was worried that Dubcek's reforms could lead to a rejection of communism in the Eastern Bloc and in the USSR itself. If Czechoslovakia pulled away, other satellite states might follow.

Events in August 1968 triggered a Soviet response...

- President Tito of Yugoslavia visited Prague. Yugoslavia had refused to sign the Warsaw Pact and had never accepted the USSR's version of communism. The trip was an ominous sign to Brezhnev that Czechoslovakia was no longer loyal to the USSR.
- The USSR received a letter from communists in Czechoslovakia, asking for help.

Dubcek wanted to reform Czechoslovakia peacefully...

In the exam, always read the question carefully and work out what it wants you to do. It's very easy to just describe what happened — but often you need to analyse events, too.

EXAM TIP

The Prague Spring

In August 1968, the USSR decided to intervene <u>militarily</u>. This led to a new <u>pro-Soviet</u> leader in power and Czechoslovakia returned to <u>Soviet-style</u> communism.

The USSR Invaded Czechoslovakia in August 1968

1) On 21st <u>August 1968</u> 500,000 Soviet troops <u>invaded</u> Czechoslovakia.

2) The Czechoslovakians responded with <u>non-violent</u> demonstrations — people took to the streets with <u>anti-invasion banners</u>, and in January 1969 a student <u>burned himself alive</u> in the street in protest.

> Czechoslovakia was keen to avoid the <u>violence</u> that erupted in the 1956 <u>Hungarian Uprising</u> (see p.120).

3) In April 1969, Dubcek was <u>forcibly removed</u> from office, and replaced with <u>Gustav Husak</u>. Husak was <u>loyal</u> to Soviet-style communism, and would ensure that Czechoslovakia <u>remained close</u> with the USSR.

Countries Criticised the USSR, but Didn't Act

There was an <u>international outcry</u> at the Soviet intervention in Czechoslovakia, but <u>no action</u> was taken.

Warsaw Pact forces enter Prague in August 1968.

- The UN <u>denounced</u> the invasion and proposed a draft resolution requesting the <u>withdrawal</u> of Soviet troops from Czechoslovakia. This was <u>vetoed</u> (rejected) by <u>the USSR</u>.
- Many countries <u>condemned</u> the Soviet action but <u>didn't intervene</u>. They were <u>wary</u> of interfering within the USSR's <u>sphere of influence</u>.
- Communist parties in the West <u>criticised</u> Brezhnev's reaction and sought to <u>distance themselves</u> from Soviet influence.

Comment and Analysis

Countries were <u>wary</u> of taking action against the USSR. The Prague Spring occurred at a time when the Cold War had <u>thawed slightly</u>. Nobody wanted to <u>re-ignite tensions</u> between the two superpowers.

> The <u>lack of reaction</u> from the UN and the West made the Western powers appear <u>weak</u>.

The Prague Spring Strengthened the USSR

1) The USSR succeeded in <u>returning</u> Czechoslovakia to <u>Soviet-style communism</u>.

2) Brezhnev used the Prague Spring as an opportunity to <u>establish his authority</u> in the Eastern Bloc. He showed he was prepared to invade a <u>friendly</u> satellite state in order not to <u>weaken</u> the anti-Western alliance. He also <u>proved</u> to the <u>USA</u> that he was a <u>strong</u> and <u>determined</u> leader.

Brezhnev Doctrine
- After the invasion, <u>Brezhnev</u> announced that in future the USSR would <u>intervene</u> in any country where <u>communism</u> was under <u>threat</u>.
- The Brezhnev Doctrine was important because it <u>strengthened</u> the USSR's <u>control</u> over its satellite states.
- It also <u>sent a message</u> to the Eastern Bloc that giving up communism <u>wasn't</u> an option — the USSR would respond <u>with force</u>.

3) Soviet-American relations continued to be <u>strained</u>. Despite recent moves towards <u>reducing</u> the nuclear threat (see p.124), both countries still <u>distrusted</u> one another.

4) The incident reminded both superpowers that the Cold War <u>wasn't over</u>. Brezhnev had proved he was still <u>willing to risk conflict</u> to uphold communism in the Eastern Bloc.

The USSR regained control — the Cold War got chillier...

Look back at pages 121-126. Make a timeline of the main crises that occurred in the Cold War between 1958 and 1970, and summarise what happened in each one.

Détente — Easing of Tensions

In the 1970s there was a period of 'détente' — an easing in tension between the two superpowers.

The policy of Détente was Practical

Détente wasn't just goodwill — it was also a sensible policy for both countries.

1) The 1960s were marked by crises, including some of the most tense moments in the Cold War (p.121-126). Both the USA and the USSR wanted to avoid other near misses.

2) Boosting military power hadn't succeeded in reducing tensions. Both countries recognised that a new strategy was needed.

3) Both countries were also keen to reduce their military spending — the arms race was extremely expensive and led to falling standards of living.

Comment and Analysis

The USSR was especially worried about falling living standards in the Eastern Bloc. In 1970, there were riots in Poland in response to high living costs.

The Superpowers agreed to Reduce Arms and Cooperate

The two superpowers developed closer relations under détente. In 1975, Soviet and American spacecraft docked together in space. However, the most significant progress was achieved through diplomacy.

The First Strategic Arms Limitation Treaty (SALT 1) 1972

1) SALT 1 was a treaty signed in 1972 by the USA and the USSR. It limited the number of ABMs (anti-ballistic missiles) each country could have and placed a temporary limit on the numbers of ICBMs (Intercontinental Ballistic Missiles) on both sides.

2) ABMs were designed to intercept incoming missiles and had the potential to upset the delicate 'nuclear balance' between the USSR and the USA.

3) In the short term, the treaty was a success because it slowed down the arms race.

Comment and Analysis

By limiting the number of ABMs each country could have, SALT 1 reduced the likelihood of one country holding an advantage over the other.

If one side could use ABMs to destroy the other side's missiles then the threat of retaliation would be gone. The side with ABMs could launch a first strike and then just destroy the missiles that were fired back towards it.

The Helsinki Agreement 1975

1) The Helsinki Agreement in 1975 was a pact between the USA, the USSR, Canada and most of Europe. All countries agreed to recognise existing European borders and to uphold human rights.

2) Both superpowers accepted the division of Germany and the USSR's influence over Eastern Europe.

3) The West viewed the USSR's agreement to uphold human rights as great progress, but the USSR didn't stick to its word. It didn't grant freedom of speech or freedom of movement to its citizens. This undermined the Helsinki agreement and made the USA distrust the USSR.

The Second Strategic Arms Limitation Treaty (SALT 2) 1979

1) The SALT 2 Treaty was signed in 1979. The treaty banned the USA and the USSR from launching new missile programmes and limited the number of MIRVs (Multiple Independently targetable Reentry Vehicles) each country could have.

2) However the treaty was never ratified (approved) by the US Senate, so it didn't come into effect. See p.128 for more information.

MIRVs are weapons which can carry several missiles at once and deploy them to different targets.

The superpowers took important steps towards limiting their nuclear arms during détente, but both countries continued to hold vast stockpiles of weapons.

You'd better learn this, or I'll put you in détente-tion...

1) Jot down a quick summary of why both powers wanted to pursue détente.
2) Write out a table listing the successes and failures of détente.

The Soviet Invasion of Afghanistan

The Soviet War in Afghanistan was a <u>turning point</u> for détente in the 1970s — it demolished the <u>trust</u> that had been so carefully built up between the USA and the USSR.

The USSR got bogged down in a War in Afghanistan

1) In 1978, a <u>civil war</u> broke out in Afghanistan. Rebels were protesting at <u>new radical reforms</u> brought in by the <u>Afghan communist government</u>, which had <u>close ties</u> to the Soviet Union.

2) The Afghan government requested <u>help</u> from the <u>USSR</u>, which <u>invaded</u> Afghanistan in December 1979.

3) This decision turned out to be a <u>disaster</u> — the USSR found itself in a seemingly <u>unwinnable</u> conflict.

4) It had to fight in difficult <u>mountainous terrain</u> against determined opposition, who were supplied with <u>weapons</u> by the <u>USA</u>.

> **Comment and Analysis**
>
> The USSR used the <u>Brezhnev Doctrine</u> (see p.126) to justify the invasion. It was also concerned by the idea of an <u>anti-Soviet</u> government in Afghanistan, as the countries shared a <u>border</u>.

> Around <u>1 million Afghan</u> civilians were killed and over <u>6 million</u> became <u>refugees</u>.

The War was Disastrous for the USSR

1) <u>15,000</u> Soviet troops were killed and the government spent huge amounts of money, but the USSR <u>couldn't win</u>.

2) The Soviet-Afghan War led to a <u>loss</u> of public support in the USSR for the communist regime. The Soviet people were <u>angry</u> at falling living standards, which had <u>deteriorated</u> as a direct result of <u>high spending</u> in Afghanistan.

> **Comment and Analysis**
>
> When <u>Mikhail Gorbachev</u> came to power in 1985, he admitted that the USSR <u>couldn't afford</u> to keep fighting. In <u>1988</u>, he began <u>withdrawing</u> Soviet troops from Afghanistan (see p.130).

> **It didn't work out too well for Brezhnev internationally, either...**
> - The war was an <u>embarrassment</u> for Brezhnev and <u>undermined</u> the USSR's strong military reputation, which was essential for keeping its satellite states under <u>control</u>.
> - In January 1980, the UN <u>condemned</u> the invasion. It proposed a resolution demanding Soviet withdrawal, but the resolution was <u>vetoed</u> (rejected) by the USSR.
> - In <u>1980</u>, the USA and over 50 other countries (including Canada and West Germany) <u>boycotted</u> the Moscow Olympic Games, in <u>protest</u> at the Soviet-Afghan War.

The Superpowers began to Move Away from Détente

The war caused <u>tension</u> between the USSR and the USA to <u>resurface</u>. The situation was as <u>dangerous</u> as ever.

1) Soviet intervention in Afghanistan was <u>interpreted</u> by the USA as an act of <u>communist expansionism</u>. In 1979, US President Jimmy Carter was so alarmed he stopped the <u>SALT 2 Treaty</u> (see p.127) being debated by the US Senate, meaning it could never come into effect. Instead he called for an <u>increase</u> in the <u>defence budget</u>.

2) The USA was also worried that the USSR was trying to <u>gain influence</u> in the <u>Persian Gulf</u>, close to the Afghan border. The oil-rich area had formed close economic ties with the West, and Carter thought Soviet influence in Afghanistan <u>threatened US interests</u> there.

3) Carter warned that the USA would <u>use force</u> to prevent the USSR from <u>gaining control</u> of the Gulf region. This warning became known as the <u>Carter Doctrine</u>.

> The <u>Carter Doctrine</u> was the <u>first threat</u> of <u>aggression</u> between the superpowers since détente.

The USSR bit off more than it could chew...

If you're asked about the importance of an event, think about its knock-on effects, e.g. the Soviet invasion of Afghanistan contributed to the end of détente and harmed Brezhnev's popularity.

The Second Cold War

Cold War tensions were <u>resurrected</u> during the 1980s, in a period now known as the 'Second Cold War'.

Reagan Boosted American Defences

After the Soviet invasion of Afghanistan, the policy of <u>détente</u> was badly damaged. It was in even more danger when US President Carter was <u>succeeded</u> by President <u>Ronald Reagan</u> in January 1981.

1) Ronald Reagan was a hardline <u>anti-communist</u>. His speeches were often full of anti-Soviet rhetoric and he called the USSR an '<u>evil empire</u>'. This increased hostility between the two superpowers.

2) Reagan <u>didn't believe</u> in the policy of détente. He was willing to <u>negotiate</u> with the USSR, but only from a position of <u>strength</u>.

3) This meant he wanted to <u>increase American defences</u>. American intelligence gathered in 1976 also suggested that the USA had <u>underestimated</u> the USSR's nuclear strength, and the USA felt it had to <u>catch up</u>.

> This worried the USSR — it couldn't afford to <u>match</u> Reagan's spending.

Reagan started the biggest arms build-up in American history...
- In the 1980s the USA spent <u>$550 billion a year</u> on conventional and nuclear weapons.
- Reagan also <u>re-authorised</u> some weapons programmes that had been <u>abandoned</u> during détente. The USA began to develop the <u>neutron bomb</u>, which was designed to cause <u>maximum</u> loss of life and minimum damage to property.

The USA Launched the Strategic Defence Initiative

Relations between the superpowers <u>worsened</u> when Reagan announced his <u>Strategic Defence Initiative</u> (<u>SDI</u>).

1) In March 1983, Reagan announced the development of the Strategic Defence Initiative, nicknamed '<u>Star Wars</u>'.

2) The program would develop weapons that would be <u>deployed</u> in <u>space</u> and that could destroy nuclear missiles <u>after</u> they had been launched.

3) It would be the <u>ultimate defence system</u> — even nuclear missiles already heading towards the USA could be stopped.

4) If successful, the SDI would <u>shift the balance</u> of the Cold War in the USA's <u>favour</u>.

5) By 1983, détente was truly <u>over</u>.

Comment and Analysis

The SDI is a typical example of the <u>differing perspectives</u> that kept the Cold War going. For the USA, the SDI was a means of <u>defence</u>. But the USSR viewed it as an act of <u>aggression</u> — the USA would theoretically be able to attack the USSR <u>without</u> fear of retaliation.

There were anti-nuclear demonstrations as old fears resurfaced. This demonstration took place in Vienna in 1983. The banner reads 'create peace without weapons'.

Reagan's attitude Changed after 1985

> Gorbachev's leadership brought about a <u>thaw</u> in Cold War tensions, and <u>the return</u> of détente.

1) When <u>Mikhail Gorbachev</u> became leader of the USSR in March 1985, Reagan <u>reassessed his attitude</u> towards the USSR.

2) Gorbachev proposed <u>radical reforms</u> and was far <u>more open</u> towards the West than previous Soviet leaders. Reagan recognised that the USSR was being steered in a <u>new direction</u>.

3) The USA realised that this change could be good. Although initiatives like the SDI weren't scrapped, Reagan thought <u>negotiation</u> was now the best way to protect American interests.

4) Importantly, the two leaders <u>got on well</u>, creating a <u>better relationship</u> between the superpowers.

In the early 1980s, the Cold War Rea-ganed momentum...

Give an account that analyses the role that Reagan's attitude played in the ending of détente. You could mention his fears about the USSR and the Strategic Defence Initiative. [8]

EXAM QUESTION

Gorbachev's 'New Thinking'

Mikhail Gorbachev came to power in the USSR and radically changed Soviet policies. This was one of the biggest turning points in the Cold War — it laid the foundations for the collapse of the USSR.

The Cold War created a Crisis in the USSR

1) The arms race with the USA and the war in Afghanistan were hugely expensive and the Soviet economy just couldn't support this level of spending.

2) Soviet goods were poor quality and Soviet farming was inefficient — there wasn't enough food and millions of tonnes of grain had to be imported from the USA.

3) The communist government was becoming more corrupt and was unable to give the Soviet people the same high living standards as people had in the West.

> By the 1980s, Soviet citizens were becoming increasingly discontent.

Gorbachev introduced Radical Reforms

1) In 1985, Mikhail Gorbachev became General Secretary of the Communist Party. He was more open to the West than previous leaders and he admitted that the Soviet system had problems.

2) He introduced two major policies — 'perestroika' and 'glasnost'.

> Perestroika and glasnost were part of what is known as Gorbachev's 'New Thinking'. Changes to foreign policy were part of it too.

Perestroika means 'restructuring'...
- Gorbachev wanted to make the Soviet economy more efficient.
- He moved away from the centralisation of industry — the government no longer told businesses exactly what they had to produce.
- Gorbachev also allowed private business ownership and allowed Soviet businesses to trade with the Western powers.

Glasnost means 'openness'...
- Gorbachev gave the Soviet people new rights.
- Thousands of political prisoners were released.
- Free speech was allowed and censorship was relaxed.
- In 1989, Gorbachev created the USSR's first elected parliament — Communist Party officials were chosen by the public for the first time.

Comment and Analysis

Gorbachev didn't want to end communism — he wanted to modernise it. He hoped that reform would revive the USSR's struggling economy, which was falling further behind the USA's.

Gorbachev changed Foreign Policy

1) Gorbachev improved relations with the West. He met with US President Reagan several times, for example at the Geneva Summit in 1985. Gorbachev's open attitude softened Reagan's hard approach.

2) In 1987, a disarmament treaty was signed — the INF Treaty (Intermediate-Range Nuclear Forces Treaty). The USA and the USSR agreed to remove medium-range nuclear missiles from Europe within three years.

3) The first missiles were dismantled in 1988. The INF Treaty was a milestone in American-Soviet relations — both countries actively reduced weapons for the first time.

4) Gorbachev reduced the scale of the USSR's commitments abroad. In 1988, he announced that all Soviet troops would withdraw from Afghanistan.

5) In 1988, he also announced the immediate reduction of the USSR's weapons stockpile and the number of troops in the Soviet armed forces.

> Gorbachev's decrease in military spending and his decision to withdraw from Afghanistan greatly defused tensions between the superpowers.

> In 1988, Gorbachev decided to abandon the Brezhnev Doctrine (see p.126). He told the United Nations that Eastern Europe now had a choice — the USSR wasn't going to control it any longer.

Gorbachev wanted to improve communism...

Draw a table with three columns labelled 'perestroika', 'glasnost' and 'foreign policy'. Put each of Gorbachev's 'New Thinking' policies into the table under the correct heading.

Eastern Europe Pulls Away

Gorbachev's 'New Thinking' was intended to <u>modernise</u> communism, but actually sparked its <u>decline</u>.

The satellite states No Longer Feared the USSR

Gorbachev's decision to abandon the <u>Brezhnev Doctrine</u> led to the USSR <u>losing control</u> of its satellite states.

- Gorbachev stated the USSR would <u>no longer use force</u> to uphold communism in its satellite states. In 1988, he announced the <u>withdrawal</u> of Soviet troops, tanks and aircraft from <u>Eastern Europe</u>.
- It was <u>fear</u> of Soviet military intervention that had kept opposition movements <u>under control</u> within the USSR's satellite states. Without it, they had a chance to <u>act</u>.

'New Thinking' Energised Opposition

1) The nature of Gorbachev's new policies <u>encouraged</u> reformist movements within Eastern Europe.

2) Gorbachev's 'New Thinking' also caused <u>splits</u> in the Soviet Communist Party, making control of Eastern European countries from Moscow more <u>difficult</u>.

> Some members thought that Gorbachev's reforms <u>weren't</u> radical enough, and others worried they were <u>too</u> radical.

The Berlin Wall Fell in November 1989

1) In May 1989, communist Hungary <u>opened its border</u> with non-communist Austria. This let East Germans <u>travel</u> through Hungary to Austria, and then into West Germany.

2) Between August and September 1989, thousands <u>left</u> East Germany for West Germany. The East German government was <u>unable to control</u> the situation, and received <u>no help</u> from the USSR.

3) In October 1989, there were <u>mass protests</u> against the <u>communist regime</u>. The East German government finally agreed to <u>open</u> the border between East and West Berlin in November 1989. <u>Free elections</u> were promised and the wall was <u>torn down</u>.

4) The fall of the Berlin Wall showed that the relationship between East and West was <u>transforming</u>, and that the USSR was <u>losing its grip</u> over communist territory.

As news of the decision to open the wall spread, Berliners gathered at the wall. Here, East German officials wait for orders.

Communist governments in Eastern Europe started to Collapse

1) <u>Free elections</u> were also held in <u>Poland</u> in June 1989. In 1990, a new <u>non-communist</u> government came to power. The USSR <u>didn't intervene</u>.

2) In December 1989, communist governments <u>collapsed</u> in <u>Czechoslovakia</u>, <u>Bulgaria</u> and <u>Romania</u>. Hungary's Communist Party suffered a large <u>defeat</u> in <u>free elections</u> in March 1990.

In <u>October 1990</u>, communist East Germany and democratic West Germany <u>rejoined</u> to form a single state again. For many people this was a <u>powerful symbol</u> that the communist experiment was <u>over</u>.

Comment and Analysis

The <u>reunification</u> of Germany and the <u>decline</u> of communism in the USSR's satellite states symbolised a <u>new thaw</u> in the Cold War. Europe was no longer <u>ideologically divided</u> between East and West.

The satellite states eventually got a bit of space...

Look back at the information on Gorbachev's 'New Thinking' and the effect it had on Europe. Make a timeline of events between 1988 and 1990.

REVISION TASK

The Collapse of the Soviet Union

Despite the fall of communist regimes in Eastern Europe, the Cold War wasn't over until the USSR collapsed.

The Republics of the USSR Wanted Independence

As the USSR lost its grip on its satellite states, it was undergoing a national crisis.

1) In early 1990, some important regions in the Soviet Union demanded independence, especially the Baltic republics — Latvia, Lithuania, and Estonia.

2) They were encouraged by the recent success of revolutions across Eastern Europe (see p.131) and by Gorbachev's policy of 'glasnost' (openness), which gave greater power to individuals and encouraged constructive criticism of Soviet policy.

3) Gorbachev didn't want to lose the Republics. He granted them more power — but it wasn't enough.

4) The leaders of the Soviet republics no longer listened to Gorbachev, and he lacked the authority to make them comply with Soviet wishes.

> The USSR was made up of 15 republics. Each republic had its own parliament, but was centrally controlled by Moscow.

- Lithuania declared itself independent in March 1990. Soviet troops were sent to Vilnius, the capital of Lithuania, in January 1991, and several civilians were killed in the violence that followed. But this only strengthened the independence movement.
- In April 1991, Georgia declared its independence, followed by the Ukraine's declaration in August.

> Military intervention no longer deterred protests, it escalated them.

> As Gorbachev's authority weakened, independence movements gained in strength.

There was a Political Crisis in the USSR

By 1990, Gorbachev faced opposition from within his own party and the public. The Communist Party was divided — some members wanted more drastic reform and others wanted a return to former Soviet policies. The public were unhappy because Gorbachev's reforms hadn't lived up to their high expectations.

1) More traditional Soviet communists were worried that the Communist Party was so divided it was going to split up.

2) They thought Gorbachev's reforms had gone too far and plotted a coup against the government in August 1991.

3) They arrested Gorbachev, tried to force him to resign, and sent tanks onto the streets of Moscow to deter protesters.

4) The coup didn't go to plan — it was condemned by Boris Yeltsin, a Soviet politician who opposed Gorbachev and wanted the USSR to adopt capitalism.

5) Yeltsin went onto the streets to rally opposition against the coup. There were mass protests in major cities, showing that Soviets had clearly rejected communism. The coup failed.

Economic reforms hadn't worked

- The USSR's economy hadn't improved, and in 1990 a quarter of its population was living below the poverty line.
- Economic corruption was still rife.
- Inflation was high and basic goods were in short supply.
- The huge costs of the arms race and the war in Afghanistan hindered the reforms too.

The Soviet Union Collapsed

1) On Christmas Day 1991, Gorbachev resigned.

2) The USSR was dissolved on the 26th December.

3) The republics that made up the Soviet Union had become independent states. These included Latvia, Lithuania, Estonia and Belarus.

4) The biggest of the republics was Russia. Yeltsin was elected leader and adopted capitalism.

> As more and more countries declared their independence from the USSR, they also declared their intentions to pull out of the Warsaw Pact (p.118). This made it weaker and it eventually ended in July 1991.

The dissolution of the USSR marked the end of the Cold War...

Give two consequences of Communist Party divisions in 1990-1991. Explain your points. [8]

Revision Summary

That pretty much sums up the Cold War — now all you have to do is check it's all sunk in.
- Try these questions and <u>tick off each one</u> when you <u>get it right</u>.
- When you've done <u>all the questions</u> for a topic and are <u>completely happy</u> with it, tick off the topic.

The Origins of the Cold War, 1941-1958 (p.115-120) ☑

1) What was the Grand Alliance?
2) Describe the different ideologies followed by the USA and the USSR.
3) Why was the USSR in a position of influence over Eastern Europe after the Second World War?
4) What did Churchill mean when he said an 'Iron Curtain' divided Europe?
5) Why were the Long and Novikov Telegrams important?
6) What was the Truman Doctrine?
7) What was the Cominform? What did it do?
8) Describe the events of the Berlin Airlift.
9) Give two consequences of the 1948-49 Berlin Crisis.
10) What is meant by an 'arms race'?
11) What did Khrushchev mean by 'peaceful co-existence'?
12) Give two consequences of the Hungarian Uprising.

Cold War Crises, 1958-1970 (p.121-126) ☑

13) Why was Berlin a source of tension between the superpowers?
14) Describe Khrushchev's 'Berlin Ultimatum' of 1958.
15) How did the Paris and Vienna Summits affect the USSR's attitude towards Berlin?
16) Give two consequences of the establishment of the Berlin Wall.
17) Describe the main events of the Cuban Missile Crisis. How did it alter the course of the Cold War?
18) Why did the USSR end the Prague Spring?
19) How did other countries react to the Soviet invasion of Czechoslovakia?
20) What was the Brezhnev Doctrine?

The End of the Cold War, 1970-1991 (p.127-132) ☑

21) What does 'détente' mean?
22) Name three treaties signed by the superpowers in the 1970s.
23) How did the Soviet invasion of Afghanistan change relations between the USA and the USSR?
24) What was US President Reagan's attitude towards détente?
25) What was the SDI?
26) When did Mikhail Gorbachev become leader in the USSR?
27) What were 'perestroika' and 'glasnost'?
28) How did Gorbachev change Soviet foreign policy?
29) Why did opposition to communism rise in Eastern Europe after 1988?
30) Why was there a political crisis in the USSR by 1990?
31) Describe the events that led to the collapse of the Soviet Union from 1990-91.

Exam Skills

These pages cover the <u>main skills</u> you'll need to tackle some of the most common types of exam question.

Learn the Facts about the Periods you've studied

You'll be asked to <u>describe</u> or <u>outline</u> some <u>features</u> of the period you've studied to test your <u>knowledge</u> of the <u>facts</u>. Make sure your points are <u>clear</u> and <u>accurate</u>.

> Give two aspects of education in Elizabethan England, 1558-88. [4 marks]

For the <u>Thematic Study</u>, you might have to compare <u>two aspects</u> of your period — this means describing how a <u>key feature</u> of your period <u>developed</u> by explaining <u>similarities</u> or <u>differences</u> over time.

> Give one way that beliefs about the spread of disease in the fourteenth century were similar to those in the seventeenth century. Explain your answer. [4 marks]

You'll be asked to Analyse Features, Events and Developments

1) Some questions will ask you to explain the <u>causes</u> of something, or the <u>reasons why</u> it happened. Consider what <u>triggered</u> certain developments and <u>why</u> the changes were <u>fast</u> or <u>slow</u> to happen.

2) You could be asked about <u>why</u> a change or event was <u>important</u> or <u>significant</u> — think about how the development influenced <u>attitudes</u> and <u>later events</u>, and link the event or development to <u>wider issues</u>.

3) If you're asked to write about the <u>consequences</u> of a change or event, think about its <u>impact</u> and <u>what changed</u> as a result of the development.

> Explain how important the formation of NATO (1949) was to relations between the Soviet Union and the USA. [8 marks]

4) Use <u>detailed</u> and <u>relevant</u> information to <u>support</u> your points. Including specific dates, names and statistics shows you have a good <u>knowledge</u> and <u>understanding</u> of the period.

You need to know how Analyse a Statement or Interpretation

1) Some questions will give you a <u>statement</u> or <u>interpretation</u> and ask you <u>how far you agree</u> with it.

2) Decide your opinion <u>before</u> you start writing and state it clearly at the <u>beginning</u> and <u>end</u> of your answer.

3) Even if you <u>agree</u> with the statement in the question, you still need to analyse some <u>counter-arguments</u> — this shows you've considered all of the evidence and looked at <u>different sides</u> of the argument.

> 'Commercial rivalry was the most important reason for the outbreak of war with Spain in 1585.' Do you agree with this statement? Explain your answer. [16 marks]

For example, if you're answering a question like this one, it's a good idea to consider <u>other reasons</u> why war broke out with Spain. You could talk about other <u>long-term causes of tension</u> (e.g. Elizabeth's religious settlement) or <u>short-term factors</u> (e.g. Elizabeth's decision to sign the Treaty of Nonsuch). You need to say whether the other factors you've mentioned were <u>more</u> or <u>less important</u> than the reason in the question.

4) You could also be asked to look at <u>how</u> or <u>why</u> something <u>changed</u> in the period you've studied.

5) You'll be given <u>two factors</u> to discuss and you'll have to <u>argue</u> in favour of one of them.

> What was the most important reason why Hitler became Chancellor in 1933: Hitler's popularity or economic problems? Explain your answer, referring to both reasons. [12 marks]

6) Write about <u>both</u> factors and explain how they're <u>linked</u>. You don't need to bring in other factors for this question type, but you should still use your <u>own knowledge</u> to support your argument.

Exam Skills

These sample answers will show you how to analyse historical <u>statements</u> and write a <u>summary</u> or <u>account</u>.

Here's a Sample Answer that Analyses a Statement

This sample answer shows you how to answer questions that ask you <u>how far you agree</u> with a statement.

'The discovery of anaesthetics was an important development in surgery between c.1700 and c.1900.' Explain how far you agree.   [16 marks]

This gives a <u>basic answer</u> to the question <u>straight away</u>.

I agree that the discovery of anaesthetics was an important development. Before anaesthetics were discovered, many patients died from the trauma of pain in surgery. Anaesthetics like chloroform, whose effects were discovered by James Simpson in 1847, improved surgery by removing pain. They also allowed surgeons to carry out longer and more complicated procedures.

This explains how things <u>used</u> to be, to show that the development of anaesthetics was <u>significant</u>.

The answer gives examples of how anaesthetics <u>improved</u> surgery.

It's important to give <u>counter-arguments</u> to show you've considered <u>all</u> the evidence.

However, the importance of anaesthetics was limited at first because they also caused a rise in death rates in the short term. The period between 1846 and 1870 is known as the 'Black Period' of surgery because surgeons used anaesthetics to perform more complicated operations, which caused greater bleeding and infection. While anaesthetics saved some lives, they also caused more deaths because of the way they were used by surgeons, meaning their impact was limited at first.

This is a <u>shortened example</u> — in the exam, you'll need to make <u>several more points</u> for <u>both sides</u> of the argument.

It's good to end by clearly stating your <u>overall opinion</u> in the conclusion.

Overall, I agree that the discovery of anaesthetics was an important development in surgery because they meant patients were in a lot less pain and made it easier for surgeons to operate. Although they contributed to more deaths in the short term, anaesthetics (combined with the use of antiseptics) had improved surgery by 1900.

You might be asked to write a Summary of Something

This sample answer shows you how to write an <u>account</u> or a <u>summary</u> of events in your period. <u>Explain</u> what happened and <u>analyse</u> it by using concepts such as cause, consequence and change (see p.1).

Give an account that analyses the key events between 1985 and 1989 that led to the fall of the Berlin Wall.   [8 marks]

This <u>evidence backs up</u> the point.

In 1985, Mikhail Gorbachev became General Secretary of the Communist Party and changed Soviet policy. He created closer ties with US President Reagan, e.g. at the Geneva Summit in 1985, and began withdrawing Soviet troops from Afghanistan in 1988. This helped to reduce tensions between East and West, and brought hope that relations could improve further.

In 1988, Gorbachev abandoned the Brezhnev Doctrine, which had promised that the USSR would intervene in any country where communist regimes were threatened. This meant that countries in Eastern Europe no longer had to fear Soviet aggression if they chose to turn away from communism.

This analyses the <u>impact</u> of the event that took place by explaining how it <u>affected other countries'</u> attitudes.

This makes it clear that <u>one event led to another</u>.

As a result, Hungary felt it could open its border with Austria in May 1989 without fear of military consequences. This caused chaos for the East German government, as thousands of East Germans crossed the border to travel to West Germany. Public opposition to the government grew — in October 1989 there were anti-communist protests in East Germany. As the USSR was now unwilling to support struggling communist regimes, the government was forced to give in to public pressure, and opened the Berlin Wall in November 1989.

It's important that you make <u>connections between different events</u>.

Exam Skills

Here are some lovely tips on how to write about <u>interpretations</u> and <u>sources</u> in the exam.

You'll be asked to Analyse and Compare historical Interpretations

1) You'll be asked to <u>compare interpretations</u> and explain <u>why</u> two interpretations are <u>different</u>. Here are some <u>tips</u> on how to approach these questions:

- When you're working with <u>interpretations</u>, you need to figure out what the author is trying to <u>say</u> — look at what <u>information</u> they give, what their <u>tone</u> is and if they <u>emphasise</u> anything in particular.
- If the interpretation is <u>visual</u>, think about what's <u>happening</u> in the picture and what <u>emotions</u> are shown. Use your <u>own knowledge</u> to decide whether any important details have been <u>missed out</u>.

2) If you're asked to decide <u>how convincing</u> an interpretation is or explain <u>how far you agree</u> with it, then you need to consider the <u>event</u> or <u>issue</u> that it is discussing and decide whether you think it describes it <u>accurately</u>. <u>Explain</u> your decision using your <u>own knowledge</u> and refer to the interpretation.

Here's a Sample Answer to help you Analyse Interpretations

This sample answer will give you an idea of how to explain <u>why</u> two interpretations are <u>different</u>.

Interpretation 1

To describe Hitler's thinking as an ideology is really to flatter it. It lacked coherence and was intellectually superficial and simplistic. It was not even a rational system of thought. It was merely a collection of ideas not very cleverly pieced together. Although the combination was unique, it was not in any positive sense original.

Extract from 'Access to History: Germany: the Third Reich 1933-45' 2nd ed., by Geoff Layton, published in 2000.

Interpretation 2

Nazism contained... wholly 'modern' types of appeal offering social mobility, a society of equal chances where success came from merit and achievement, and new opportunities to thrive and prosper through letting youth and vigour have its head at the expense of the old... and the decayed.

Extract from 'The Nazi Dictatorship: Problems and Perspectives of Interpretation', by Ian Kershaw, published in 2015.

Give one reason why these interpretations give different opinions on what the Nazi Party offered the German people. [4 marks]

> **Give a <u>clear reason</u> in your <u>first</u> <u>sentence</u>.**

> **Use <u>evidence</u> from the text, then <u>explain</u> what it shows.**

Interpretations 1 and 2 may have different opinions about what the Nazi Party offered the German people because they focus on different aspects of the party. Interpretation 1 focuses on the 'collection of ideas' behind the Nazi Party — it's emphasising the lack of originality in Nazi ideology. However, Interpretation 2 looks at the new opportunities the Nazis seemed to offer. It doesn't examine ideology, but instead considers how the party seemed to provide new ways for Germans to 'prosper' in society.

> **Discuss <u>both</u> <u>interpretations</u>.**

> **Explain how looking at <u>different aspects</u> of the party could have affected the <u>authors' views</u>.**

There'll be some questions about Sources too

1) Some sources questions will ask you to <u>evaluate</u> what a <u>visual</u> or <u>written</u> source is saying.
2) Other source questions will ask you to <u>analyse sources</u> and say <u>how useful</u> they are.

- When working with <u>sources</u>, it's not just a case of describing what you see or read. You need to <u>analyse</u> the source and use it to <u>draw conclusions</u> about the period you've studied.
- When you're analysing the <u>usefulness</u> of a source, always look at <u>what</u> it's saying and <u>where</u> it's from. Use the source and your <u>own knowledge</u> to decide if the source is <u>reliable</u> and if the content is <u>relevant</u>.

Exam Skills

Long essay questions can seem tricky at first, but you'll get the hang of them if you put these skills into action.

Have a look at this Sample Answer

This sample answer will help you to assess the usefulness of a source.

Source A

An English cartoon by John Leech, published in 1858. Its title is, 'Father Thames Introducing his Offspring to the Fair City of London'. It shows figures representing diphtheria, scrofula and cholera rising from the river.

© The Art Archive / Granger Collection

Look at Source A. Using the source and your own knowledge, explain how useful Source A would be to a historian studying cholera. [8 marks]

> The first sentence directly addresses the question.

Source A was published in 1858 and is useful because it shows the fear surrounding cholera in Britain at the time. The corpse-like figures rising out of the water suggest that cholera symbolised death, and that Londoners were under attack from the disease.

> Details from the source are used to back up points.

Indeed, an epidemic in 1848 killed 53,000 people. The source therefore gives historians an idea of people's views of cholera, but doesn't reveal much about other aspects of the disease, e.g. its impact on London.

> The answer talks about why it might not be useful.

> Using your own knowledge shows a good level of understanding.

Source A is also useful because it gives historians an insight into people's beliefs in 1858 about how cholera was spread. The figure of cholera is rising from the river, which is clearly polluted — dead animals have been washed ashore. The link the cartoonist makes between pollution and cholera suggests people's continued belief in the 'miasma theory' — the idea that inhaling bad smells caused disease.

> This refers back to the source for evidence.

> This is a shortened example — in the exam, you'd need to finish this paragraph and make more points

Remember these Four Tips for Answering Questions

Don't Spend Too Long on Short Questions

The more marks a question is worth, the longer your answer should be. Don't get carried away writing loads for a question that's only worth a few marks — leave time for the higher mark questions.

Stay Focused on the Question

1) Directly answer the question and back up your points with relevant facts. Don't just write everything you know about the period.

2) Be relevant and accurate — e.g. if you're writing about the rise of the Nazi Party, don't include stories about a London camel called George who moved rubble during the Blitz.

3) It might help to try to write the first sentence of every paragraph in a way that addresses the question, e.g. 'Another way that better living conditions led to improved public health is...'

Use a Clear Writing Style

1) Essay answers should start with a brief introduction and end with a conclusion. Remember to start a new paragraph for each new point you want to discuss.

2) Try to use clear handwriting — and pay attention to spelling, punctuation and grammar (see p.138).

Plan your Essay Answers, but Not the Others

1) You don't need to plan answers to the shorter questions in the exam. That will waste time.

2) For longer essay questions, it's very important to make a quick plan before you start writing.

3) Think about what the key words are in the question. Scribble a quick plan of your main points — cross through this neatly at the end, so it's obvious it shouldn't be marked.

Exam Skills

In some papers, the examiner will be marking you partly on your spelling, punctuation and grammar (SPaG). SPaG is worth nearly 5% of your overall mark, so don't forget to write nicely (as my mum would say).

Remember to Check your Spellings

1) You should leave about five minutes at the end of the exam to check your work.

2) Check as many questions as you can, but make sure you read over the questions which award SPaG marks especially carefully. (Marks are shown very clearly at the end of each question.)

3) 5 minutes isn't long, so there won't be time to check everything thoroughly. Look for the most obvious spelling mistakes...

> If you're not confident with any of these things, learn them now.

where / wear / were   your / you're   silent letters, e.g. know, science, could

names of historical figures or places, e.g. Roanoke, Khrushchev, Scutari   there / their / they're   to / too / two   of / off

effect / affect   double letters, e.g. aggression, success   don't confuse 'past' with 'passed'   though / thought / through / thorough

You need to Punctuate Properly...

1) Always use a capital letter at the start of a sentence. Use capital letters for names of particular people, places and things. For example:

> All sentences start with capital letters.

> In 1985, Gorbachev was made General Secretary of the Communist Party.

> The name of a person.   A title.   The name of an organisation.

2) Full stops go at the end of sentences, e.g. 'General Custer was killed in June 1876.' Question marks go at the end of questions, e.g. 'How successful was the Nazi propaganda?'

3) Use commas when you use more than one adjective to describe something, or to separate items in a list:

> Elizabeth I was intelligent, confident and powerful.

4) Commas can also join two points into one sentence with a joining word (such as 'and', 'or', 'so' or 'but'):

> The work of Galen was central to medieval medical teachings, so doctors found it difficult to disagree with him.

5) Commas can also be used to separate extra information in a sentence:

> The Civil Rights Act, which was enacted in 1870, was opposed by President Andrew Johnson.

...and use Grammar Correctly

1) Don't change tenses in your writing by mistake:

> The mountain men explored the West first — they hunted animals for their skins.

> Both verbs are in the past tense — which is correct. Writing 'hunt' instead of 'hunted' would be wrong.

2) Write your longer answers in paragraphs.

- A paragraph is a group of sentences which talk about the same thing or follow on from each other.
- You need to start a new paragraph when you start making a new point.

> You show a new paragraph by starting a new line and leaving a gap (an indent) before you start writing:

> From 1933, Hitler started a programme of public works, such as the building of huge new motorways. This gave jobs to thousands of people.
> Even though there was increased employment, the Nazis altered the statistics so that things looked better than they were. Wages were also poor.

That's that, then — all that's left to do now is to sit the exams...

Good SPaG is a great way to get marks in the exam. So make sure you've learnt all the stuff on this page, and also everything about anything that's ever happened in all of history, and you should be okay.

Index

Index